Praise for *The Financial Times Guide to Mentoring*

'As one who had the privilege to be a mentee and, later, a mentor during my long United Nations career, I can attest to how critical it can be. To have a mentor who will give you frank advice and guidance is invaluable. And to pass that knowledge and experience on is a gift. *The Financial Times Guide to Mentoring* by Ruth Gotian and Andy Lopata makes a compelling and inspiring case for mentoring in the workplace.'

Gillian Sorensen, United Nations Assistant Secretary-General (ret.)

'Gotian and Lopata's book delivers a masterclass in mentoring. With their expert guidance, readers can expect to enhance their mentoring relationships and create opportunities to learn their way through almost anything while growing both personally and professionally.'

Pamay Bassey, Chief Learning and Diversity Officer, The Kraft Heinz Company

'*The Financial Times Guide to Mentoring* is a comprehensive dive into the art and science of mentorship that's as accessible as it is profound. Ruth and Andy bridge the gap between academic research and practical application, offering a dynamic learning experience that's rich with resources, from worksheets to real-world case studies. Their approach speaks to mentors and mentees alike, providing a valuable assessment tool to gauge and grow your mentoring relationships. Whether you're starting out or looking to deepen your mentoring skills, this book is a treasure trove of insights. I wholeheartedly endorse it for anyone serious about making a meaningful impact in their career and the lives of others.'

Dr. Marshall Goldsmith, *Thinkers50* #1 Executive Coach and *New York Times* bestselling author of *The Earned Life*, *Triggers* and *What Got You Here Won't Get You There*

'In my experience, mentoring plays a key role in leadership development and business success. Ensuring that valuable expertise and experience is captured and shared makes a significant positive difference to individual performance and team skill development. Defining a successful approach to mentoring requires a clear strategy and careful implementation. Through this book Andy Lopata and Ruth Gotian provide a comprehensive and well-researched guide to mentoring. This book provides an excellent approach to how an organisation can encourage more people to engage in the activity and to equip people to be better mentors and to get more value as mentees.'

Kevin Gaskell, former CEO of Porsche, Lamborghini and BMW; author and world record-holding adventurer

'Mentoring is often seen as a critical component of effective career development, but is rarely fully understood or supported effectively within organisations. Whether you are a mentor, a mentee or a HR professional seeking to design mentoring for organisational impact, Ruth and Andy have put together a remarkable guide to mentoring, bringing together all of the advice you will need.'

Brian Murphy, Senior Director, Employee Skilling, Microsoft

'Dr Ruth Gotian and Andy Lopata's book beautifully unravels the transformative power of mentorship. I've not only witnessed the magic that mentorship can bring to one's journey, but I credit much of my success on Broadway and in Hollywood to my own mentors that have radically changed my life for the better.'

Telly Leung, Disney's *Aladdin* on Broadway, *Rent*, *Godspell*, *Glee*

'This book is an indispensable roadmap for crafting a meaningful career. Read it to unlock the full potential of mentorship in the modern business world.'

Dorie Clark, *Wall Street Journal* bestselling author of *The Long Game*; Executive Education Faculty, Columbia Business School

'This book is a fantastic resource for mentors and mentees alike. It provides practical insights and strategies to foster both professional and personal growth. As someone who has benefited from mentoring, I can attest to the value of this guide.'

Tendai Wileman, Chief of Staff and Director of Organisational Change, Guys and St Thomas' NHS Foundation Trust

'If you're eager to grow and thrive, Ruth Gotian and Andy Lopata's mentoring guide is essential reading. This new book provides invaluable insights for nurturing effective mentorship relationships and jumpstarting your personal and professional growth.'
Amy C Edmondson, Novartis Professor of Leadership, Harvard Business School; author of *Right Kind of Wrong: The Science of Failing Well* Financial Times/Schroders Business Book of the Year 2023, Thinkers50 ranked #1 Management Thinker in the World

'My new go-to mentoring manual! Comprehensive and brilliantly written, if you want to supercharge mentoring in your organisation, go no further.'
Joe Tidman, Head of Learning and Development, DLA Piper UK LLP

'In today's rapidly changing and complex world, mentoring makes the difference between getting noticed and being missed. I recommend *The Financial Times Guide to Mentoring*, where Gotian and Lopata have crafted a comprehensive roadmap for both mentors and mentees. Their engaging insights will lead you to creating meaningful and impactful relationships!'
Eileen M. Collins, Colonel, USAF, Ret; former NASA astronaut and first woman space shuttle pilot and commander

'How do you open the world of opportunities to others? How do you enable people to develop the skills and confidence to maximise their talents? How do you practically encourage people to seize their day? Mentoring provides a powerful answer to these important challenges. It is both practical and universal, something which many of us have already benefitted from. In *The Financial Times Guide to Mentoring* the mechanics and magic of mentoring are clearly and powerfully described by Ruth Gotian and Andy Lopata. For anyone who wishes to understand more about mentoring, to be a mentor or be mentored this is truly required reading.'
Stuart Crainer and Des Dearlove, founders of Thinkers50

'*The Financial Times Guide to Mentoring* is an invaluable resource for those seeking profound insights into mentorship, bridging the worlds from the court to the C-suite. With their extensive expertise, Gotian and Lopata deliver a

comprehensive guide that goes beyond conventional mentoring boundaries. It's a must-read for both emerging leaders and seasoned professionals.'
RC Buford, CEO, San Antonio Spurs; two-time National Basketball Association (NBA) Executive of the Year

'This essential guide is a gift for all on what it means to be mentored, what an effective mentoring relationship looks like and the ways you can add mentoring to your future successes. It is equally valuable for mentors and mentees alike.'
Dr Kirstin Ferguson AM, former Deputy Chair, Australian Broadcasting Corporation; bestselling author of *Head and Heart: The Art of Modern Leadership and Thinkers50*, Distinguished Leadership Award winner

'Thank you, Ruth and Andy for highlighting how mentoring can change the workplace for everyone! *The Financial Times Guide to Mentoring* offers practical strategies and real-world examples that can be implemented in the workplace. Dive into the pages of this book to unlock the power of collaborative empowerment in the workplace, fulfilling futures through mentorship. The motto of The Mentor Project is "Mentors change lives. Mentors change the world." Now, we know mentorship changes the workplace!'
Dr. Deborah Heiser, Co-Founder and CEO, The Mentor Project

'Practical and insightful content on all aspects of mentoring brought to life with authentic examples. A must read for anyone exploring and engaged in mentoring, especially mentors and organisations offering mentoring programmes, for whom this provides powerful and important guidance.'
Kerrie Dorman, Founder of the Association of Business Mentors

'Ruth Gotian and Andy Lopata's *The Financial Times Guide to Mentoring* is a game-changer for anyone aspiring to reach the pinnacle of success, much like the journey to the Olympics. As a two-time Olympic medalist, I can attest that mentorship is the driving force behind realising one's full potential, and this book is an invaluable guide on that transformative journey.'
Ori Sasson, two-time Olympic Medalist in Judo

'Even though Gotian and Lopata admit in the first few pages of their new book that "mentoring is not an exact science", this book comes as close as any out there to providing a protocol. They eloquently make the case for why mentoring is important and how to become a not just a good mentor, but an exceptional one. A must-read for everyone who supervises or is supervised!'

Ushma S. Neill, PhD, Vice President, Scientific Education and Training, Memorial Sloan Kettering Cancer Center

'This is a rallying cry in the form of a book.

Some development practices are as old as time began, mentoring is one of them. When done well, there are few things as impactful. Having had the benefit of being a mentee in my career, I have paid it forward and provide mentor relationships. I wish I had access to this book when I started both roles.

This pragmatic and easy-to-digest book is peppered with real examples and frameworks. It lifts the lid on effective practices and pitfalls, ensuring that the application is as effective and meaningful as it can be. An excellent reframe on an underused development resource.'

Barbara Thompson, Learning and Development Leader, FTSE Retailer

'Mentoring tends to be the least understood development tool, and yet the most powerful, if done right. This book will equip your leaders and organisation with the knowledge and know-how to make that difference.

Steven D'Souza, Senior Client Partner, Korn Ferry EMEA; author of the *Not Knowing* trilogy

'*The Financial Times Guide to Mentoring* is a profound resource that not only showcases the authors' deep understanding of mentoring but also their commitment to fostering growth and development. An essential read for all leaders.

Not before reading Gotian and Lopata's book had I realised how essential mentorship is – and why I better get my act together, securing a mentor or two. *The Financial Times Guide to Mentoring* is simply a game-changer for anyone seeking to make the most out of mentorship.'

Martin Lindstrom, *New York Times* and *Wall Street Journal* best-selling author of *The Ministry of Common Sense* and *Buyology*

'We all have people in our lives who have made a difference for us. They are in our story. But the real question is, whose story are we in? Whose life have we

made a difference for? Mentoring is the way to make a difference and this book will help you do that.'
      Dr. Ivan Misner, *New York Times* **bestselling author; Founder, BNI**

'Mentoring is an important part of the journey to leadership and this book provides a thoroughly comprehensive guide to help business leaders support their successors effectively and to help people engage in mentoring at all levels, to create the best possible impact.'
      Phil Jones MBE, Managing Director, Brother UK

'Mentoring is probably one of the most beautiful practices a human being can offer.

Simply, wisdom shared at the most opportune time. Dr. Ruth Gotian and Andy Lopata have brought together the best practices and real-world advice for both mentors and mentees, making it an essential guide for anyone interested in personal and professional development.'
      Scott Hamilton, Olympic and World Champion in figure skating

'Most successful high-performance organisations recognise the importance of learning and the value of mentorship in maintaining a culture which strives for personal and organizational achievement. I highly recommend *The Financial Times Guide to Mentoring* by Dr. Ruth Gotian and Andy Lopata as a transformative resource for navigating your journey through personal and professional fulfillment. As I look back on my career as a NASA research engineer and astronaut, I realise how truly blessed I was to have great mentors during both totally different career paths. This book will help optimise the process.'
      Charles Camarda, PhD, NASA Astronaut (Ret)

The mentoring landscape has been transformed by Dr. Ruth Gotian and Andy Lopata's expertise. 'The Financial Times Guide to Mentoring' is an indispensable guide for those looking to harness the power of mentorship for personal and professional advancement.
      Darek Lenart, EVP, People and Capability, Americas and Strategic Growth, Mastercard

THE FINANCIAL TIMES GUIDE TO MENTORING

Pearson

At Pearson, we believe in learning – all kinds of learning for all kinds of people. Whether it's at home, in the classroom or in the workplace, learning is the key to improving our life chances.

That's why we're working with leading authors to bring you the latest thinking and best practices, so you can get better at the things that are important to you. You can learn on the page or on the move, and with content that's always crafted to help you understand quickly and apply what you've learned.

If you want to upgrade your personal skills or accelerate your career, become a more effective leader or more powerful communicator, discover new opportunities or simply find more inspiration, we can help you make progress in your work and life.

Every day our work helps learning flourish, and wherever learning flourishes, so do people.

To learn more, please visit us at **www.pearson.com**

The Financial Times

With a worldwide network of highly respected journalists, *The Financial Times* provides global business news, insightful opinion and expert analysis of business, finance and politics. With over 500 journalists reporting from 50 countries worldwide, our in-depth coverage of international news is objectively reported and analysed from an independent, global perspective.

To find out more, visit **www.ft.com**

THE FINANCIAL TIMES GUIDE TO MENTORING

A COMPLETE GUIDE TO EFFECTIVE MENTORING

FIRST EDITION

DR. RUTH GOTIAN
ANDY LOPATA

Pearson

Harlow, England • London • New York • Boston • San Francisco • Toronto • Sydney
Dubai • Singapore • Hong Kong • Tokyo • Seoul • Taipei • New Delhi
Cape Town • São Paulo • Mexico City • Madrid • Amsterdam • Munich • Paris • Milan

PEARSON EDUCATION LIMITED
KAO Two
KAO Park
Harlow CM17 9NA
United Kingdom
Tel: +44 (0)1279 623623
Web: **www.pearson.com**

First edition published 2024 (print and electronic)
© Pearson Education Limited 2024 (print and electronic)

The rights of Ruth Gotian and Andy Lopata to be identified as authors of this work have been asserted by them in accordance with the Copyright, Designs and Patents Act 1988.

The print publication is protected by copyright. Prior to any prohibited reproduction, storage in a retrieval system, distribution or transmission in any form or by any means, electronic, mechanical, recording or otherwise, permission should be obtained from the publisher or, where applicable, a licence permitting restricted copying in the United Kingdom should be obtained from the Copyright Licensing Agency Ltd, Barnard's Inn, 86 Fetter Lane, London EC4A 1EN.

The ePublication is protected by copyright and must not be copied, reproduced, transferred, distributed, leased, licensed or publicly performed or used in any way except as specifically permitted in writing by the publishers, as allowed under the terms and conditions under which it was purchased, or as strictly permitted by applicable copyright law. Any unauthorised distribution or use of this text may be a direct infringement of the authors' and the publisher's rights and those responsible may be liable in law accordingly.

All trademarks used herein are the property of their respective owners. The use of any trademark in this text does not vest in the authors or publisher any trademark ownership rights in such trademarks, nor does the use of such trademarks imply any affiliation with or endorsement of this book by such owners.

Pearson Education is not responsible for the content of third-party internet sites.

ISBN: 978-1-292-72668-7(print)
        978-1-292-45843-4(ePub)

British Library Cataloguing-in-Publication Data
A catalogue record for the print edition is available from the British Library

Library of Congress Cataloging-in-Publication Data
Names: Gotian, Ruth, 1970- author. | Lopata, Andy, author.
Title: The Financial Times guide to mentoring: a complete guide to
   effective mentoring / Ruth Gotian, Andy Lopata.
Description: First edition. | Harlow, England; New York: Pearson, 2024. |
   Includes bibliographical references and index.
Identifiers: LCCN 2023056769 | ISBN 9781292726687 (paperback) | ISBN
   9781292458434 (epub)
Subjects: LCSH: Mentoring in business. | Employees--Coaching of. |
   Mentoring.
Classification: LCC HF5385 .G67 2024 | DDC 658.3/124--dc23/eng/20240119
LC record available at https://lccn.loc.gov/2023056769

10 9 8 7 6 5 4 3 2 1
28 27 26 25 24

Cover design by Michelle Morgan
Cover design © Peter Steiner/Alamy Stock Photo

Print edition typeset in 9.5/14 Stone Serif ITC Pro by Straive
Printed by Ashford Colour Press Ltd, Gosport

NOTE THAT ANY PAGE CROSS REFERENCES REFER TO THE PRINT EDITION

Both of us have lost parents in the last three years.

Ruth has lost both her mother and father, and Andy lost his father.

We would like to dedicate this book in memory of our first and ultimate mentors ... our parents.

Arthur J. Ginsburg, z"l
Dina D. Ginsburg, z"l
Harvey Lopata

And Claire Lopata, who continues to support, guide and inspire Andy.

CONTENTS

About the authors — xvi
Authors' acknowledgements — xviii
Publisher's acknowledgements — xxi
Foreword — xxiv
Preface — xxvi
Introduction — xxviii

PART 1
THE CASE FOR MENTORING — 1

1. Why mentoring is so important — 3
2. What does effective mentoring look like? — 15
3. Formal v informal mentoring — 27
4. Why mentoring is not coaching — 39

PART 2
BEING A MENTOR — 49

5. Why should you mentor other people? — 51
6. Responsibilities of a mentor — 65
7. The ingredients of an effective mentoring relationship — 77
8. How to deliver the best value — 103
9. How do you know and what should you do if the relationship is not working? — 115
10. Why do mentoring relationships go wrong? — 129

PART 3
SUPPORTING MENTORING AS AN ORGANISATION — 139

11 Who is responsible for leading the programme and who needs to support it? — 141

12 How do you identify and match mentors and mentees? — 149

13 How will you measure success? — 157

PART 4
BEING MENTORED — 165

14 Why it's never too late to be mentored — 167

15 How do you find the right mentor for you? — 173

Conclusion — 187
Index — 191

Pearson's Commitment to Diversity, Equity and Inclusion

Pearson is dedicated to creating bias-free content that reflects the diversity, depth and breadth of all learners' lived experiences. We embrace the many dimensions of diversity including, but not limited to, race, ethnicity, gender, sex, sexual orientation, socioeconomic status, ability, age and religious or political beliefs.

Education is a powerful force for equity and change in our world. It has the potential to deliver opportunities that improve lives and enable economic mobility. As we work with authors to create content for every product and service, we acknowledge our responsibility to demonstrate inclusivity and incorporate diverse scholarship so that everyone can achieve their potential through learning. As the world's leading learning company, we have a duty to help drive change and live up to our purpose to help more people create a better life for themselves and to create a better world.

Our ambition is to purposefully contribute to a world where:

- Everyone has an equitable and lifelong opportunity to succeed through learning.
- Our educational products and services are inclusive and represent the rich diversity of learners.
- Our educational content accurately reflects the histories and lived experiences of the learners we serve.
- Our educational content prompts deeper discussions with students and motivates them to expand their own learning and worldview.

We are also committed to providing products that are fully accessible to all learners. As per Pearson's guidelines for accessible educational Web media, we test and retest the capabilities of our products against the highest standards for every release, following the WCAG guidelines in developing new products for copyright year 2022 and beyond. You can learn more about Pearson's commitment to accessibility at:

https://www.pearson.com/us/accessibility.html

While we work hard to present unbiased, fully accessible content, we want to hear from you about any concerns or needs regarding this Pearson product so that we can investigate and address them.

- Please contact us with concerns about any potential bias at: https://www.pearson.com/report-bias.html
- For accessibility-related issues, such as using assistive technology with Pearson products, alternative text requests or accessibility documentation, email the Pearson Disability Support team at: disability.support@pearson.com

ABOUT THE AUTHORS

A specialist in professional relationships and networking for 25 years, **Andy Lopata** was called "one of Europe's leading business networking strategists" by the *Financial Times* and "a true master of networking" by the *Independent* and **Forbes.com**.

A very experienced international speaker and podcast host, this is Andy's sixth book. In addition, he has been quoted in a number of other business books and regularly quoted in the international press and writes a regular blog for Psychology Today.

Andy is a former President of the Fellows Community, a two-time Board Member of the Professional Speaking Association UK & Ireland (PSA) and a Fellow of the Learning and Performance Institute as well as a Member of the Meetings Industry Association and Association of Business Mentors. He is also one of just 32 recipients of the PSA's top honour, the 'Award of Excellence'. To learn more about his work, visit **www.andylopata.com**

Dr Ruth Gotian is the Chief Learning Officer and Associate Professor of Education in Anaesthesiology and former founding Assistant Dean of Mentoring and Executive Director of the Mentoring Academy at Weill Cornell Medicine. She has been hailed by the journals *Nature* and the *Wall Street Journal*, as well as Columbia University, as an expert in mentorship and leadership development and was recently recognised as one of the top 20 mentors in the world by the International Federation of Learning and Development.

In 2021, Thinkers50, dubbed the Oscars of management thinking, ranked her the #1 emerging management thinker in the world, describing her as a "prolific mentor and educator, leading important research into the secrets of success." In 2023, LinkedIn named her a top voice in mentoring. She was also a semi-finalist for the *Forbes* 50 Over 50 list. In addition to publishing in top academic journals, she is a contributor to *Harvard Business Review, Forbes* and *Psychology Today*. As a social-scientist, her research is about the mindset and skillset of peak performers, including Nobel Prize winners, astronauts and Olympic champions, which she writes about in her best-selling book, *The Success Factor*. To learn more about her work, visit **www.ruthgotian.com**

AUTHORS' ACKNOWLEDGEMENTS

In the journey from vision to execution, we were far from alone. We begin by expressing our gratitude to our mentors, both formal and informal, whose guidance has been invaluable.

Andy extends his heartfelt thanks to Tim Farazmand, Alan Stevens, Paul McGee, Charlie Whyman, Kathie O'Donoghue, Barbara Thompson and Christine Clacey and his many trusted advisors, many of whom are members of the Professional Speaking Association and its international counterparts.

Ruth is deeply grateful to her team of mentors, especially Drs Marie Volpe, Bert Shapiro, and Marshall Goldsmith, who encouraged her to always explore less-travelled paths. She's also indebted to her incredible colleagues at Weill Cornell Medicine, especially Drs Hugh Hemmings and Kane Pryor, for their unwavering support as well as the Women's Mentoring Circle. To all her high-achieving friends, your support when she needed it most means the world.

We have also had great support from the mentoring community, many of who reviewed an early version of this book and offered profound insights, including Georgina Waite and Simon Fordham from The Association of Business Mentors (ABM), the ABM's Founder Kerrie Dorman, Chelsey Baker, Founder of National Mentoring Day, Dr Deborah Heiser, Co-founder and CEO of The Mentor Project, Max Fellows and Melissa Noakes from Elevate, Dr Chaveso 'Chevy' Cook, Co-founder and Executive Director of Military Mentors and Dr Christine Pfund, Director, Center for the Improvement of Mentored Experiences in Research (CIMER). Your contributions and wisdom have greatly enriched our work.

Thank you to everyone who contributed to the book. Your expertise and stories really helped to bring the topic alive and help us to dive deeper into such an important topic. Sadly, space dictated that we couldn't include everybody's insights, but be on the lookout for articles and videos with their nuggets of wisdom and profound experiences.

AUTHORS' ACKNOWLEDGEMENTS

When word got out about our book, we were humbled by the generosity of people who opened their networks to us. Special thanks to Robert Kenward, Margaret Heffernan, Des Dearlove, Stuart Crainer and many others who offered encouragement, partnerships, stories and wise counsel.

It has been a pleasure working with Pearson and FT Prentice Hall, the second time for Andy and the first for Ruth. Thank you to Eloise Cook for being there for us from the very beginning of the project, helping us to craft a book that we hope is a fitting addition to the excellent *Financial Times* series, and giving valuable advice and guidance throughout. Thanks also to the rest of the FT team, Yashmeena, Priya, and Amer, for your input and support and to Mick Lowe for his help with the graphics.

This has been a project lasting the best part of two years with support and friendship from more people than we can count. We know we run the risk of inadvertently omitting people, and the guilt is there, but know that we value every ounce of guidance you have offered us along the way, and we apologise for any omissions.

Andy would like to add his thanks to Claire and Sara Beth for their support and patience throughout this process, arranging interviews and calls and creating the space for Andy to devote the time needed to this project.

Ruth would like to give an extra special shout-out to Amnon, Benjamin, Jonathan and Eitan, her pillars of strength, the ones who always believe that impossible simply means I'm possible. Anything can be done with the focus and vision needed (and tech support, offered by her in-house IT squad, and ample amounts of coffee). Of all the high achievers she's interviewed, her family are those who inspire her the most, each and every day. Thank you for the time, quiet, encouragement, laughter, joy and funny text messages. To her brothers, Ron and Daniel, thank you for your patience. To her mother, Dina z"l, who was with us until we were halfway through this project. Ruth's wish is that her mother and father (Arthur z"l) could have seen the final masterpiece.

Finally, co-authoring a book is not a straightforward venture. You may think that it halves the workload, but it doesn't quite present itself like that! Andy last co-authored a book in 2006 and, while Ruth has co-authored academic papers and co-edited a textbook, this is her first co-authored book. Add the cultural and language differences (Andy writes in British English while Ruth writes in American English), and it becomes a continuous learning experiment. We entered into this project with confidence that we had the chemistry and complementary styles to make the partnership work well, but not necessarily the certainty that it would be an easy journey. We based it on trust.

It has, in fact, been a very enjoyable and rewarding experience. Believe it or not, we had never met in person until November last year, after this book had been submitted to our editors. Yet we found a way to collaborate and support each other, across multiple time zones. As we have mentioned in the book, while we broadly share the same views on and approach to mentoring, we don't always agree. Where our opinions clashed, we discussed and accommodated each other's views in a way that we hope enriched the text. At no point did disagreement turn into an argument. In fact, we feel the difference of opinion made us look deeper into a subject, peeling away assumptions that blocked our full vision of an idea and topic. The civil discourse made for a more robust book while enhancing our thinking about the topic.

Andy and Ruth express their gratitude to each other for this remarkable journey. We hope the final product reflects the power of collaboration, but the judgement is yours to make.

PUBLISHER'S ACKNOWLEDGEMENTS

Text credits

26 Nicole Stott: Quoted by Nicole Stott; 26 Jay Honeycutt: Quoted by Jay Honeycutt; 38 Andy Homer: Quoted by Andy Homer; 4 Simon Fordham: Quoted by Simon Fordham; 9 Melissa Mensah: Quoted by Melissa Mensah; 11 John Wiley & Sons: Faucett, E.A., Brenner, M.J., Thompson, D.M. and Flanary V.A. (2022). "Tackling the minority tax: a roadmap to redistributing engagement in diversity, equity, and inclusion initiatives." Otolaryngology–Head and Neck Surgery 166(6):1174–1181. doi:10.1177/01945998221091696.; 12 Dr. Heather Melville: Quoted by Dr. Heather Melville, OBE, Chancellor of The University of York; 15 Zaza Pachulia: Quoted by Zaza Pachulia; 18 Luca Signoretti: Quoted by Luca Signoretti; 24–25 Patrice Gordon: Quoted by Patrice Gordon; 28 Academy of Management: Ragins, B. R. and J. S. Miller (2000). "Marginal Mentoring: The Effects of Type of Mentor, Quality of Relationship, and Program Design on Work and Career Attitudes." The Academy of Management Journal 43(6).; 31 Flatiron Books: Syed, M. (2021). Rebel Ideas. New York, NY, Flatiron Books.; 36 Margaret Heffernan: Quoted by Margaret Heffernan; 39 John C. Crosby: Quoted by John C. Crosby; 41 Anonymous Proverb: Anonymous Proverb; 44 Simon Fordham: Quoted by Simon Fordham; 45–46 LaTonya Kilpatrick-Liverman: Quoted by LaTonya Kilpatrick-Liverman; 47 Francesca Lagerberg: Quoted by Francesca Lagerberg; 47 Francesca Lagerberg: Quoted by Francesca Lagerberg; 51 Shonali Devereaux: Quoted by Shonali Devereaux; 53 Caroline Flanagan: Quoted by Caroline Flanagan; 54 Caroline Flanagan: Caroline Flanagan; 53–54 Caroline Flanagan: Quoted by Caroline Flanagan; 56–57 Nicholas Davies: Quoted by Nicholas Davies; 59 Matthew Lewis: Quoted by Matthew Lewis; 60 Vanessa Vallely OBE: Quoted by Vanessa Vallely OBE; 61 Lord David Young.: Quoted by Lord David Young.; 61 Chelsey Baker: Quoted by Chelsey Baker; 62 Springer: Woolston, C. (2019). "A message for mentors from dissatisfied graduate students." Nature 575(7783):551–552. doi: 10.1038/d41586-019-03535-y. PMID: 31748721.; 80 Emerald Publishing Limited: Ployhart R. E., Bliese P. D. (2006).

Individual adaptability (I-ADAPT) theory: conceptualizing the antecedents, consequences, and measurement of individual differences in adaptability, in Understanding Adaptability: A Prerequisite for Effective Performance Within Complex Environments, Vol. 6, eds Burke C. S., Pierce L. G., Salas E. (St. Louis, MO: Elsevier Science;), 3–39; 82 Luca Signoretti: Quoted by Luca Signoretti; 83 Megan Reitz: Quoted by Megan Reitz; 84 Megan Reitz: Reitz Megan, "How your power silences truth", Tedx Hult Ashridge; 85 Alison Wood Brooks: Quoted by Alison Wood Brooks; 85 Panoma Press: Lopata, Andy. (2020) Just Ask: Why Seeking Support is your Greatest Strength'. Panoma Press; 86–87 Vanessa Hall: Quoted by Vanessa Hall; 87–88 Lindsey Pollak: Quoted by Lindsey Pollak; 89–90 Samantha Hiew: Quoted by Samantha Hiew; 89 Samantha Hiew: Samantha Hiew: ADHD girls; 91 Simon & Schuster: Carnegie, Dale (1936) How to Win Friends and Influence People. Simon & Schuster; 91 Bob Lefkowitz: Quoted by Bob Lefkowitz; 92 Pegasus Books: Robert Lefkowitz, Randy Hall (2021) A Funny Thing Happened on the Way to Stockholm, Pegasus Books; 93 The Times: Syed, M. (2017). "Why leaders must be encouraged to speak their mind." The Times, 27 September.; 105 Pegasus Books: Lefkowitz, Robert and Hall, Randy. A Funny Thing Happened on the Way to Stockholm. Pegasus Books.; 106 Simon and Schuster: Covey, S. R. (1989). The seven habits of highly effective people: restoring the character ethic. New York, Simon and Schuster.; 106 Evergreen podcasts: Landherr, Daniela (2023) "Fail Fast, Learn Fast", The Connected Leadership Podcast.; 108 Bob Lefkowitz: Quoted by Bob Lefkowitz; 110 Forbes Media LLC: Gotian, R. (2023). "Agility in basketball: An interview with 2x NBA champion Zaza Pachulia." Forbes; 110 Roberto Forzoni: Quoted by Roberto Forzoni; 111 Bleacher Report: Bleacher Report (2023). "Giannis calls out reporter in heated response: 'There's no failure in sports.'." from https://www.youtube.com/watch?v=n2QCiJC06y4; 115 Kluwer Academic Publishers.: Tiberius Richard, Sinal Joanne, Flack Edred, (January 2002) 'The Role of Teacher-Learner Relationship in Medical Education'. International Handbook of Research in Medical Education; 118 Yes Magazine: Adapted from Drago-Severson, E., Leading Adult Learning; Supporting Adult Development in our Schools. Thousand Oaks: Corwin/Sage Publications, (2010). www.yesmagazine.org/51facts for additional citations; 146 Max Fellows: Quoted by Max Fellows; 146 Mel Noakes: Quoted by Mel Noakes; 154 Peter Brown: Quoted by Peter Brown; 167 Annetta Marion: Quoted by Annetta Marion; 169 Andy: Quoted by Andy; 170 Brian Chernett: Quoted by Brian Chernett; 175 Miranda Brawn: Quoted by Miranda Brawn; 107 John Wiley & Sons, Inc: Brookfield, S. and S. Preskill (2005). Discussion as a Way of Teaching. San Francisco, CA, Jossey-Bass.

Image credits

COV Alamy Images: Peter Steiner/Alamy Stock Photo; 16 Lee Allison Photography: Lee Allison Photography; 11 Chelsey Baker: Chelsey Baker; 44 The Association of Business Mentors: ABM/Nicholson 2021; 101 Shutterstock: nikiteev_konstantin/Shutterstock; 189 The Association of Business Mentors: The Association of Business Mentors.

FOREWORD

When I became the head coach of the Golden State Warriors in 2014, I began a job that I had never done before. I had played basketball professionally for 15 years in the NBA, but other than two seasons at the helm of the San Diego Wildcats – my son's 7th- and 8th-grade club basketball team – I had never coached a team. For many years, I had known I *wanted* to become a coach, but I didn't know how or where to start. So I spent time preparing for a potential opportunity. I sought out advice. I visited with coaches from different sports, observing practices, reading books and trying to put together a coherent plan for a job I hoped might materialise.

One of the coaches I visited was Pete Carroll. Coach Carroll had been a hugely successful football coach at both the collegiate and professional levels for decades, and though I had never met him, I had admired him from afar. A mutual friend connected us, and just a month or so before my first practice with the Warriors, I headed to Seattle to watch Pete at work with his team, the Seahawks. I sat in on meetings, watched practices and visited with players. It was exhilarating witnessing the passion, energy and cohesion of the coaches and players. I was thrilled to be in Seattle getting a bird's eye view of the defending Super Bowl champions, and their head coach was giving me the red carpet treatment. It was amazing! After a couple of days, Pete called me into his office. "How are you gonna coach your team?" he asked. I responded, "You mean like what offense are we going to run?" He said, "No, that stuff doesn't matter. How are you gonna COACH your team?"

I realised then that I had no idea what I was doing. And that I'd better figure it out in a hurry! I had lots of plans and ideas in my head about offensive sets, defensive schemes and practice drills, but I couldn't answer Pete's basic question – how was I going to coach my team?

Over the next couple of days, Pete told me his entire story how he had gone from a college football player to a young coach, to working his way up the ranks to eventually coaching in college and the NFL. He told me that despite coaching for decades, it had taken him a long time to figure out what coaching was really about – not the Xs and O's, but the culture that takes shape under a coach's influence. We talked about values and how leadership is really about instilling and displaying personal values that your team *feels* every day when they walk into the gym and the locker room. And that those values represent authenticity and help guide a team through success and adversity. In a few short days, Pete shared his DECADES of experience with me to help me prepare for my first coaching job, all while he was preparing for his own daunting job of trying to win another championship. I was blown away. Pete had become my mentor, whether he knew it or not!

Nearly a decade has passed, and led by Steph Curry, the Warriors have won four NBA championships, featuring a values-based culture of joy and competition that has defined the team but was originally spawned by someone who took the time to be a mentor. Pete and I have stayed close, visiting each other's teams, chatting, texting and even hosting a podcast together during the pandemic. But for me, he will always be the man who mentored me at a time when it was desperately needed. I needed his help, and he offered up decades of experience to help me get my coaching career off the ground. His wisdom and advice are on my mind all the time as I coach the Warriors. The values we share as a team are the guiding principles in our culture. They have helped me to make sound decisions and avoid serious pitfalls over the course of our team's run. And now that I have enjoyed a measure of success as a coach, I am frequently approached for advice myself. I try to pay it forward by offering mentoring to people who ask. The more wisdom we can share with each other, the more people are impacted in a positive way, the better society becomes. That's why mentoring is so important.

And that's also why I recommend this book. Dr Ruth Gotian and Andy Lopata have written a book about mentoring that shows how powerful a force it is. For those who want to succeed, a mentor is a pivotal member of your team. But there's no reason to stop there; you can help someone else by paying it forward and becoming a mentor yourself. Dr Gotian and Lopata have prepared the perfect playbook to bring this idea to life. Underscored by research and insights from top thought leaders, this book utilises scripts, templates and best practices to help you elevate your mentoring journey. As someone who considers learning a lifelong quest, I highly recommend this book. Enjoy.

Steve Kerr
Head Coach, Golden State Warriors & Olympic Team USA

PREFACE

Nicole Stott earned her pilot's licence before graduating from high school. She was itching to fly again by the time she graduated from college. Armed with an engineering degree, Nicole applied to the National Aeronautics and Space Administration, commonly referred to as NASA.

Nicole worked at NASA's Kennedy Space Center for nearly a decade, watching the astronauts come in regularly. She quickly realised that most of what the astronauts do is on Earth, not in Space, and some of them were engineers, just like her.

Could she? Should she? The idea of becoming an astronaut took hold in her mind, but she often dismissed it. "That's what other special people get to do," she said. No one told her she couldn't do it. It was a false narrative she was telling herself.

Jay Honeycutt, the former director of NASA's Kennedy Space Center, took Nicole under his wings. "Pick up the pen and fill out the application," he told her. He didn't tell her how difficult it would be or that the chances of acceptance were slim. He focused on having her control what she could control, which, in this case, was filling out the application to become a NASA astronaut. She couldn't be an astronaut if she didn't take the first step of applying.

Like many who apply, Nicole was not accepted to become an astronaut on her first try, and her mentor pushed her to reapply. "Here's how we can, not why we can't," exclaimed Jay Honeycutt. Having affirmation from someone she respected was pivotal in this process.

Ultimately, Nicole was accepted and spent 104 days in space on two missions. She was the tenth woman to perform a spacewalk, the first astronaut to operate the space station's robotic arm to capture a free-flying cargo spacecraft and, as a personal highlight, was the first astronaut-artist to paint with watercolours in Space. Later, after retiring from NASA, she appeared in a Super Bowl commercial for Girls Who Code, and discovered her next mission in life as a founder of the Space for Art Foundation. She didn't just become an astronaut; she became a role model for an entire generation of future engineers.

Nicole Stott would never have applied to be an astronaut if it was not for her mentor, Jay Honeycutt. Decades after he first encouraged her to fill out the application to become an astronaut, Nicole and Jay are still great friends. His message of "Here's how we can, not why we can't" sits on an engraved sign on her desk.

INTRODUCTION

What you can expect from *The Financial Times Guide to Mentoring*

Who this book is for

Mentoring is for everyone. From school students who need additional help with their studies, through young adults finding their way in life, to participants in their company's 'Rising Leaders' programme and beyond – all the way up to the C-Suite. As we discuss later, everybody stands to benefit from the guidance, insights and support of those who have expertise and experience to share.

When writing *The Financial Times Guide to Mentoring*, we have had two particular audiences in mind: more senior leaders with the opportunity to mentor others and those who are responsible for introducing and successfully implementing mentoring programmes within organisations.

This doesn't mean, of course, that anyone who has an interest in mentoring or being mentored can't find something to support them within these pages. Much of the information we share should help you on your journey. We should also stress that we don't only see senior leaders in organisations as potential mentors. Anyone has the potential to mentor others, as we will discuss.

We do have a focus on mentoring within organisations but also share examples and stories from small business owners. Mentoring is an important part of a career journey whether you work for a multinational giant, you're in public service or work for yourself. Other than where we focus on the challenges inherent within institutional settings, much of the advice we offer is fully applicable to different environments.

We would encourage you to read the book with your own situation in mind and apply the ideas as they are relevant to you.

How the book is organised

The book is divided into four clear sections:

Part 1: The case for mentoring
We outline why we think mentoring is so important and distinguish between different types of mentoring and between mentoring and other business support.

Part 2: Being a mentor
This forms a large part of the book, partly to avoid too much duplication later on. We explore why you should mentor other people, the responsibilities of mentors and the ingredients of an effective mentoring relationship.

We also look at how you can deliver the best value as a mentor, as well as why things don't always go according to plan, how to respond when they don't and how to recognise when it's the right time to move on.

Part 3: Supporting mentoring as an organisation
Predominantly written for people who are responsible for running mentoring programmes within organisations, this is also an important section for senior management teams who might not deal with the logistics but whose support is essential.

In this section we discuss where responsibility for running a programme lies, how to match mentors and mentees effectively and how to measure success.

Part 4: Being mentored
Good mentors get mentored, we don't believe it's a choice between one or the other. Much of the advice we give in Part 2 will help you get the most out of the relationships where you are the mentee. In Part 4 we add to the discussion with a look at how to approach being mentored and how to find the right mentor for you.

Our approach to writing *The Financial Times Guide to Mentoring*

In writing this book, we wanted to strike the right balance between an academic text and a business book that is enjoyable, practical and easy to read. We have sought to back up our own insights with those of other experts we have interviewed, together with reference to rigorous research conducted in the field.

The two of us share years of experience and expertise as mentors, as mentees and as people who have written and presented on the topic globally. We've added to that mix Ruth's academic discipline as an Associate Professor, Chief Learning Officer and former founding Assistant Dean of Mentoring at an Ivy League medical school, and stories and insights from experts in the field, experienced mentors and people who have felt the impact of mentoring on their professional lives.

We've also been grateful for the support of other experienced mentors and experts on the topic from our networks who have reviewed the text and provided pointers on how to make sure this book is as comprehensive as possible.

Ultimately, mentoring is not an exact science. There are different approaches and schools of thought. Even as co-authors, we have found areas of disagreement on the 'right' approach, maybe because there isn't necessarily a right or wrong. We present best practice as we see it and we hope to inspire you through our ideas to try new things, to focus more on your mentoring and to help you to make a bigger impact on your own career and those of the people around you.

Research has repeatedly shown that adults take in and process information differently. To ensure a comprehensive and dynamic learning experience for you, we've gone beyond the traditional text-based teaching method. In addition to the content within the book's pages, you will find a wealth of supplementary resources that are designed to fortify your learning process. These include worksheets, questionnaires, case studies, user-friendly step-by-step guides presented, curated resource lists, interactive activities and indispensable checklists. With this multifaceted approached, we hope to actively engage and empower you on your mentoring journey. But that's not all.

In a few places we use the abbreviation LGBT+. We are aware that there are a number of different formats used to recognise this community. We have taken advice from our connections in this community and have settled on this as a globally recognised and inclusive format.

At the end of the book, we share an assessment we have created to help you measure the current state of your mentoring relationships, whether as a mentor or mentee. We have shared this as a tool at the end as we feel that you might like to understand our suggested approach to mentoring first. But if you plan to apply lessons as you go, you might like to skip forward and take the assessment before you start reading and then revisit it once you have had a chance to apply your learnings, to see how much your relationships have improved.

Whichever approach you choose, happy mentoring!

Andy and Ruth

Why we wrote *The Financial Times Guide to Mentoring*

The power of mentoring

The term 'mentor' has been with us since ancient times; it has its earliest origins in Greek Mythology, in Homer's *Odyssey*. When Odysseus went to fight in the Trojan War, he entrusted his son, Telemachus, to Mentor (who was really the goddess Athena in disguise) to teach him skills, protect him and guide him during his father's absence. The role of mentors has long been valued and respected but, in more modern times, it is increasingly recognised as a powerful tool for talent acquisition, retention and development, personal career success and problem solving; a perception that is borne out by much research, as we will share.

That doesn't mean, however, that everyone believes in the power of mentoring or that its qualities are fully understood and leveraged.

Delivering and receiving impactful mentoring is often an enigma. We know it when we see it, but often don't know how to deliver or receive it effectively. As Nicole Stott's story shows us, the right mentor can ensure that your career goes stratospheric; beyond what you thought, or gave yourself permission to believe was possible. But how many individuals get or take the opportunity to benefit from the potential that a great mentor can offer?

Over the course of this book we will be showcasing just why mentoring is so powerful, for mentees, for the organisation they serve and, in fact, for the person mentoring them. We will explore the fundamental ingredients of a successful mentoring relationship, what makes those relationships tick and what can make them implode; we'll look at the importance of mentoring for an organisation and the role the organisational culture plays in making that impact; and we look at why it's vital to continue being mentored, even when you mentor others.

According to research from Olivet Nazarene University, 76% of people understand the importance of mentoring but only 37% actually have a mentor.[1] We will explore ways to close this gap.

---

[1] Olivet Nazarene University (2020). "Study explores professional mentor – mentee relationships in 2019."

The authors of this book believe that there are a number of challenges to overcome to ensure that we can see mentoring take its rightful place at the heart of academia, government, commerce, third sector and elsewhere. Mentors, mentees and organisations all stand to benefit from a more considered approach to the practice, as do the wider societies in which we live.

This book is predominantly written for leaders who have the opportunity to mentor others and who want to make the most of that opportunity. Not to just tick the box of a regular meeting but to make a real impact on those individuals' lives and to inspire them to greater achievements. This book seeks to transform mentoring from something that is nice to have, to something you must have. And if you are going to do it, you might as well try to maximise your impact.

But it's not just about leaders imparting their wisdom. Everybody has the potential to be both a mentor and a mentee, whatever their experience. Young people at the early stages of their careers can guide wizened leaders through generational shifts, increased focus on sustainability and the digital world, while even those at the very top need somebody to confide in, to bounce ideas off and for further guidance. Mentoring becomes that fertile ground to deepen understanding and relationships while fighting off isolation.

We will be exploring the different models of, and approaches to, mentoring, giving you a choice of the format and approach that will best suit you and your needs.

We want you, as a reader of this book, to gain insights on how to learn and develop more as a mentee as well as how to be a more effective mentor. In the meantime, if you are an organisational leader, Human Resources (HR) professional or volunteer for an employee resource group, you will be able to gain valuable guidance on creating a much more impactful mentoring environment in your organisation, with greater visibility, uptake and more demonstrable results.

Why isn't mentoring achieving its potential?

So why isn't mentoring taking its rightful place at the heart of our talent development programmes and company cultures right now? Here are some of the challenges that we see getting in the way of a more effective approach to mentoring, some of which are specific to different groups while others are universal.

Universal challenges

Universal challenge 1 – How to ensure your mentoring relationships are focused

In his book and TEDx talk, Simon Sinek famously talked about the importance of Starting with 'Why'[2,3] and the answer to so many areas of underperformance can be the lack of clarity of a desired outcome. For organisations, mentors and mentees, failing to truly understand the ideal outcome of a mentoring relationship will lead to dissatisfaction on all parts.

We know mentoring is important, so many people talk about the impact of mentors on their careers and encourage others to find a good mentor. Inspired by such stories, ambitious and driven staff will seek out a mentor, leaders will agree to play the role and HR departments will put a programme in place. There needs to be an open and honest conversation first though and it's not happening often enough.[4,5,6]

Many of the issues with mentoring programmes can be traced to this lack of clarity about the desired outcome. Mentees find themselves paired with the wrong mentor, who may lack the experience or expertise they need and who doesn't ask the right questions, simply because nobody has had the conversation. People don't know how to measure whether the mentoring relationship is on track to be successful because of the failure to identify and articulate what success will look like.

Similarly, at an organisational level, a lack of focus on what a mentoring programme is designed to achieve will inhibit attempts to attract both mentors and mentees. The most successful mentoring programmes are generally geared toward future leader programmes because there is a clear outcome in mind and everybody knows what they are trying to achieve.

Mentoring opportunities should not, however, be restricted just to those who manage to get onto such fast-track initiatives. That process is filled with a bias

---

[2] Sinek, S. (2009). "How great leaders inspire action," TEDxPugetSound, Puget Sound, WA, 18 September https://www.ted.com/talks/simon_sinek_how_great_leaders_inspire_action?language=en
[3] Sinek, S. (2009). *Start with Why: How Great Leaders Inspire Everyone to Take Action* New York, Portfolio.
[4] Johnson, W. B. (2002). "The intentional mentor: Strategies and guidelines for the practice of mentoring." *Professional Psychology Research and Practice* 33: 88–96.
[5] Johnson, W. B. (2003). "A framework for conceptualizing competence to mentor." *Ethics and Behavior* 13: 127–151.
[6] Allen, T. D., et al. (2009). *Designing Workplace Mentoring Programs: An Evidence-based Approach*. New York, Wiley-Blackwell.

toward those who already benefit from having access to good education and support networks. The number of people who can participate in typically very select programmes is simply too small. A failure to make mentoring more widely available means that a lot of potential talent will either not be identified or will drift off to other organisations where they feel better valued.

Universal challenge 2 – Coping with time management issues

A lack of clarity about what success looks like naturally leads to the next challenge – time. A perceived lack of time can often be found as the main challenge, or excuse, for any work activity that is not deemed as core to the relevant person's job description. And mentoring is no exception.

Most of us are busy at work; as shared in the book, *The Success Factor*,[7] the more successful or ambitious you are, the less control you have over your calendar. You might feel unsure about asking somebody with too much time on their hands to mentor you – the perception, rightly or wrongly, being that they are not successful enough to give you the boost you need.

Everybody has the same number of hours available to them and successful people find time both to mentor others and to seek support for themselves. In fact, they make it a priority. And this is where it is linked to a lack of focus. If you know *why* you are mentoring, being mentored or running a mentoring programme and you understand the impact of a successful mentoring programme on you or those around you, then you will find it much easier to prioritise and make the time you need to achieve those objectives.

If mentoring sessions are important to both key parties (mentor and mentee) and there genuinely isn't time in the working day to fit it in, then – with an eye on the impact of the outcome – reimagine what that time well spent might look like.

For more junior people in the organisation, prioritisation isn't solely down to them. This is where the organisational culture is so important. If the organisation values mentoring throughout its DNA, then line managers and colleagues will support and value team members who take time away from their responsibilities for a mentoring session.

On the other hand, if mentoring is left to the individual or is only made available to a select few, colleagues will resent the time taken for mentoring and

---

7   Gotian, R. (2022). *The Success Factor: Developing the Mindset and Skillset for Peak Business Performance*. Kogan Page.

it will be harder to justify. If mentoring is not embedded into the company culture, it will create a divide between the haves and have-nots. When it is a natural part of the week, it is more likely to get done, and done well.

Universal challenge 3 – Matchmaking is unfocused

The third challenge that impacts all groups is the process used to match mentors and mentees. Mentors want to work with mentees who respect and value them, whom they can believe in, feel they can inspire and who are well-placed to benefit from their experience. Mentees want someone who understands and listens to them, has the expertise most suited to their needs and whose advice they can trust.

Yet too many internal programmes leave the matching process to chance. Many approaches are unscientific, with matches based on who is available, selected by looking for something that resonates in biographies on a webpage, people paired because of random shared interest or partnered at a 'speed mentoring' event where they get a couple of minutes to meet each other before moving on to the next person and making a choice.

In the worst cases, which sadly are all too common, there's little follow-up beyond these half-hearted attempts to match pairs. Mentors and mentees are rarely offered training showing them how to make the most of the relationship and there's insufficient follow-up to see how the programme is progressing or key metrics examined to determine success. In the minority of cases where there is follow-up, the mentoring meetings become transactional, checking off items on a checklist.

Challenges faced by mentors

Beyond the challenges discussed above, mentors face a number of challenges of their own if the relationship is to be successful.

Mentors' challenge 1 – How to inspire mentees

A good mentor is never satisfied sharing advice, sitting back and considering the job to be done. They want to see their mentee full of renewed energy, curiosity and enthusiasm for the task ahead, itching to take action and reporting back on successful progress. A positive mentoring relationship is marked by reviewing genuine progress since the last conversation and discussing next steps, rather than going back over old ground because no action has been taken.

The challenges listed above, however, such as pressures on time and a lack of clarity of outcome, can lead to a lack of progress between sessions and dwindling enthusiasm for the process from both participants.

In a perfect world, mentoring meetings should be charged with energy, although the levels of energy should match the personality styles of the participants. The mentee should welcome challenge and be ready to respond with creative ideas or well-considered justification. Mentors should be hearing enthusiastic reports of progress, ideally not just in those meetings but on a regular basis between sessions as well.

That's the ideal. The challenge for mentors is to build a strong enough relationship with their mentees to ensure that it happens.

Mentors' challenge 2 – How to navigate conflict

The course of mentoring relationships does not always run smooth. There are a number of potential clashes with mentees that a mentor may need to navigate, some of which are beyond their control but others they definitely will be able to address.

In their *Journal of the American Medical Association (JAMA)* article,[8] Drs Vineet Chopra, Dana Edelson and Sanjay Saint outline the passive and active practices that lead to anxiety-riddled mentorship. Ranging from the mentor who is too busy to meet to the one who blocks a mentee from collaborating with others, these toxic mentoring patterns can leave deep scars and disjointed careers.

Learning how to avoid these toxic behaviours is critical for positive mentorship and the organisation's health. Teaching mentees how to counteract these poor behaviours is equally important.

It is important to avoid, or at least acknowledge, conflicts of interest in mentoring relationships. Many people initially consider their line managers as possible mentors, but we strongly recommend[9] that mentors within an organisation should be outside the direct line of management. Mentors need

---

[8] Chopra, V., Edelson, D.P. and Saint, S. (2016). "A PIECE OF MY MIND. Mentorship malpractice." *JAMA* **315**(14): 1453–1454. doi: 10.1001/jama.2015.18884. PMID: 27115263.

[9] Gotian, R. (2020). "Why your boss shouldn't be your mentor." *Forbes*. **https://www.forbes.com/sites/ruthgotian/2020/10/16/why-your-boss-shouldnt-be-your-mentor/** Accessed 15 November 2023.

to be able to take an objective view of challenges and mentees' goals. It's hard to do so if you have a stake in the outcome. If you do have potential conflicts, plan for them by agreeing how you will respond before issues arise.

Mentees will not always want to follow a mentor's advice,[10] nor should they. Ultimately, it's the mentee's career that's at stake and they should be comfortable with the path they choose to take. Just because the mentor feels that something is the right choice, doesn't make it so.

A mentor needs to be comfortable and, dare we say, excited with their advice being challenged and even not taken up. As long as it's properly considered, that should be enough.

More concerning is the fear of giving inappropriate or bad advice. Mentors may hold back for a fear of being wrong. There's a fine balance between considering whether your advice is the best fit for the mentee and holding it back completely. A mentor won't be serving their mentee well if they always play it safe.

Mentors challenge 3 – Scaling your mentorship

When you become a great mentor, everyone wants your wise counsel. You have become that mentor who inspires[11] and helps their mentee reach heights they never knew existed. You have a line out your door and an overflowing inbox. At some point, it becomes unmanageable and starts to impact your work. This is especially true for women and those underrepresented in certain ranks. Everyone wants a mentor who looks like them. This is when it is time to start considering scaling your mentorship.

In addition, mentoring one-to-one can both be isolating for the mentee and mentor, and both parties are restricted to the knowledge and ideas in the room. The mentor might feel they need to have all of the answers. When a mentor is in demand, there is scope for more peer-learning, bringing new perspectives into the conversation. But this opportunity is often missed.

Scalability allows the mentor to reach more people and offer cascading mentorship, where the benefits have a ripple effect.

---

[10] Drago-Severson, E. (2009). "How do you 'know'." *Yes!*. Fall 2009. https://www.yesmagazine.org/wp-content/uploads/pdf/51/51JustTheFacts.pdf Accessed 15 November 2023.
[11] Gotian, R., et al. (2022). "Becoming an inspiring mentor." https://www.linkedin.com/learning/becoming-an-inspiring-mentor/the-business-case-for-mentoring?autoplay=true

Challenges faced by mentees

Mentees challenge 1 – Support from managers and peers

As indicated above, one of the biggest challenges facing mentees is getting support from their colleagues and line management to invest time in development through mentoring. Unless there is an organisational culture of supporting learning, they can come under pressure to prioritise task-oriented activities over and above time out for mentoring sessions and follow-up.

If a mentoring programme isn't widely available and embraced, such pressure may be insidious rather than overt but it can have the same negative effect, turning the mentee away from committing fully and enthusiastically to the process.

Mentees challenge 2 – Balancing conflicting advice and demands

A lack of a communication and alignment can also lead to conflict in advice and guidance to the mentee. While their mentor, looking from a long-term and more holistic perspective, might suggest they take one path, a line manager focusing on short-term results and targets may want to see them take a different action and prioritise elsewhere. They are unable to see or appreciate benefits which may be several steps beyond their current task.

A lack of communication between mentor and manager can confuse and demoralise the mentee, who might feel caught in the middle and dragged in different directions.

This isn't just applicable in workplace mentoring relationships. Experienced mentor Andy Homer of Merryck, firmly believes that a mentoring relationship should be strictly sacrosanct. He stressed, "The anchor point for a good mentoring relationship is trust, pure and simple. To achieve this the mentor must be completely aligned with their mentee. Multiple mentoring relationships complicate the development of the mentee. It is hard enough to build a single and effective mentoring relationship and this in itself takes time and mutuality."

During the course of the book, we are going to recommend the creation of mentoring teams, relying not on just one mentor. But Homer still has a valid point, that multiple mentoring relationships can lead to conflicting and confusing advice. This is something that you need to be able to manage.

Mentees challenge 3 – When the mentor becomes a tormentor

Often, a mentoring relationship starts off beautifully but disintegrates over time. The mentor turns into a tormentor, leaving the mentee with endless angst and self-doubt. Finding a way out of this toxic relationship requires finesse and guidance. When the mentor holds power in a relationship, this is especially difficult.[12]

As actor Tyler Perry famously reminds us,[13] some people are only meant to be in our life for a certain amount of time. Just as a space shuttle sheds its power boosters after take-off because they have fulfilled their purpose, some people need to be removed from our mentoring circle as they start to weigh us down.

Challenges faced by organisations

Organisational challenge 1 – When the mentoring programme is a best kept secret

Perhaps the most common issue we see with organisational mentoring programmes is that nobody seems to know they exist. Or they may be vaguely aware that there is one but not know how to participate or even who to talk to.

Mentoring has sadly been left on the shelf in too many organisations. It's worrying, considering the benefits and potential impact of mentoring on developing and retaining top talent. There is confusion over whose responsibility it is, programmes can be targeted solely to small groups of employees, or left to untrained volunteers to implement.

Part of the issue is that mentoring is considered a discipline apart from a general talent development programme. If mentoring becomes an accepted and expected tool within any growth intervention, effectively systemic, the confusion and mystery will disappear.

Organisational challenge 2 – Attracting good mentors

Senior leaders are busy but they are the 'Headline Artists' of any mentoring programme. If staff see the top tier of management committing fully to the mentoring scheme, they will be more enthusiastic about participating.

---

[12] Davila, J.S. and Gotian, R. (2023). "Tormentor mentors, and how to survive them." *Nature* 16 March. doi: 10.1038/d41586-023-00821-8. Epub ahead of print. PMID: 36928402.

[13] https://youtube.com/shorts/oBxoXAMBqIQ?si=dC0uAMufSGRZ0rNI

The challenge is not just attracting the right people to volunteer as mentors but encouraging them to commit to the process. Not to just paying lip service and attending a couple of meetings, but taking on the responsibility of supporting at least one mentee and sticking with them throughout the process – finding time to meet with them, showing a genuine interest in their success and using their network and knowledge to help their mentee to succeed.

Organisational challenge 3 – Confusing mentoring and coaching

Mentoring and coaching are often confused. This means that, if a coaching programme is already in place, mentoring will be dismissed as unnecessary. We will explore in this book the key differences between mentoring and coaching, as well as sponsorship and role models, and how mentors and coaches can and should co-exist in the same organisations.

Organisational challenge 4 – Making mentoring appealing

As we've touched on here and we'll explore in more detail in the next chapter, strong mentoring programmes can have a huge impact on an organisation's bottom line. Repeated studies in multiple industries historically show[14,15,16,17] that effective mentoring leads to lower staff attrition, particularly of top talent, higher internal mobility, greater productivity, greater job and career satisfaction, lower burnout and higher retention.

Yet, as we demonstrated earlier, take up is low.

At the time of writing, we have not come across post-COVID studies to look at how the changing work environment has had an impact, but we don't envisage much of a shift.

Mentoring needs to be made more attractive and the benefits sold well to both mentors, mentees and the organisation as a whole. And it's not just getting

---

[14] Eby, L.T., Allen, T.D., Evan, S.C., Ng, T. and DuBois, D. (2008). "Does mentoring matter? A multidisciplinary meta-analysis comparing mentored and non-mentored individuals." *Journal of Vocational Behavior* 72(2): 254–267.

[15] Allen, T., Eby, L., Poteet, M., Lentz, E. and Lima, L. (2004). "Career benefits associated with mentoring for protégés: A meta analysis." *Journal of Applied Psychology* 89(1): 127.

[16] Burke, R. J. (1984). "Mentors in organizations." *Group and Organizational Studies* 9: 353–372.

[17] Malmgren, R., Ottino, J. and Nunes Amaral, L. (2010). "The role of mentorship in protégé performance." *Nature* 465: 622–626. https://doi.org/10.1038/nature09040

people to sign up for mentoring programmes that's needed, but developing an understanding of what each party needs to contribute to the process to ensure that mentoring pays off, and ensuring that mentors and mentees are trained on how to be effective and inspiring in these roles.

Making mentoring appealing isn't just about promoting the benefits but educating people about how to achieve them and encouraging them along the way. That's a conversation to which we aim to contribute with this book.

PART 1
THE CASE FOR MENTORING

CHAPTER 1
WHY MENTORING IS SO IMPORTANT

Simon Fordham was introduced to George Rumball, the owner of the London City franchise of Kall Kwik, a well-known UK printing company. George was struggling with the effects of COVID on his business and, having worked with mentors and coaches in the past, was looking for some support.

Initially, George was hesitant to seek advice from Simon, as he believed that only someone with knowledge of the printing industry could truly understand his challenges; however, Simon assured him that his expertise lay in business and helping people, rather than specific industries, and that may well be what was needed. They sat down for a conversation and immediately hit it off. George was impressed by Simon's ability to understand his struggles and provide fresh insights and invited him to mentor him on an ongoing basis.

George shared more details about the challenges he was facing, which included a significant loss of customers due to COVID-19, a decrease in revenue and an overwhelming workload. Simon listened attentively and acknowledged that he didn't possess a magical solution. Instead, he offered to analyse the business, discuss aspirations and provide guidance based on his own extensive business experience.

Throughout their mentorship, Simon and George worked together to identify opportunities for improvement. They examined the business operations and its relationship with the franchisor, and addressed personnel issues. Simon challenged George to move away from doing things as they had always been done, encouraging him to explore alternative approaches and opening up his own network to introduce potential new clients, helping to rebuild his confidence.

The impact of Simon's mentorship has been profound. George experienced a shift in his mindset, transitioning from exhaustion to excitement about his business once again. Simon's guidance led to positive changes in the business, including improved website functionality, better customer relationship management and a more effective staff structure. Additionally, George began networking and collaborating with other print companies, creating new opportunities within the City of London and, at the time of writing, he was in talks to buy another business within the franchise.

Overall, Simon's involvement as a mentor allowed George to overcome the challenges posed by COVID-19 and regain his passion for the business. They tackled various aspects of the business together, ultimately leading to increased traction and success and a fourfold increase in turnover from when they began working together.

Simon stressed the key to their success lay in the trusted relationship between the two of them. He told us, "George is now in a place where he almost feels that he has me sitting on his shoulder as he goes through his working day, asking himself 'What would Simon suggest?'.

"I've helped him to grow as a person and as a leader, as well as helping him develop the business, because they're inextricably linked. The most important thing in mentoring is that they know you are sitting at their side, you don't sit opposite them. You go through their challenges with them and they're no longer alone."

George experienced the true impact mentoring can make, with Simon's expertise helping to transform his business. Yes, as we declared in the preface to this book that we believe that mentoring is often underestimated as a tool for organisational and personal development and that mentoring programmes are often delegated away or organised half-heartedly as an afterthought.[18] At the outset, it is met with great promise and enthusiasm, but quickly dwindles to barely a spark.

Mentoring is universally recognised as a pathway to success. This is perhaps why two-thirds of Fortune 500 companies have a mentoring programme.[19] The challenge is that they are often a one size fits all approach and rarely are they as effective as they could be. Reams of research underscore that for mentoring relationships to be effective, the conversations need to be contextual and intentional, focusing on specific areas of development.[20]

---

[18] DeLong, T. J., et al. (2008). "Why mentoring matters in a hypercompetitive world." *Harvard Business Review* (January 2008).
[19] Gutner, T. (2009). "Finding anchors in the storm: Mentors." *The Wall Street Journal*. New York, NY.
[20] Stoeger, H., Balestrini, D.P. and Ziegler, A. (2021). "Key issues in professionalizing mentoring practices." *Annals of the New York Academy of Science* 1483: 5–18. https://doi.org/10.1111/nyas.14537

Organisations naturally want their employees to deliver the best version of themselves, preferably while staying with that organisation for a large portion of their career. Meanwhile, ambitious and driven individuals also want to achieve the best they can, whether in their chosen field or climbing the ladder to senior leadership.

It is very hard to achieve your full potential on your own. You don't know what you don't know and can't see beyond the horizon. Knowing the key players, opportunities and landmines to avoid is pivotal to your career success. A mentor can help open those doors you never knew existed, protect you from the politics that plague every organisation and cheer you on when things did not go as planned. Other people are a key component of personal success, sharing their expertise, experience and ideas or simply encouraging the next step forward.

Mentoring relationships move that support to another level, beyond what you thought possible, making it even more accessible and, from an organisational perspective, ensuring that those who have achieved success already play an active role in pulling up others after them. When those who have achieved success can help others reach previously unattainable levels of achievement, the organisation has a healthy culture of accomplishment and collaboration. It sends a strong message when people realise that a light shone on one person does not detract from the light on everyone else.

If mentoring was more widely embraced, organisations and individuals would achieve so much more. The Olivet Nazarene study we mentioned in the introduction revealed that 76% of people recognised the importance of having a mentor, yet only 37% actually had a mentoring relationship in place.[21] As a society, we seem to place great emphasis and effort on mentoring youth, in such programmes as the Boys and Girls Clubs in the US or The Prince's Trust in the UK, but fail to carry that momentum into the workplace.

A recent view of mentoring in academic medicine showed that while medical students are heavily mentored, that effort seems to dissipate once they advance to the ranks of faculty.[22,23] There is a disconnect between the espoused and

---

[21] Olivet Nazarene University (2020). "Study explores professional mentor-mentee relationships in 2019."
[22] Sambunjak, D., Straus, S. E. and Marusić, A. (2006). "Mentoring in academic medicine: A systematic review." *JAMA* **296**: 1103–1115.
[23] Buddeberg-Fischer, B. and Herta, K.D. (2006). "Formal mentoring programmes for medical students and doctors: a review of the Medline literature." *Medical Teacher* **28**: 248–257.

enacted actions associated with mentoring. If so many people understand and believe in the power of mentorship, why do so few people have one?

The statistics don't stop there but go on to tell a compelling story about just why mentoring is so important both for organisations and individuals within them.

Mentoring by numbers

Those who are mentored out earn and outperform those who are not. They are happier in their jobs, get promoted more often and show greater loyalty to their employer. It's a win-win. The CNBC/SurveyMonkey Workplace Happiness Survey illuminates what begets loyalty to an employer.[24] This is an important study, as replacing someone can cost twice as much as their salary.[25,26] Nearly 8,000 US-based employees were studied and helping employees find a mentor was one of the top five ways recommended to improve retention. This is no surprise and the statistics tell a fascinating story. At a time when employee engagement is at an all-time low and retention of employees is at the top of everyone's mind, mentoring might be the answer to these ongoing woes.

- Ninety percent of those who are mentored are satisfied with their jobs, and more than half (57%) are 'very satisfied.'
- Those who have a mentor aren't just earning more, 79% recognise that they are well paid.
- Eighty-nine percent of those mentored feel their contributions are valued by their colleagues.
- Seventy percent of those mentored share that their company offers them excellent or good opportunities for advancement, while just 47% of those without a mentor share the same sentiment.

---

[24] Wronski, L. and Cohen, J. (2019). "CNBC/SurveyMonkey Workplace Happiness Survey" from **https://www.surveymonkey.com/curiosity/cnbc-workplace-happiness-index/**

[25] (2017). "How much does employee turnover really cost?" Retrieved 12 February 2023, from **https://www.huffpost.com/entry/how-much-does-employee-turnover-really-cost_b_587fbaf9e4b0474ad4874fb7?utm_source=link_wwwv9&utm_campaign=item_236051&utm_medium=copy**

[26] Cascio, W.F. (2006). *Managing Human Resources: Productivity, Quality of Work Life*, Profits (7th ed.). Burr Ridge, IL: Irwin/McGraw-Hill. Mitchell, T.R., Holtom, B.C. and Lee, T.W. (2001). "How to keep your best employees: developing an effective retention policy." *Academy of Management Executive* **15**, 96–108.

- More than 4 in 10 workers who do not have a mentor admit to having considered quitting their job in the last three months, while only 25% of those with a mentor felt the need to leave.
- Despite the contemporary thinking that mentors need to be assigned, the Olivet Nazarene study showed that only 14% of mentoring relationships commenced by asking someone to be their mentor. The vast majority, 61% of mentoring relationships, developed organically.

A case study at Sun Microsystems[27] revealed other interesting insights, namely that mentoring programmes positively impact both the mentees and mentors.

- Employees who actively engaged in the mentoring programme were five times more likely to advance in pay grade, and the mentors six times more.
- Retention rates for mentored employees was 72%, while those who were not mentored had a paltry 49% retention rate. The programme benefited the mentors as well who achieved a 69% retention rate.

Mentoring has a powerful impact on diversity, even greater than traditional Diversity, Equity and Inclusion (DEI) programmes. A study out of Cornell University found that mentoring programmes improved minority representation at the management level by 9%–24%, compared to 2%–18% with other diversity initiatives.[28]

The broader benefits of mentoring

Creating a culture that elevates and embraces mentoring is not just a win for individuals and the organisations they serve, but for wider society too. The numbers shared above show the positive impact that mentoring relationships can have, and it doesn't take a vivid imagination to see how those benefits can extend further afield.

---

[27] https://knowledge.wharton.upenn.edu/podcast/knowledge-at-wharton-podcast/workplace-loyalties-change-but-the-value-of-mentoring-doesnt/

[28] Conboy, K. and Chris, K. (2016). "What evidence is there that mentoring works to retain and promote employees, especially diverse employees, within a single company?", Cornell University, School of Industrial and Labor Relations. Retrieved on 12 February 2023. https://hdl.handle.net/1813/74541

Mentoring should not just be for a select few. Broadening its scope and appeal can lead to an upskilling of a large portion of the workforce. New talent can be identified, which might otherwise have been missed, and individuals can be encouraged to take risks and try new things which will lead them along paths that might otherwise have passed them by. Astronaut Nicole Stott's story in the preface is a great example of this.

That new talent can come from all parts of society, creating greater social mobility. As we will see throughout this book, mentoring programmes play a key role in DEI initiatives,[29] and mentoring can be targeted to break privilege and knock down overt and covert barriers by extending a helping hand to sections of society that have traditionally been overlooked.

As a society brings through new talent and casts the net for that talent across a wider pool, the benefits can be felt in innovation and creativity. Bringing new perspectives and backgrounds into sectors like technology, manufacturing, government and academia can breathe fresh new ideas into key discussions and lead to new solutions.

This combination of greater social mobility, a wider talent pool and fresh innovation can only impact the bottom line positively. As organisations grow, innovations take root and new businesses are formed, GDP will naturally grow, benefitting society as a whole.[30]

Who is mentoring for?

When she was at university and starting to look at possible careers, Melissa Mensah identified a career in PR as the most likely way forward for her, combining her interest in creative work with recognition of an industry populated mainly by women. She wanted to learn more about the industry and options available to her, so she started to look for people to whom she could turn for advice.

---

[29] National Academies of Sciences, Engineering, and Medicine; Policy and Global Affairs; Board on Higher Education and Workforce; Committee on Effective Mentoring in STEMM. *The Science of Effective Mentorship in STEMM*. Dahlberg, M.L. and Byars-Winston, A. (eds) (2019). Washington (DC): National Academies Press (US); 30 October PMID: 31958221.

[30] Grossman, G.M. and Helpman, E. (1994). "Endogenous innovation in the theory of growth." *Journal of Economic Perspectives* 8: 23–44.

Most of the people Melissa identified as role models didn't feel approachable to her as a young black woman from the London suburbs. She told us, "All of the people I originally saw were women but none of them looked like me. I instinctively felt, rightly or wrongly, that they were already five notches up."

Then Melissa started following Ronke Lawal, a young black woman who was running a PR agency that had values that aligned to Melissa's and was clearly making an impact. Melissa wanted to know more about this woman who looked like her, boasted a similar background and who seemed successful, yet felt approachable because of her online personality.

Melissa took a few weeks to observe Ronke's activity on Twitter before reaching out. When she did engage, she made sure to mention what she had picked up from Ronke's tweets and why she was interested in speaking to her. This thoughtful and engaging approach impressed Ronke and she agreed to meet with Melissa.

Melissa didn't formally ask Ronke to mentor her; she stressed to us that she has never made such a formal request. Instead, she offered to work with Ronke voluntarily, identifying what she could do to support Ronke and learn from her at the same time. In return, Ronke helped Melissa understand more about the opportunities open to her within PR but also beyond, worked with her to develop her practical skills such as presenting herself, took her along to events with her and opened up her network by making key introductions and briefing her ahead of meetings.

The support that Ronke gave, alongside those other mentors throughout her career, including her uncle who has had a profound influence on her personal development journey, has helped Melissa to align with true passion and transfer her skills as a creative in film and TV. Some of the advice she has received has had an immediate benefit; in other cases the support of her mentors has helped to shape her as a person and as a professional.

Melissa summed up the support she has received over the years, "The advice from my mentors have been like seeds planted over a period of time. But then it rains and it rains and it rains, with plenty of setbacks and failure. But those seeds were there and being watered. It's like a bamboo tree, which takes ages to grow but eventually, when you're ready to receive the information, that knowledge flourishes."

One of the reasons for the under-utilisation of mentoring is that it is typically introduced at key moments on career journeys. More junior people are only likely to be offered mentoring support if they find themselves on a fast-track programme, or as part of a DEI initiative. Otherwise, support tends to be offered to people who are on the verge of, or new to, executive positions.

Once people have reached and established themselves in the senior ranks, they traditionally change hats and become mentor rather than mentee.

However, as Melissa's experience above and George Rumball's story at the beginning of this chapter illustrate, to follow this model is to misunderstand the potential that mentoring offers. Mentoring is not just for people working for large organisations, and even in such an environment, why would you wait until someone has established themselves as having senior leadership potential before offering them the support they need?

By having a robust mentoring programme open to anyone with ambition or who just want support in their role, organisations will be more likely to uncover the diamonds in the rough, junior employees who have enormous untapped potential. By developing these employees early, you are building your company's pipeline. As already mentioned, mentored employees are more loyal to the organisation, so there is a higher likelihood that not only will they become your best employees, but they will also stay and attract their talented friends to join you as well.

A good mentor will uncover and nurture the passion or talent that has previously lain dormant. Investing in mentoring for the wider workforce will give many more employees the opportunity to excel in their role or to find the niche that is the perfect fit for them.

As the statistics earlier in this chapter illustrate, just by showing that faith in and support for people, they are more likely to stay with the organisation for a longer period of time. Loyalty grows and attrition falls.

How does your relationship with mentoring change when you become a senior executive?

At the other end of the career spectrum, just because you have reached a senior level, it doesn't mean that you have all of the answers. You should certainly be able to handle challenges better than somebody who doesn't have your experience but you can still benefit from different perspectives and insights. Becoming an executive can be isolating. None of your reports necessarily understand, nor care about, the pressures you are facing. That is where a mentor is critical.

Even the world's leading athletes have coaches to fine-tune their approach and to help them achieve even better results.

Mentoring doesn't always need to come from people more senior than you either. In the next chapter, we will look at different mentoring models, including peer and reverse mentoring. An increasing number of senior leaders are embracing reverse mentoring, learning from those junior to them, which is particularly important in a world where up to five generations work in the same office, digital tools change by the minute and priorities shift with the challenges facing our planet and society.

You do need to overcome that complacency that you have 'made it' and no longer need support. You also, however, need to be able to find the time to support others at a moment when new pressures, expectations and demands are placed on you and uncertainty in your role is amplified as you deal with unfamiliar responsibilities.

The burden of the 'minority tax'

Once you are seen as a success, others will want to learn from you. This is amplified if you represent a minority group. Everybody who identified themselves in you will want you to be their mentor, particularly if that group is underrepresented at senior levels. This can be a particular challenge for women and people from other minority groups such as ethnic minorities, veterans and first – generation college and university graduates. This dilemma is often referred to as the 'minority tax'.[31,32]

As she progressed through a successful career in financial and professional services, with companies such as IBM, Royal Bank of Scotland and PwC,

---

[31] Faucett, E.A., Brenner, M.J., Thompson, D.M. and Flanary V.A. (2022). "Tackling the minority tax: a roadmap to redistributing engagement in diversity, equity, and inclusion initiatives." *Otolaryngology–Head and Neck Surgery* **166**(6):1174-1181. doi:10.1177/01945998221091696.

[32] Rodríguez, J.E., Campbell, K.M. and Pololi, L.H. (2015). "Addressing disparities in academic medicine: What of the minority tax?" *BMC Medical Education* 15:6. doi: 10.1186/s12909-015-0290-9. PMID: 25638211; PMCID: PMC4331175.

Dr Heather Melville, OBE, Chancellor of The University of York, started to mentor other women because she couldn't see many people who looked like her in leadership positions. She recognised that she was fortunate to have had amazing leaders and sponsors who believed in her, and she wanted to provide the same support and guidance to others who may not have the same opportunities.

Heather believes that everyone should know that they can achieve success, even if they have been told otherwise. She has a clear passion for helping Black women specifically, as she can see that there is a lack of support and representation for them. She told us, "It's about the lived experience. If you haven't had the lived experience, you will not know how to help someone."

Heather estimates that she has mentored around sixty people over the last decade and the journey continues. She's recently launched Nebula, a programme for Black women who are two years away from a C-Suite role and who need opportunities, networks and support to get to the boardroom. She does, however, admit that the constant call on her to mentor other women has a price.

"The increased demand for my time as a mentor has certainly been a challenge. I've had to learn to prioritise my commitments and set boundaries to ensure I can manage the demand effectively and maintain a healthy work–life balance and think about my own health. One of the things I used to do to manage the toll was group mentoring sessions. I'd say to people, 'I'm available on a Thursday afternoon between 5pm and 7pm', or put people into mentoring groups.

"As times have got even busier, I'm really clear to people that if they are not mentoring somebody else and they tell me they're too busy to do so, then they don't deserve my time. If I can give you an hour of my time, then you need to be able to give your time to someone else. It's all about paying it forward. Really paying it forward.

"So the one caveat that I say is, 'Who are you mentoring?'"

Despite the challenges, Heather remains committed to mentoring women, particularly those from underrepresented communities. She stressed, "I think it's made me realise that we've got to invest in the change that we want. There's no point just talking about wanting to see more women on boards. If you're a Black person and you're in a position where you can help, you've got to help until we've got the majority that look like us.

"Sadly, sometimes people are too busy, or they think that if they are shown to be taken an interest in this, it might have an impact on their careers. We need to get away from that. We have to make time for this because it's the future. My legacy must be that, when I turn around, I see a room full of different people that look like me, instead of me going into a room where I'm always the minority."

Mentoring matters

The statistics and the stories shared in this chapter should illustrate just why we felt it was so important to write this book. Mentoring has a huge impact, and not just on the people being mentored. Mentors learn by giving; organisations thrive by supporting and raising their staff; and society gains as more people become equipped to achieve greater things.

If you're not being mentored, find people who can guide and support you.

If you're not mentoring, find people you can help and lift up.

If you're not encouraging others to get involved in the same way, start shouting about the power of mentoring from the rooftops and be an advocate of mentoring throughout your career.

CHAPTER 2
WHAT DOES EFFECTIVE MENTORING LOOK LIKE?

"If you stop learning and growing, someone else will pass you," remarks two-time National Basketball Association (NBA) Champion Zaza Pachulia. At 19, Zaza, originally from the country of Georgia, landed as a young teen in Orlando, Florida, about to embark on his professional basketball career. Everything was foreign to him – the country, language and professional association he would later call home. For sixteen years, three times the national average for NBA athletes, Zaza played over 1,000 games in the NBA, running many miles up and down the court.

When he landed in the United States, he knew little about professional basketball and living in America. He counted on the other few international professional NBA basketball players to help him get acclimatised. So Zaza would know what to expect, they taught him the unwritten rules, expectations and assumptions that are never formally communicated or conveyed, often known as a hidden curriculum.[33] From off court expectations to US taxes, the more senior players took Zaza under their wing.

From investing their now significantly larger salaries, to social media etiquette, NBA players are supported and advised. As he developed into a more senior player in the league, Zaza saw it as his duty to mentor the junior players, manage their expectations and tell them what to watch out for. He warned them of temptations, taught them how to block out distractions and guided them on staying focused on being the best. No one told him to do it, he just knew it had to be done. It was the expectation he had of himself and the unspoken culture of the team.

Organisational culture is found in the daily behaviours seen at work. When the people within the organisation start mentoring others of their own accord, without being prompted to do so, that is a sign of a healthy culture. Everyone is paying it forward because they want to, not because they have to.

---

[33] Alsubaie, M.A. (2015). "Hidden curriculum as one of current issue of curriculum." *Journal of Education and Practice* **6**(33).

Mentors can help you develop skills, consider new perspectives and can share access to a broad and influential network. There are multiple types of mentoring paradigms to consider, from the traditional top-down hierarchical mentoring structure to peer and reverse mentoring relationships, as well as group and mentoring in different formal and informal formats.

Over the course of the next two chapters, we will break down the different options and explain the merits and drawbacks of each, as shown in Figure 2.1.

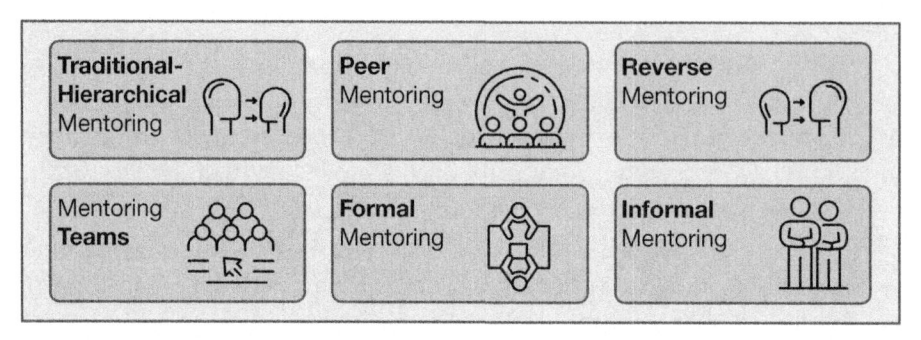

Figure 2.1 Types of mentoring relationships

Types of mentoring relationships

Traditional-hierarchical mentoring

When you hear the word 'mentoring', what do you picture?

The chances are, particularly if you are new to mentoring, that the image your mind summons is of a grey-haired, wizened, senior executive, likely male, imparting the knowledge and experience they have gleaned from years climbing the ladder, to someone on a lower rung, looking up.

That sage figure will carry the title of 'Mentor', whether or not you have formally discussed or assigned the label, and have a formal or unspoken agreement to share their insights with the ambitious and upwardly mobile party sitting at their feet.

Of course, many *traditional-hierarchical* mentoring relationships of this kind exist, to different degrees of efficacy. And they certainly make sense in theory, but they are also limiting in several respects.

Probably the first source of support people look for when working towards an objective is people who have already successfully achieved something similar.

"I want what they have" is familiar thinking. The experience, expertise and lessons successful people have learned on their journey can be invaluable, helping the mentee to choose the right path and avoid repeating mistakes already made.

A mentor may not always have all the answers, but they will save you an enormous amount of time. They know what works and what doesn't, and they can steer you in the direction of what has greatest impact, efficiency or return on investment.

The traditional-hierarchical mentor will often be a senior executive in the same organisation (in larger businesses and institutions) or someone from elsewhere in the same sector. Based on statistics alone, those at the highest levels of the corporate structure in most industries are of a certain vintage, gender and ethnicity;[34] they are predominantly white males. As such, they are often looked up to as mentors for the rising generation of leaders. But they do not corner the market on mentoring, as you will see in subsequent sections and chapters of this book.

Furthermore, only having these people mentor you can put you at a disadvantage, as you will also soon learn.

Both individual organisations and industry associations have a vested interest in nurturing future leaders and developing succession plans.[35] Mentoring programmes should be an obvious way to encourage this and, in theory, benefit the organisations who adopt them, although we feel that they fall short much of the time. Such programmes should provide a great launching point to establish and develop mentoring relationships when finding a suitable mentor seems like an insurmountable task.

However, formal mentoring programmes should not replace the organic mentoring relationships which occur over spontaneous conversations in hallways, meetings and break rooms.

It is who you connect and jive with in such a way that make the conversations flow easily. You look forward to the conversations with anticipation and excitement. These great mentors push you outside your comfort zone, as that

---

[34] Wilkie, D. (2023). "How DE&I evolved in the C-Suite." *SHRM Executive Network*. Retrieved 15 March from **https://www.shrm.org/executive/resources/articles/pages/evolving-executive-dei-diversity-c-suite.aspx**

[35] Heffernan, M. (2023). "Succession is painful but it doesn't need to be." *Financial Times*.

is where true learning occurs. They offer an appropriate level of challenge and support so that you are stretched to new heights, without feeling overwhelmed. We will explore formal and informal mentoring in Chapter 3.

A strong relationship with a mentor fuels the loyalty and connection you feel towards the organisation who brought you together. You want to continue working with your mentor and continue to see the benefits as you rise through the ranks. While the company certainly benefits from the mentorship relationship, it also positively impacts the mentor and mentee – as we will discuss.

When people consider mentoring for their own development, or pick up on the suggestion made to them, the most obvious place for them to start looking is within the higher ranks of their own employer. Some will look to their immediate line manager to mentor them, but this is not something we recommend, as we discuss in Chapter 14. In larger organisations, there can be plenty of other candidates to approach. Not all mentors need to be senior to you, as we will review in this chapter.

Traditional-hierarchical mentors don't have to come from the same company or sector, as there are benefits to having diverse perspectives. Sometimes the lessons learned are not directly related to the specific role or function but to the journey they have taken and the lessons they've learned upon reflection.

Oftentimes, problems pervasive in one industry are solved in another. For example, the safety checklists used in operating rooms around the globe were copied from the checklists pilots use. Healthcare borrowed a solution from aviation. You can do the same. If you want a solution to closing more deals, presenting in front of stakeholders, or leading a team, there is nothing stopping you from looking outside your company and industry for people who can guide you.

Luca Signoretti, Leadership Expert and Director, BBA program at IAE Nice School of Management, told us "The nature and complexity of the challenges that leaders must face today are increasingly broad. Thus, it's less probable that the individual leader possesses valuable experience and expertise in all these new domains.

"The mentoring here is not along the junior-senior axe but rather among leaders in the same role (for example, Chief Operating Officer), across different industries. Each has a specific expertise and set of solutions for challenges they have faced in their own industry that are instead uncharted ones for the other leader.

"For example, a car manufacturing industry leader can be more experienced with disruption of the supply chain than a consumer product industry leader, because of the complexity and high dependency on suppliers of the car manufacturing industry. On the other hand, the consumer goods leader is probably much more expert with rapid change in consumer attitudes and social expectations and can provide mentoring to the car manufacturing leader on that.

"You can still read this mentoring activity within the junior-senior framework but where the seniority here is about the experience with a specific set of challenges, not the number of years of a career. They mentor each other because one is more 'senior' in facing and solving a specific problem (more frequent in their industry) than the other, and the role may be inversed with a different challenge."

Traditional-hierarchical mentoring is not the only approach to consider. Limiting a search for the best advice only to people more senior than you will leave a lot of opportunities missed. The further someone escalates up the hierarchy, the more limited and filtered conversations they have with those more junior who may be introduced to cutting edge methodologies and technologies.

In a rapidly changing world, what was successful on your mentor's journey to the top may be less effective, or even irrelevant, in the modern commercial or public sector landscape. Meanwhile, that single mentor's experience will have been shaped by their own peer group, challenges faced, personality type and events that unfolded on that journey.

Your path may well be very different and similar approaches less effective. No two people can have the same upbringing, opportunities and challenges, and cultural and other beliefs. Believing that one person can be the answer to all of your questions and woes is unrealistic.

"You are a young version of me," or "I see me in you," can be dangerous phrases. Be wary of mentors who try to create a 'mini-me,' meaning they want to mould you into a miniature version of themselves. You are your own person with your dreams, wishes and goals, which may not be shared or recognised by your mentor. Look for and accept guidance, but if all the recommendations are identical to your mentor's journey, question whose career is the focus – yours or the mentor who is trying to create their legacy.

Peer mentoring

While not dismissing traditional-hierarchical mentors entirely, we need to consider additional approaches to getting the support and input we need. This stage of your career has nuances, struggles and challenges which might be unfamiliar or a distant memory to someone who is more senior.

Peer mentors are those who are at a similar stage of their careers, whether or not they are in your organisation or industry. There is a common bond and empathy which ebbs and flows between you. If one person is struggling, a peer can be the listening ear. Sometimes, we just want to be heard, and that's okay. A judgement-free peer mentor can offer that supportive role, provide additional perspectives and let you know of opportunities they have seen in their network which may not be on your radar.

As shared in *The Success Factor,* Drs Lynn Perry Wooten and Erika James are best friends, and each other's peer-mentors, or as Ruth calls them, 'friendtors'. They met as classmates in graduate school at the University of Michigan and have become close friends and supporters of each other's work, even collaborating on several research projects on crisis leadership and their latest book, *The Prepared Leader.*[36]

As they ascended in their careers, they supported each other. They talk to each other daily on their way to work. Peers rise together, and Lynn and Erika were not going to be graduate students forever. Lynn is now the President of Simmons University in Boston and Erika is Dean of Wharton, the business school at the University of Pennsylvania.

Even to this day, having reached such exalted positions in their field, they continue to support and co-mentor each other.

We are all part of different social and professional networks, which allows us to tap into and hear of different opportunities. One friend might hear of a job prospect, which may not be suitable for them, but which they share with their peer. They can help you with mock interviews and practise how you will craft some key statements. Alternatively, we each have our individual strengths. My strength might be your weakness and vice versa. As a peer, I can ask for your help with something knowing I will not be judged.

---

[36] James, E. and Wooten, L.P. (2022). *The Prepared Leader: Emerge from Any Crisis More Resilient Than Before.* Wharton School Press.

When Andy first started speaking at events internationally, working with audiences who did not speak English, or have English as a first language, he turned to fellow speakers who were experienced in this area. They shared some invaluable tips on how to engage with interpreters, to both make the interpreters' work easier and to ensure that they conveyed his message more effectively.

Andy has since supported other speakers in the same position with similar advice.

Peers can mentor each other in a one-on-one relationship as well as in a group environment. One popular approach is for two people on a similar career track or at similar stages of their career to *Co-Mentor* each other, as Drs Wooten and James did. Rather than one person being the giver in the relationship and the other receiving, the co-mentors provide each other with reciprocal support and encouragement, meeting regularly and talking through challenges with each other. Sometimes it's enough to talk through new ideas or strategies, consider opportunities or provide perspectives as problems arise.

Peer group mentoring

Breaking the traditional vision of the single mentor sharing their wisdom opens up new possibilities. For example, *peer group mentoring* is a powerful alternative or addition to the two models outlined above. Typical examples of peer group mentoring include action learning sets, mastermind groups or mentoring circles, where small groups of people, typically between five and seven participants, most commonly at a similar stage of their career, will get together to explore solutions to a common issue, or to each other's challenges.[37]

Action learning sets would usually be found within the same organisation, often focused on a particular business challenge or training programme, whereas mastermind groups are often made up of people from across the same profession or a completely diverse group, all from different organisations and each facing different problems. Their skillsets will often be complementary, giving a different range of expertise and diversity of perspectives to each challenge.

Both are similar in approach. Each meeting, either someone else takes centre stage to focus on a problem they need help solving and the group weighs in with

---

[37] Bustillo, M. and Gotian, R. (2020). "A mentoring circle supports women anaesthesiologists at every career stage. "*British Journal of Anaethesia* **124**(3): e190-e191. doi: 10.1016/j.bja.2019.12.014. Epub 2020 Jan 22. PMID: 31982113.

the sole intention of helping the person in the spotlight solve their challenge, or the group explores a common business challenge together.

Mentoring circles follow a similar path and were initially inspired by Sheryl Sandberg's book *Lean In*.[38] They have grown in popularity since. Unlike mastermind groups or action learning sets, where this is optional but not essential, they do rely on a dedicated mentor facilitating the conversation.

The approach in all of these cases is typically structured around sharing the challenge, a period of enquiry where questions are asked, to allow the group to understand the challenge and its context in greater depth, then solutions and suggestions are offered.

Mastermind groups were discussed in detail in *Just Ask* and the steps you need to take to establish and run such groups are detailed in Figure 2.2.[39]

Flash mentoring (hallway mentoring in the US)

Flash mentoring originated from the demands of Millennials, who had expressed their need for short, sharp mentoring conversations centred around specific projects at the time they need the support the most. Flash mentoring is made up of one-off conversations with the right mentor for a particular challenge at the right point in time, without the need for a long-term commitment.

Flash mentoring is similar to speed mentoring, which we'll take a brief look at in Chapter 12, but the mentoring conversations would typically be for a longer duration, allowing mentor and mentee to explore the challenge in more depth.

Reverse mentoring

When challenging the traditional-hierarchical model, we shouldn't just question the predominance of a single mentor but also the hierarchical relationship between mentor and mentee, beyond suggesting that peers can support each other.

Reverse mentoring has gained in popularity over recent years, although in the purest form of mentoring, it likely existed for much longer. Businesses are facing

---

[38] Sandberg, S. (2015). *Lean In: Women, Work, and the Will to Lead*. WH Allen.
[39] Lopata, A. (2020). *Just Ask: Why Seeking Support Is Your Greatest Strength*. Panoma Press.

2 WHAT DOES EFFECTIVE MENTORING LOOK LIKE?

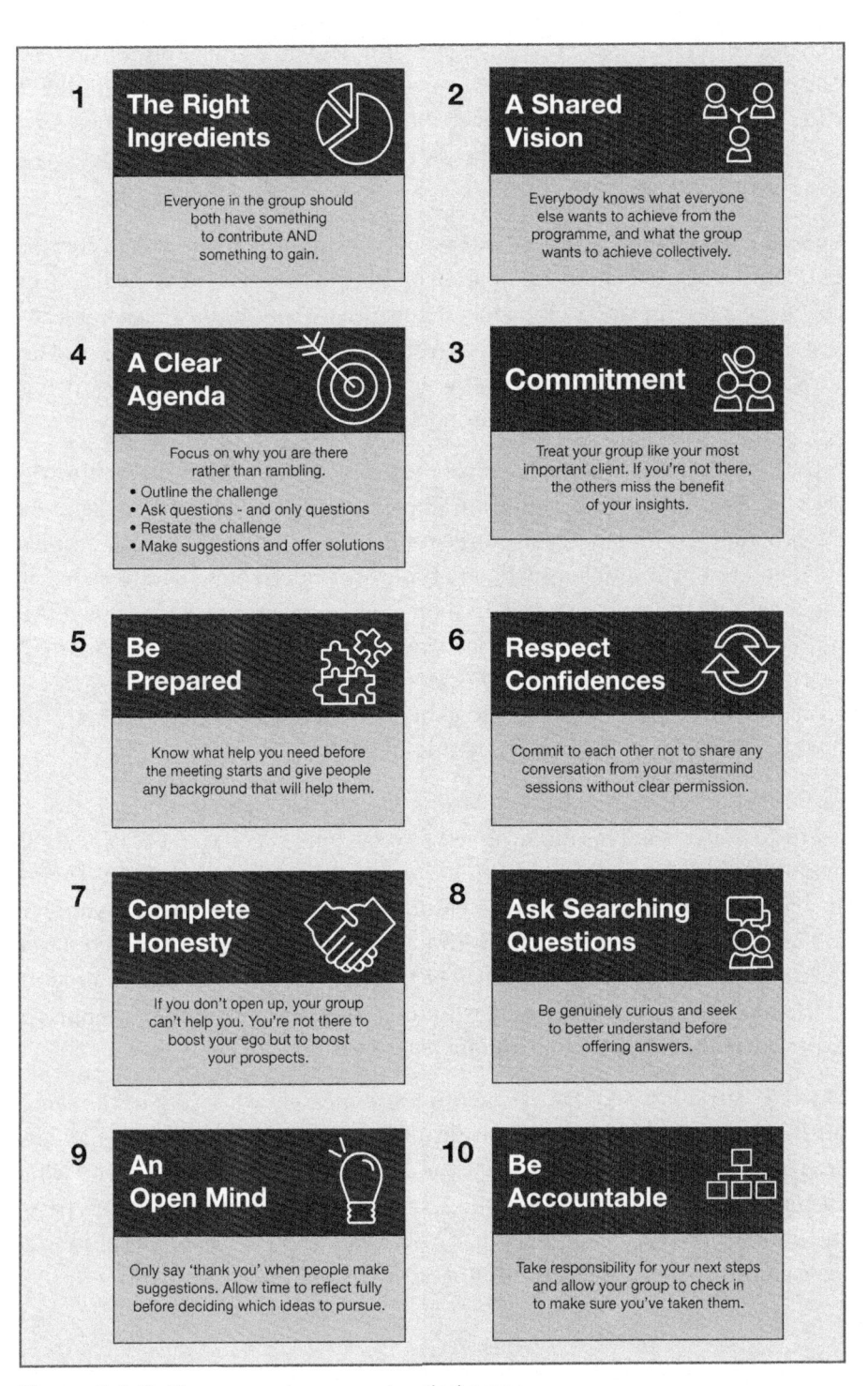

1 The Right Ingredients
Everyone in the group should both have something to contribute AND something to gain.

2 A Shared Vision
Everybody knows what everyone else wants to achieve from the programme, and what the group wants to achieve collectively.

4 A Clear Agenda
Focus on why you are there rather than rambling.
- Outline the challenge
- Ask questions - and only questions
- Restate the challenge
- Make suggestions and offer solutions

3 Commitment
Treat your group like your most important client. If you're not there, the others miss the benefit of your insights.

5 Be Prepared
Know what help you need before the meeting starts and give people any background that will help them.

6 Respect Confidences
Commit to each other not to share any conversation from your mastermind sessions without clear permission.

7 Complete Honesty
If you don't open up, your group can't help you. You're not there to boost your ego but to boost your prospects.

8 Ask Searching Questions
Be genuinely curious and seek to better understand before offering answers.

9 An Open Mind
Only say 'thank you' when people make suggestions. Allow time to reflect fully before deciding which ideas to pursue.

10 Be Accountable
Take responsibility for your next steps and allow your group to check in to make sure you've taken them.

Figure 2.2 Setting up your own mastermind group

challenges in fast-paced areas such as technology and social responsibility. With five generations currently in the workforce simultaneously, generational differences are substantially changed today from where they were when senior leaders joined their organisations, or even since they entered management positions.

A grey-haired senior executive is not necessarily in the best position to mentor a Millennial or Generation Z employee on how to leverage social media effectively, the likely impact of artificial intelligence (AI) on the business or how to best consider the environmental responsibilities impacting their decisions. The advice will more likely flow the other way, with the more junior employee being more connected to current thinking and future trends.

Patrice Gordon was the first reverse mentor at Virgin Atlantic, mentoring the CEO, and she now specialises in implementing bespoke reverse mentoring programmes for a range of companies. Leaders on Patrice's programmes are mentored by individuals who are typically underrepresented in terms of gender, ethnicity, sexuality and disability, with a view to breaking down the similarity bias that exists at senior leadership team tables, where decisions may lack impact and challenge due to the homogeneity of the group. In these cases, reverse mentoring allows leaders to gain alternative viewpoints and perspectives, leading to more impactful decision-making.

Patrice believes that establishing trust is crucial in leadership, and it is easier to trust people who are similar to us. To overcome this natural bias, reverse mentoring encourages leaders to, in her words, "put themselves in the vulnerable position of a novice" and be mentored by individuals who are dissimilar to them. This creates an initially awkward but valuable relationship that starts from a point of difference but ultimately, through conversation and the growth of the relationship, creates an understanding based on trust, shared interests or experiences that might not be immediately apparent.

Much of Patrice's work involves mentors and mentees who work in the same organisation, and it can have a significant impact where there is a strong hierarchy and change is necessary. Frontline employees who interact directly with customers can share their insights and pain points with senior leaders, bypassing multiple layers of management. This accelerates change and promotes an agile culture, which is vital in a fast-paced and volatile environment.

While reverse mentoring can have numerous benefits, it is essential to acknowledge potential pitfalls. One key factor is the level of organisational trust. If trust is low within the organisation, implementing a reverse mentoring programme may not be successful, as it can be met with scepticism. In such cases, it is crucial for organisations to focus on building trust before introducing reverse mentoring initiatives.

Patrice believes that reverse mentoring can potentially have a big impact beyond the initial mentoring conversations. She told us, "If reverse mentoring is done really well, it means that a longer-term relationship is established, and that those two individuals can tap into each other at a future point in time. It also means that if a senior leadership team does not have an understanding of how their discussions might impact a certain group, they can go back to their mentors and ask them for their insights."

CHAPTER 3
FORMAL V INFORMAL MENTORING

Whether you are looking at a traditional or less conventional mentoring model, you will need to consider just how structured and set your mentoring relationships should be.

Formal mentoring programmes are officially supported and sanctioned by a company or organisation. There are clear structures, policies and support systems. The organisation is at the helm to nurture these relationships.[40] Today, about 70% of Fortune 500 companies have mentoring programmes[41] but their effectiveness is a mixed bag. How mentors are chosen is often not based on skill or competence, rather availability or those who were told to do so; they were 'voluntold'.[42] Just because you are good at your job doesn't mean you are a good mentor.[43]

The mentees pose another challenge – as previously stated, while three out of every four people understand that mentoring is crucial, only one actually has a mentor. Among those who do have a mentor, only a quarter had them formally assigned to them.[44]

As we have already mentioned, many organisations will have formal mentoring programmes in place, but research has shown few formal in-house mentoring programmes are effective or meeting their intended goals.[45] Some employees report favourable outcomes, but a significant portion report minimal benefit,

---

[40] Baedke, L. K. (2023). *Mentor Coach Lead*. Chicago, IL, Health Administration Press.
[41] Gutner, T. (2009). "Finding anchors in the storm: Mentors." *The Wall Street Journal*. New York, NY.
[42] Gotian, R. (2023). "9 signs you've been voluntold." *Forbes*.
[43] Gotian, R. (2016). "Mentoring the mentors: Just because you have the title doesn't mean you know what you are doing." *College Student Journal* 50(1): 1-4.
[44] Olivet Nazarene University (2020). "Study explores professional mentor-mentee relationships in 2019." Retrieved 6 February 2021, from **https://online.olivet.edu/research-statistics-on-professional-mentors**
[45] Ragins, B.R. and Miller, J.S. (2000). "Marginal mentoring: The effects of type of mentor, quality of relationship, and program design on work and career attitudes." *The Academy of Management Journal* 43(6).

let alone meaningful engagement. The programmes are performative; organisations may have a mentoring programme on paper, but their impact is debatable. It's an outcome that's been coined, 'marginal mentoring.'[46]

Perhaps the greatest challenge is with the pairing – they are often completely random and are based on some small commonality in background such as education or hometown. Just as not everyone who attended the same school has the same avatar, likes the same things or has the same level of ambition, it is preposterous to think that such a random pairing could be effective. At best, it is ineffective. At worst, it is toxic.[47,48]

The longer-term detrimental consequence of the failure of formal mentoring programmes is that as the mentoring relationship sours, there is often no exit plan. Both mentor and mentee are often committed for an agreed period.

In varying fields, research indicates that poor mentoring is worse than no mentoring.[49] The scarred mentee will often not look for a new mentor, thinking that mentoring as a process is ineffective, even though research shows the opposite to be true. Poor mentorship therefore ruins retention, loyalty and workforce development – the exact goals that mentorship tries to inculcate in the first place.

Responsibility for formal mentoring programmes normally lies within a Human Resources (HR) department, with Learning and Development (L&D) if a mentoring programme is designed to accompany a particular training programme, such as a fast-track scheme, or will be voluntarily led by the committee of an Employee Resource Network (ERG), such as the Women's Network, LGBT+ Network or an ERG for minority ethnic groups.

The latter schemes are, by their very nature, only available for selected members of the workforce, whether people selected for that training programme or members of the ERG. As they are run by volunteers, their growth and reach are often in direct correlation to the organisers' bandwidth. There are often limits to the

---

[46] Ragins, B.R. and Miller, J.S. (2000). "Marginal mentoring: the effects of type of mentor, quality of relationship, and program design on work and career attitudes." *The Academy of Management Journal* **43**(6).
[47] Chopra, V., Edelson, D.P. and Saint, S. (2016). "Mentorship malpractice." *JAMA* **315**(14): 1453–1454. doi:10.1001/jama.2015.18884.
[48] Davila, J.S. and Gotian, R. (2023). "Tormentor mentors, and how to survive them." *Nature* 16 March. doi: 10.1038/d41586-023-00821-8. Epub ahead of print. PMID: 36928402.
[49] Scandura, T.A. (1998). "Dysfunctional mentoring relationships and outcomes." *Journal of Management* **24**(3): 449–467. **https://doi.org/10.1177/014920639802400307**

resources available, which means they can fail to have the intended impact, despite the right intentions.

Many company-wide schemes with open access suffer from poor visibility and take-up, getting lost in the noise of other communications to the workforce as a whole. Due to conflicting schedules and work demands, often the smallest of minorities of the organisation's workforce take part in these offerings. Those who do participate are randomly assigned to mentors whose only experience and training is their own lived experience, as good or bad as it may have been. They haven't been trained in any way on effectively using key power skills such as listening, communication skills and empathy.[50]

If in-house mentoring programmes are to be successful, the approach needs to be rethought. Impetus needs to begin at Board level, with a serious conversation about the benefits to the business that a robust mentoring programme will bring and clarity about the business goals by which such a programme will be measured over time, realising that the benefits of mentorship are seen long term. This is not an easy exercise, but it is something that we will explore in Chapter 13.

Responsibility then needs to be delegated to someone with the time, resources and leverage to make a real impact in the business and to get buy-in from across the senior leadership team. It is imperative that the people running these programmes have the responsibility and authority to impact change.

That senior leadership team are the key. They are both essential advocates for the programme, ensuring its prioritisation and availability to members of their departments, and important participants in the scheme, primarily as mentors but potentially as mentees too (senior leaders would benefit greatly from peer mentoring groups). They will also ensure there is funding to support this programme, including the training of mentors and mentees so that they may both optimise the relationship.

Sector-wide mentoring

The inadequate strategic thinking given to mentoring programmes within organisations means that the scope is often limited to pairing mentors and

---

[50] Johnson, W.B., et al. (2020). "Why your mentorship program isn't working." *Harvard Business Review*.

mentees in-house. Often, but not always, this will even mean creating partnerships within the same office in a multinational company rather than between participants from different countries and regions.

By restricting the focus to just within the organisation, or even office, itself, an opportunity is missed. Into the void have sprung a number of *sector-wide mentoring* schemes, more often run by third-party organisations such as industry associations. There are many examples of these, and they are now prevalent in many industries. For example, Women in Banking and Finance offer a six-month mentoring programme to all of their members, with new intakes starting every month,[51] the Managing Partners Forum in the professional services sector bring together leaders from different firms across the sector to mentor each other through a 'Mentor Match' programme,[52] while Elevate is a free mentoring programme designed to support and inspire professionals within the creative and events industry.[53] We'll look at Elevate in more detail in Chapter 11.

Cross-sector mentoring

Taking the step beyond learning from others within the same profession or sector, we are big fans of programmes where the participants learn from mentors who work in different sectors.

This may take the form of people within the same role mentoring each other and be run by a professional association, or mentoring programmes offered as part of DEI initiatives with participants from across the work spectrum. But there's a strong argument for organisations to develop a mentoring programme in conjunction with one or two other organisations from different industries. Rather than simply matching people with senior people in their own firm, cross-pollinate mentors and mentees between the participating companies.

When you keep mentoring in-house or even in-sector, you run the risk of reinforcing the messages of the echo chamber. Many communities have their

---

[51] Women in Banking and Finance. Retrieved 1 February 2023, from **https://www.wibf.org.uk/mentoring/**
[52] Managing Partners' Forum. "Mentor match programme." Retrieved 1 February 2023, from **https://www.mpfglobal.com/mentor-match-programme.aspx**
[53] Elevate. Retrieved 1 February 2023, from **https://www.elevateme.co/**

way of doing things that rarely get challenged and will continue in that vein if other voices are not invited into the conversation. By cross-mentoring with organisations in completely different sectors, with a different way of doing things, that conventional thinking is more likely to be challenged and new ideas introduced.

In his book *Rebel Ideas*, Matthew Syed argues that "Solutions to complex problems typically rely on multiple layers of insights and therefore require multiple points of view. The trick is to find people with different perspectives that usefully impinge on the problem at hand."

Syed goes on to discuss 'perspective blindness'. He explains, "We are oblivious to our own blind spots. We perceive and interpret the world through frames of reference but we do not see the frames of reference themselves. This, in turn, means that we tend to underestimate the extent to which we can learn from people with different points of view."[54]

Creating mentoring relationships with people who have different frames of reference means that you are more likely to challenge invisible perceptions that might be holding individuals, teams and their organisations back and identify new and innovative solutions. Ones that, ironically, are taken for granted elsewhere.[55]

Informal mentoring

We mentioned in Chapter 1 that, according to a study by Olivet Nazarene, 61% of effective mentoring relationships evolved organically. Repeated research of graduate students has shown time and again that informal mentoring relationships tend to be more effective than formal mentoring pairings.[56,57] It's important to recognise that formal mentoring approaches are not the only way

---

[54] Syed, M. (2021). *Rebel Ideas*. New York, NY, Flatiron Books.
[55] National Academies of Sciences, Engineering, and Medicine (2019). *The Science of Effective Mentorship in STEMM*. Washington, DC: The National Academies Press. **https://doi.org/10.17226/25568**
[56] Clark, R.A., et al. (2000). "Mentor relationships in clinical psychology doctoral training: Results of a national survey." *Teaching of Psychology* 27: 262–268.
[57] Tenenbaum, H.R., et al. (2001). "Mentoring relationships in graduate school." *Journal of Vocational Behavior* 59: 326–341.

forward and, at the moment certainly, far from the most common spur for mentoring relationships.

When encouraging organic growth of mentoring relationships, we must bear in mind that this is not always equitable; it's easier for people from certain backgrounds to find qualified mentors among their extended network than for others, as we will explore later. This is where formal mentoring programmes can help to level the field; alternatively we need to better equip less fortunate groups to find the right mentors to help them grow.

In informal mentoring relationships, the individuals launch and sustain these mentoring connections. They are often developed spontaneously[58] and may not even carry the title. There are enough labels thrown around to identify people, so we really don't need any more. A mentor is a guide by your side who believes in you more than you believe in yourself. As such, the title of mentor is earned, and bestowed by the mentee. You should not call yourself a mentor if your mentee doesn't see you in that vein. In other words, you are not a mentor until your mentee calls you one.

While the traditional view of a mentor is of someone who will accompany you on a particular journey, often career-focused, informal mentors may come into and out of your life (from a support perspective at least) based on their relevance to what you are working on at the moment. If you have a new client in a sector you haven't worked with before, you might need to reach out for advice to help you find your feet initially. But that mentoring relationship is very much short-term and project-focused and doesn't need a formal footing.

Communities of practice

A lot of informal mentoring will happen within communities of practice, formal and informal groups of people with an underlying similarity such as objectives or challenges, geography, gender or occupation. *The Mentor Project*, for example, is a collective of experts and educators who come together to mentor students worldwide, while the authors of this book are members of various professional associations in the worlds of speaking, training, mentoring, events and academia. You likely belong to communities of practice already. Consider the professional associations you are a member of.

---

[58] Baedke, L.K. (2023). *Mentor Coach Lead*. Chicago, IL, Health Administration Press.

In addition to having a common thread that unites the people in the community of practice, there has to be a way to communicate with each other. Each of these communities of practice has its own forums on platforms such as Facebook, WhatsApp, Slack and LinkedIn. They may have conferences or other ways to convene and share ideas. Even if the primary aim of membership might be something other than mutual support, there's no doubt that one of the key benefits lies in the co-mentoring members offer each other informally.

Questions are posted on a regular basis, on some forums even daily or hourly, with members asking for advice on a range of challenges. *I'm thinking of implementing X . . . what should I know?* Or *What are the best resources on Y that I should look into? Does anyone have a template for a survey or form on Z?* are common questions in these types of communities of practice.

It's also a great way to find promising talent. Sharing an open position on your team now gets into the ear of others who know who you are and what you do. They can therefore tap into their network to help you fill a role. While some members might mentor each other in private (formally or informally), on these forums anyone can offer their advice and insights. It might be less structured than how we traditionally see mentoring but can be just as valuable.[59]

Is formal mentoring the best approach?

Formal programmes need to be improved and become more effective but they are essential. It is important that employers take responsibility for their employees' development; mentoring is a key component of that. The research shared in Chapter 1 underscores the benefits to organisations of taking mentoring seriously and being seen to do so.

More often than not, voluntary mentoring programmes tend to attract those who need mentorship least as they independently seek it out.[60] In addition, research has shown many people won't seek mentoring, or know where to start, without the right support from their employer. This challenge disproportionately impacts women and underrepresented minority groups.[61] Having a formal

---

[59] Gotian, R. (2019). "Why you need a support team." *Nature* 568: 425–426.
[60] Bischof, J. (2021) "Should your company start a mentorship program?" *Quartz*.
[61] Sandvik, J., Saouma, R., Seegert, N. and Stanton, C.T. (2021). *Treatment and Selection Effects of Formal Workplace Mentorship Programs* (No. w29148). National Bureau of Economic Research.

mentoring programme in place gives people somewhere to find the support they need, but such programmes do, on the whole, need to be better designed, offer more training to both parties, and be much more positively promoted to all employees.

There is great debate on whether a formal agreement is necessary or effective. Those in favour of it argue that when there is a formal agreement in place between mentor and mentee, there is likely to be more accountability and a clearer agenda. Both parties understand the reason for their conversations and will put small talk to one side when appropriate and dive more deeply into the development conversation. Proponents of formal mentoring arrangements would also argue that such relationships are likely to be more robust, with more frequent meetings at least for a set period.

Those who don't favour formal agreements or, as they are often called, compacts or contracts, feel they are constrained, and without enforcement by a third party, the agreement holds more stress than purpose. It also alludes to a different dynamic which is more formal and is based, some might argue, on a lack of trust. Not an ideal way to start a mentoring relationship. When trust does not exist, the relationship won't flourish.

Even the two authors of this book argue about the purpose and validity of these agreements. Ultimately, you need to decide what works for you. Neither of the authors have formal agreements in place for their own mentoring relationships, other than those provided as a commercial service. If you choose not to use an agreement, it is still important that mentors and mentees identify and align expectations and communicate with each other regularly about them.

If you do decide to put a formal agreement into place, sample agreements are available on the internet but you should consider how you would enforce such an agreement, particularly in a collegiate environment.

In such an agreement, we would suggest that you consider including the items shown in Figure 3.1.

Unless it is part of a commercial offering, most mentors are not paid for their services. That is naturally going to affect their commitment. You cannot expect them to drive the relationship. While they might hold mentees accountable during mentoring meetings, they won't necessarily be chasing them if and when they don't hear anything outside a set appointment.

> **What should be included in a mentoring agreement:**
>
> ☑ Who is entering into this agreement?
> ☑ A statement of confidentiality.
> ☑ Stated expectations.
> ☑ Frequency of meetings.
> ☑ Length of relationship.
> ☑ Any additional agreements for the mentor and mentee.
> ☑ Signatures and dates.

Figure 3.1 What to include in a mentoring agreement

If a formal mentoring relationship has been established through a company's matching process, there is also the potential issue of continuity if a mentor leaves the organisation or moves to a different role. An informal mentor who is providing support because of a personal relationship with the mentee, is more likely to continue providing that support even when their role doesn't require it.

Of course, company programmes with limited focus given to effective matchmaking can also lead to issues where the two parties are simply not a match for each other. No one wants a mentor with whom they have no rapport, who doesn't believe in them, who doesn't buy into their objectives or have the necessary interest or understanding of their role or function.

And, of course, no mentor wants to find themselves in that situation either.

It might sound as though this is an easy challenge to avoid but company programmes are often limited in terms of how many people volunteer to mentor and who those volunteers are. You want the right people, not warm bodies. If you have a scarcity of choice, making the ideal matches becomes a major challenge.

This can be amplified by the minority tax we discussed in Chapter 1. If minority groups are underrepresented at the senior levels of your organisation, there will naturally be fewer potential mentors to whom people from those groups can relate and greater demand for their time. It also dilutes the ability for mentees to learn and hear perspectives from people who are different from them.

Margaret Heffernan, a successful business leader and author who mentors CEOs, sees important roles for both formal mentoring and having a network of informal mentoring relationships.

For Margaret, formal mentoring programmes are most effective when there is a specific issue or theme to address. Working with CEOs, she suggested that some of her most valuable and effective contributions have come when she has worked over a period of time with clients to address key challenges, such as helping a first-time CEO adapt to the role, working to address fundamental strategic changes or managing an acquisition.

Margaret explained, "CEOs typically have large agendas, having a mentor who can help them prioritise and maintain a clear direction can lead to significant progress in a short amount of time. Working on a specific area has been productive because we've had an early, clear sense of what we wanted to achieve and what it would look like if, and when, we had. It puts structure around our conversations.

"It doesn't mean that other subjects didn't come up along the way, but the focus and structure kept us heading in a particular direction."

Meanwhile, Margaret sees informal mentoring as accessible for anyone, whatever their role. Sometimes it will be instigated by organisations encouraging mentoring relationships to be formed and encouraged, but it can evolve naturally as well. Margaret told us, "I also believe that it's very helpful having informal mentors for your whole life. I think of this as a personal board of directors, which are people who I really trust on things like finance, parenting, my own mental health and well-being; people who will tell me when I'm doing too much or need a change.

"I would say there are four or five people in my life, who, if I'm going to make a really big decision, I'll sound out. They've known me for a very long time, and work in adjacent areas or industries, so they understand what I do and they have known me long enough to know that my work and my identity are pretty closely knit."

Mentoring teams

Earlier in this chapter, we discussed the importance of diversity of thought and avoiding confining mentoring relationships to people who share the same echo chamber. Anybody who wants to benefit from the insights of others to fulfil their full potential should not rely just on one person's advice, as Margaret shares above – it's good to have a trusted team behind you.

There is no right and wrong when it comes to formal versus informal mentoring, traditional-hierarchical versus reverse mentoring or company schemes versus cross-sector programmes. The onus should be on the individual to take responsibility and surround themselves with the support they need. As Matthew Syed stressed, this will come from a range of different perspectives.

Ambitious or driven individuals surround themselves with *Mentoring Teams*,[62] groups of supporters who provide all of the different expertise they will benefit from. Just as a world-class athlete will have specialist coaches for different techniques, fitness coaches, physios, nutritionists and more on their team, we all need to do the same to gain access to the support we require.[63]

If formal programmes offer suitable support, of course they should be embraced. But equally, there's nothing to stop an individual from approaching other potential mentors personally, asking for their support, whether formal or informal, over a short-, medium- or long-term period.

Those individuals should be approached because of what they offer, not because of how long they have been in a role. If that experience is relevant, then great. But, as we will discuss, it's essential that both parties know what the mentor is expected to bring to the table, particularly if the mentoring relationship is to be formalised.

Once a mentoring team is in place, it should be constantly reassessed to ensure that the right support is available for the challenges being faced now. Once you have built your mentoring team, keep reviewing the support you need, the support you have available to you and the support you are effectively accessing right now.[64]

---

[62] Berwick, I. and Smith, S. (2022). "Boost your career with a personal board of directors." *Financial Times*.
[63] Gotian, R. (2020). "How to develop a mentoring team." *Forbes*.
[64] Montgomery, B.L. (2017). "Mapping a mentoring roadmap and developing a supportive network for strategic career advancement." *SAGE Open* 7(2). **https://doi.org/10.1177/2158244017710288**

On a regular cadence, reflect on what you are trying to achieve and what is in your way and then ask yourself two simple questions:

- What support do I need to get to where I want to be?

It's important here to name your goal and what steps you will need to take to achieve it.

- Who can help me and provide that support?

Realising there are different milestones you need to hit, consider who has the expertise you can tap into.

More than anything else, those two questions will tell you to whom you want to be talking right now. Consider adding the following people to your mentoring team: people in and outside your field and industry, your community of practice, those with project experience and retirees.

Mentoring is not a life sentence and we explore how and when to end a mentoring relationship in Chapter 9. In the meantime, there are multiple mentoring paradigms to consider. You shouldn't focus on just one, say a traditional-hierarchical mentor, as it is extremely limiting. The more people you can lean on, the more expertise you will be able to tap into for varying opportunities and challenges. These guides by your side can help you envision a world you never knew existed.

CHAPTER 4
WHY MENTORING IS NOT COACHING

"A coach has some great questions for your answers; a mentor has some great answers for your questions"

John C. Crosby

The rise in the popularity of both mentoring and coaching over the last quarter century has led to a great deal of confusion between the two terms, as well as interchanging their definitions, sometimes correctly, other times less so. For example, we would view the coach of a sports team more as a mentor than as a coach, as defined below, but the title will stick. Opinions may differ but we hope that the concepts as outlined below prove both useful and applicable.

As we see it, the two disciplines are, in fact, distinct and can and should be used to complement each other. Anybody looking to benefit from the support of others may choose to have both coach(es) and mentor(s) and organisations should consider making both approaches available.

Just because they are distinct disciplines, this doesn't mean that mentors can't use coaching techniques. In fact, the ability to pivot between mentoring and coaching techniques as appropriate can be invaluable to a mentee. We will explore this in more detail later in this chapter.

Spot the difference

We should begin by exploring the differences not just between mentoring and coaching but we'd also like to bring in three related roles that others can play in supporting career and role development: role models, consultants and sponsors.

When looking at coaching from a personal, rather than professional, perspective, you might also want to explore where therapists sit in this conversation, but that lies beyond the remit of this book.

Role models

As a social-scientist, Ruth conducts in-depth interviews and focus groups for her qualitative research on high achievers. In fact, many were done in service of this book. The process is simultaneously precise and vague; the listening skills peaking and the conversation flowing based on the loops, turns, summits and crevasses the interviewee raises. As one theme emerges, you explore it in real time while waiting to see what additional topics arise. When interviewing, the process cannot appear rushed, rigid, mechanical, soulless or void of humanity. You need to make the person feel like they are the only person in the room.

As someone who studies extreme high achievers, that takes on an additional dimension as you want to discuss with them the very topics you cannot Google about them. It requires a level of vulnerability and trust.

There is one interviewer who is not technically a social-scientist, but in Ruth's opinion is the best interviewer out there – Oprah Winfrey. Whether talking to British Royalty or your next-door neighbour, she can make them feel like the only person in the room, carefully and respectfully unravelling a web of unspoken experiences. She can help raise themes that often the interviewee didn't even recognise.

It's a skill you painstakingly learn in doctoral programmes, but in Oprah's case, it is second nature. Since high school, long before Ruth knew she'd be a social-scientist conducting qualitative research, she looked up to Oprah's unique connection abilities and interviewing skills. Despite numerous unsuccessful attempts (she hasn't given up yet!), Ruth has never met Oprah, but respects and admires her exquisite interviewing skills.

Everybody has role models at some point in their life. From the young teenagers aspiring to follow in the footsteps of their favourite pop or sports star to the entrepreneur looking up to business icons, we have all had somebody whose achievements have resonated with us and whom we have dreamed of emulating.

We don't necessarily know our role models, in fact in many cases we admire from afar, but that doesn't diminish their impact on the choices we make.

We often hear stories of people who have made career choices as children because of somebody they saw on television, or the young aspiring entrepreneur who was struck by a great keynote talk and took action as a result. For a role model to have impact, they don't have to talk to us in person: they inspire through their actions, their words and their achievements.

What they do, to put it quite simply, resonates and inspires action. We buy into their philosophy and beliefs and want to replicate their style, their action, their approach and, ultimately, their success.

Consultants

Whereas the other roles we explore below are typically hired to work with an individual, consultants tend to focus across a business or division, with a specific expertise and a clear area of focus. Consultants will be hired to analyse a particular challenge, understand where you are through talking to a wide range of stakeholders and prescribe a way through that challenge. They will then help you to implement that solution.

While you would expect consultants you employ to pick up on external factors that impact the challenge that they are tasked with solving, their focus will be solely on finding answers to that challenge and telling you what action you need to take. After that task is completed, they usually depart.

Sponsors

Traditionally, sponsors were senior leaders in an organisation who created opportunities for others. Their recommendation carried significant weight. They would put their reputation on the line for someone else. This would lead to strategic high-profile assignments, promotions and special recognition.

Sadly, this is fraught with bias. Despite hard work, senior leadership is still disproportionately male. As people tend to hire and promote those who look like them, that means that the pipeline continues to be homogenous.

You will probably be aware of the saying, 'It's not what you know, it's who you know' but in many cases, it's more important to think about who knows you and what they know or say about you when you're not in the room. The larger the organisation, the more people are likely to be involved in hiring and promotion decisions. Realise that influence can come from anyone, not only those who make the final choice. It is important to have somebody in that conversation who has influence and is in your corner. That person can be your sponsor.

People tend to work with those whom they know, like and trust. Although not accessible to everyone, particularly those with a young family, golf games and after-dinner drinks traditionally have allowed senior executives to get to know potential future talent outside of the work environment. Times change, and if you can't get to know potential sponsors in an extracurricular setting, find another way to engage with them.

When you hear someone got promoted and you question *What do they have that I don't?*, the answer is simple. It's not that the person hiring or sponsoring them likes them better, it is that they *know* them better. There's a difference.

Today, anyone can and should be a sponsor, especially with the advent of social media. In its purest form, sponsorship means that someone is talking about you and your work in a positive light, when you are not even in the room. They can amplify your accomplishments on social media, nominate you for awards or promotions, introduce you to key people, recommend you for stretch assignments and create opportunities which will help you learn, stretch and grow. By having someone sponsor you, it means your work and reputation precede you.[65]

These types of amplifications and opportunities don't need to come from someone senior in the organisation or even within the organisation. If they did, entrepreneurs might never get their day in the limelight. Consider who you know within and outside the organisation. If there is an opportunity you are craving or an award you think you are eligible and competitive for, ask them if they will nominate you.

Ruth was once asked by someone senior in her organisation to nominate him for a big industry award. He made it easy for her by giving her a bio which highlighted his accomplishments relevant to the award. He also told her who she could ask for further letters of support. He made it easy for her and ultimately, he won the award.

People are usually eager to help others but don't know how to do so or where to start. Ask for what you'd like and then make it as simple as possible for

---

[65] Gotian, R. (2020). "How to amplify the voice of your mentees." *Forbes*.

them. Give them all the supporting material and plenty of time to accomplish the task.

Coaches

Coaching involves a particular skillset designed to delve deeply into challenges and help the client to find solutions. While mentoring tends to look at the bigger picture and take a more strategic view of challenges and objectives to be addressed, coaches will be more focused on short-term objectives and skills development. Coaches will use questions to move the conversation forward, listening intently to the conversation to identify prompts for further questioning and exploration. Through this mining technique, they will help their client to uncover their own blind spots and find solutions for themselves.

With the exception of people who specialise in particular niche areas, because their professional background does not need to be directly relevant to the client's role and challenges, coaches may not have or need specific expertise or experience in the industry in which their client works. If you are helping someone with behavioural change or delegation, it doesn't matter if you are a physician or accountant.

Because coaching is more typically offered as a commercial service, coaches are more likely than mentors to work with whole teams or organisations; although, similarly to mentors, their work will normally be carried out on an individual basis or with small groups.

There is a range of bodies that provide formal accreditation for coaches but the industry is not regulated and courses will range from one-day or weekend training to degree-level interventions. If exploring coaching, do your due diligence rather than taking accreditation at face value.

Mentors

Mentors have experience, expertise, vision and skills which can help you in your career. They can equally see the road travelled and path ahead. They are part career advisor, part cheerleader. They may be experienced in the role in which their mentee is working or aspires to, or have expertise or deep knowledge in an area the mentee wants to master. They may also be from a different industry entirely but have transferable skills, which they are willing to share.

Mentors don't focus on using questions to help the mentee find the answer for themselves; instead, they provide their suggestions based on their own experience or expertise. They listen to understand and advise.

Of course, life is never as black and white as that and as suggested earlier in this chapter, mentors may well use coaching techniques when working with mentees. After all, people are far more likely to take on new ideas if they have come up with those themselves. Even if a mentor feels that they know the answer, they may want to direct the conversation to help the mentee reach that conclusion.

Simon Fordham, who we met in Chapter 1 and who is Chair of the Association of Business Mentors, explained, "We move up and down this communications pyramid from coaching, which is pure listening, to consultancy, which is really telling. The business mentor floats between the two quite happily, if they're professional enough to do so. Mentors use a number of our skills, our experience and our empathy to be able to support and guide." (Figure 4.1)

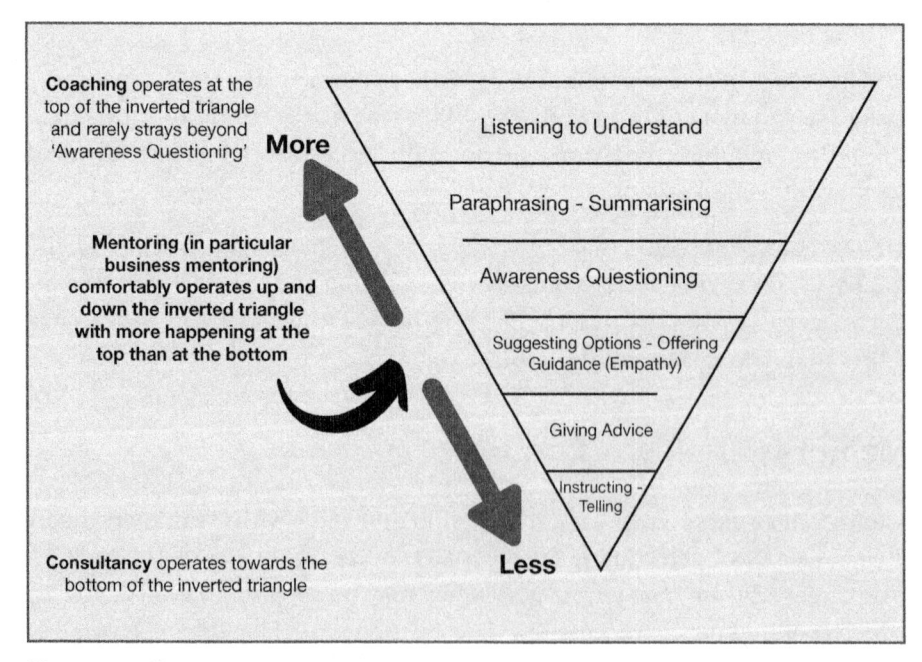

Figure 4.1 The inverted pyramid
Source: Nicholson 2021

Senior internal mentors in particular will help their mentees to recognise blind spots, particularly when reflecting back how the mentee is perceived by other people on the leadership team and around the organisation, or why certain projects aren't working or ideas being received as positively as the mentee hopes. They can motivate the mentee to persevere or tell them when they've done enough and it is time to shelve an idea.

Like coaching, mentoring is an unregulated field but unlike coaching there is, at the time of writing, very little accreditation and minimal training available for mentors. The Association of Business Mentors in the UK has introduced degree- and masters-level training that has been developed in conjunction with the Institute of Leadership and Management. The US-based Center for the Improvement of Mentored Experiences in Research (CIMER[66]) provides two-day mentor training workshops. These are two of the few mentoring qualifications at this level that we are aware of. We have listed some resources you can explore at the end of this chapter (see Figure 4.2).

It's not either/or

We've outlined some thoughts on the different roles people can play in supporting others but, as we said earlier, it doesn't have to be 'either/or', think 'and' instead.

LaTonya Kilpatrick-Liverman, PhD, Senior VP, Research & Innovation Oral Care and Global Devices at Colgate-Palmolive, recognises the value of being both coached and mentored, and the distinctions between the two approaches.

LaTonya explained that her coach excels at asking questions that require reflection rather than immediate responses. She told us, "She never accepts my first response, always asking follow-up questions to get me thinking even more deeply. With one particular issue, I thought I knew all of the answers and couldn't fail. The questions that she asked helped me to understand what was driving me to have these expectations and to become more vulnerable. I feel that I'm a better leader as a result."

In addition to working with her coach, LaTonya also has many mentors, one of whom is a former boss, someone whom LaTonya describes as a visionary, clear

---

[66] www.cimerproject.org

communicator who is not afraid to challenge organisational politics. Describing the different approach to her coach, LaTonya explained, "She doesn't ask as many questions. Instead, she shares information with me that helps me navigate company politics. She helps me with my communication skills – emphasising the importance of storytelling. I'm also trying to better learn how to be more strategic. She helps me to connect the dots to improve organisational effectiveness to deliver on strategic initiatives."

It's important that, once you understand what you are trying to achieve, you consider carefully what support you need to help you get there. But remember, you don't know what you don't know, and a mentor can shed light on opportunities, experiences you never knew existed and questions you never knew to ask.

- Will you benefit from a deep learning experience that will develop specific skills over time? Then perhaps you need a coach on your team.
- Are you looking to learn directly from people who have been on the journey you're setting out on? Find a mentor.
- Will decisions be made in rooms to which you are not invited? Who is your sponsor?
- Whose achievements or approach do you most respect? Set them up as a role model you can learn from by watching.

One person can, of course, play multiple roles but think back to our discussion of the role of mentoring teams in the previous chapter. Just as a business can bring together an advisory board of the different skillsets and areas of expertise they need to thrive, so can individuals. A team of mentors can offer multiple perspectives and remove blind spots.

A good mentor will be able to adapt to the needs of their mentee and play multiple roles. As Global CEO of the multinational accountancy firm Baker Tilly International, Francesca Lagerberg believes in the power of both mentoring and coaching and fulfils both roles for members of her team. As well as being experienced and successful in professional services, she is a fully accredited senior practitioner executive coach.[67] Francesca sees a clear distinction between the two and understands that they serve different purposes.

---

[67] Senior Practitioner accreditation – EMCC Global **https://www.emccglobal.org/**

Francesca told us, "Mentoring, in my view, is very question-led. It's about someone sharing their experience and helping others navigate through their own journeys. On the other hand, coaching has more of a tutorial element to it. It's about helping someone help themselves."

Francesca emphasised that mentoring is particularly beneficial for individuals who are early in their careers or going through significant transitions. It provides them with a sounding board and allows them to tap into the experience of others. She describes mentoring as "a moment of reflection in a mad, mad world." On the other hand, coaching takes a more proactive approach, focusing on specific scenarios or issues that individuals face throughout their career trajectory. It aims to help them improve their skills and reach their full potential.

While some people lean more towards mentoring or coaching based on their personal style, Francesca believes that they are not mutually exclusive, and the best mentors can also be excellent coaches, and vice versa. She states, "There's a place for mentoring, there's a place for coaching, but I think the reality is you share a little mixture of both." This blend of mentoring and coaching can be highly effective for individuals seeking career progression.

Francesca's approach to using mentoring and coaching varies depending on the situation. Sometimes she is specifically asked to be a mentor, while in other cases, she switches between the two techniques based on the needs of the individuals or the team she is working with. It is important to her to clarify expectations and contract at the beginning of the mentoring or coaching relationship so that both parties agree on which approach will be prioritised.

It's important that a mentor doesn't go into each meeting with preconceived ideas about what they will deliver. On the contrary, it is the mentee who drives the conversation. The mentee needs to come to the meeting with a goal and plan and the mentor can help revise the plan. Listening to their mentee and understanding what is needed is as important to *how* you deliver support as it is to what support you choose to deliver.

Nearly forty years ago, Kathy Kram, a leading thought leader and researcher on mentoring, outlined two roles of a mentor: namely, providing career guidance and psychosocial support. These fall into the categories of helping, acceptance and confirmation, problem solving and friendship. Within the career guidance spectrum, mentors offer professional development discussions and opportunities, advice, feedback, introduce mentees to people in their network, and give them stretch assignments to showcase their skills. For psychosocial support, they are the shoulder to cry on, the comforting and empathic listener, motivator and role model.[68]

Ultimately, don't worry about the labels. Whether you act as a mentor or coach, role model or sponsor, the title doesn't matter. What matters is the difference you make and the value you add. If you've set up the relationship well, you and your mentee have a clear idea of what success looks like from the beginning. Keep that end in mind and make sure you deliver on that promise.

Mentoring training and accreditation resources (correct at time of writing):

- Association of Business Mentors UK **https://www.associationofbusinessmentors.org**
- Center for Improvement of Mentored Experiences in Research (CIMER): **https://cimerproject.org**
- International Mentoring Association **https://www.mentoringassociation.org**
- European Mentoring and Coaching Council: **https://emccuk.org**
- International Authority for Professional Coaching and Mentoring: **https://coach-accreditation.services/**
- Open University – Exploring Mentoring and Coaching **https://tinyurl.com/mprv6hzs**
- The Mentoring School **https://thementoringschool.com**
- LinkedIn Learning Course (taught by Dr Ruth Gotian): Becoming an Inspiring Mentor **https://tinyurl.com/5n77e9sd**
- LinkedIn Learning Course (taught by Dr Ruth Gotian): Coach Your Team to Learn, Stretch, and Grow **https://www.linkedin.com/learning/coach-your-team-to-learn-stretch-and-grow**

Figure 4.2 Resources for mentoring training and accreditation – go to **mentoring.com** for clickable links and all resources. Please note that these are provided for information but without the endorsement of the authors.

---

[68] Kram, K. (1988). *Mentoring at Work: Developmental Relationships in Organizational Life*. Lanham, Maryland, University Press of America.

PART 2
BEING
A MENTOR

CHAPTER 5
WHY SHOULD YOU MENTOR OTHER PEOPLE?

Shonali Devereaux didn't get the support she would have wanted as she grew up, describing her upbringing as having "a front-row seat to high achievement but lacking a guide or cheerleader to help me achieve my fullest potential." As a result, she found herself navigating her own way in her career, learning through trial and error and facing daunting learning curves but eventually becoming a well-known and respected figure in the events industry. "There were many times when guidance or support would have helped me focus on what was best for me, enabling me to make better decisions about my future and accelerate my growth," she told us.

In 2019 Shonali was approached by Fay Sharpe, OBE, to become a mentor at Fast Forward 15, a leading not-for-profit mentoring scheme for women in the hospitality, events and travel sector. For Shonali it was a tremendous opportunity to offer the support to others that she had yearned for during her own journey.

Shonali told us, "Mentors wield extraordinary power. They provide a safe space for their mentees, a focus on setting and achieving goals, and the sharing of wisdom and life experiences. As a bonus, the mentorship dynamic is inherently reciprocal. It is nearly impossible to nurture the dreams of others without reflecting on and advancing one's own aspirations. I glean invaluable wisdom from each mentee, and these relationships endure far beyond their formal constraints.

"Witnessing the sustained growth and achievements of a mentee on a path we co-created brings an unparalleled sense of fulfilment. There is no greater joy than being a catalyst for another's continuous journey towards success."

As a mentor, you hold incredible superpowers. You have the ability to mould someone's career and release their greatness. This is not an obligation that should be taken lightly. Mentoring someone well is a big commitment, a huge honour and great responsibility, with enormous rewards both for the mentee and mentor.

It can be hard to turn down a request to mentor, particularly when it comes directly from the prospective mentee. We can feel flattered that our experience and skills are considered impressive enough that somebody else wants to learn from us, while the pull of being seen to 'give back' can be equally compelling.

But you won't be doing anybody any favours, least of all your mentee, if you take on board a commitment you feel ill-equipped to deliver, will struggle to meet adequately or will come to resent. Worse yet, if you do take on this role, and don't deliver, you won't be considered a mentor, rather will be labelled its evil cousin, a tormentor.[69,70]

Before saying 'yes' to any request to mentor, whether it comes directly from the mentee or from an intermediary such as your Human Resources department, understand what the programme aims to achieve, how you can serve those objectives and how mentoring others will serve you.

The latter is important, even if it looks rather mercenary in black and white. We don't mean that you should be seeking a commercial benefit, although there are some mentoring models that are paid for, or recognised when being considered for promotion. But you should know that you will get satisfaction, fulfilment and enjoyment from the experience. By no means should it be a chore or thankless task.

If you are going to be an effective mentor who has a career-long impact on your mentee's life, you need to fully commit to the process. You are far more likely to do so if you are aligned with its purpose and if doing so makes you feel anchored and positive. The act of mentoring makes you come alive with excitement; it is not just what you do, it is who you are.

Are you good enough to be a mentor?

One of the things that might stop you from putting yourself forward to be a mentor, or accepting an invitation either to mentor an individual or be a mentor on a formal programme, is impostor syndrome. Doubt about the value of your experience and achievement, together with a fear of being exposed as a

---

[69] Chopra, V., et al. (2016). "Mentorship malpractice." *JAMA* **315**(14): 1453–1454.
[70] Davila, J.S. and Gotian, R. (2023). "Tormentor mentors, and how to survive them." *Nature* 16 March. doi: 10.1038/d41586-023-00821-8. Epub ahead of print. PMID: 36928402.

fraud, might also impact the advice that you give, making you hold back from offering strong, confident opinions.

Caroline Flanagan, author of *Be the First*,[71] believes that imposter syndrome can prevent people from accepting an invitation to be a mentor, or to be mentored, in several ways. She told us, "If someone experiences imposter syndrome, they may feel unqualified to be a mentor and lack confidence in giving advice to others. They may believe that they are not worthy of being a mentor or that they don't have enough experience or knowledge to offer to others.

"Similarly, impostor syndrome may make someone feel unworthy of being mentored and make them believe that they have nothing valuable to offer as a mentee. They may feel like they're not smart enough or have enough to contribute in a mentoring relationship, and this fear may prevent them from accepting an invitation to be mentored.

"Imposter syndrome can also make people feel like they need to have everything figured out before they can be a mentor or be mentored. This pressure to be perfect and have all the answers can feel overwhelming and prevent someone from stepping into a mentoring relationship.

"Overall, imposter syndrome can hold people back from being mentors or being mentored, which can prevent them from sharing their experiences and learning from others."

Clearly, this is far from an ideal situation. If people hold back from volunteering or accepting a role in a mentoring relationship, others miss out. Mentees don't get the benefit of the experience of some highly accomplished people, while the organisation may not see their future talent pipeline reach its full potential if they don't have the confidence to take the support available to them.

Caroline offered some simple tips to help overcome imposter syndrome and be a successful mentor (Figure 5.1).

She stressed that "Being a mentor is a sign of success in itself and the fact that you have been asked to be one speaks to the talents and abilities recognised in you. By acknowledging your accomplishments, addressing your concerns through a gradual approach, and sharing your experiences authentically and

---

[71] Flanagan, C. (2021). *Be the First: People of Colour, Imposter Syndrome and the Struggle to Succeed in a White World*. Known Publishing.

> **How to Overcome Imposter Syndrome and be a Successful Mentor**
>
> **1. Recognise your achievements:** Take some time to reflect on your accomplishments, no matter how big or small they are. This will reinforce your confidence and help you to understand that you are capable of providing valuable advice.
>
> **2. Share your experiences:** As a mentor, you don't have to have all the answers. Instead, you can share your experiences, both positive and negative. This not only helps your mentee to relate to you, but also helps you to see that your own journey has been valuable.
>
> **3. Learn to say "I don't know":** It's okay not to know everything. Being honest about what you don't know can help you and your mentee to find solutions together.
>
> **4. Take small steps:** It's okay to start small and take incremental steps forward. This will help you to build confidence and momentum towards your goal of being a mentor.
>
> **5. Embrace your vulnerability:** Recognise that vulnerability is part of the growth process. Allowing yourself to be vulnerable and open with your mentee can foster an authentic relationship and help both parties to grow.

Figure 5.1 Overcoming imposter syndrome
Source: Caroline Flanagan

vulnerably, you can help yourself in overcoming those feelings of imposter syndrome while providing valuable guidance to your mentee."

Understanding your objectives

Mentoring comes from a deep and personal space. It is based on the inherent desire to pay your knowledge and good fortune forward, and to contribute something of value. Mentoring is deeply personal. Your experiences and ideas are not shared in a void. There is a person on the receiving end who is benefitting from your wisdom and your willingness to share it, thereby making the experience tangible and its success visceral.

There are a number of different factors which may influence your decision to mentor other people, which can be designated into three key categories: *personal, organisational and external*.

Personal objectives

As briefly mentioned above, while not the norm, some mentoring is offered on a commercial basis. This is more, although not exclusively, likely to be mentoring in a specific topic. For example, Andy offers mentoring in developing effective professional relationships as a core part of his commercial offering, allowing his clients to embed the learning they have gained through his talks and training. Colleagues of Andy's and Ruth's will sell mentoring in presentation skills to senior executives who need to speak to large audiences on a regular basis.

However, we envisage that most people reading this book will either already be mentoring others, or considering doing so, on a voluntary basis, as is traditionally the case. It might be that you have benefited from mentors as part of your own development and you now want to 'pay it forward' by giving similar support to somebody else. On the flip side, it could be that you never received mentoring, had to fight an uphill battle and want to ensure that others have the opportunities you didn't have.

Certain groups have had greater challenges navigating corporate culture and hierarchy. They have achieved success, but not without the significant expense of time and patience. They faced a hidden curriculum[72] – the unwritten rules, traditions and practices that certain people simply seem to know and be aware of. To help people avoid these overt and covert hurdles, leaders want to help the next generation avoid the agony, wasted time, frustration and embarrassment they were put through. This is often seen with underrepresented groups such as women, certain ethnic groups, LGBT+ and first-generation college students.[73]

Nicholas Davies had to work harder to get a foot on the career ladder than some of his current colleagues, finding his way around the education system and job market without the guidance and support that many of his peers had.

As a first-generation student from a state school with lower grades, Nicholas faced obstacles in his journey to higher education. However, he was determined to succeed and pursued his studies at Queen Mary's University in London as a mature student after completing an access course.

---

[72] Alsubaie, M.A. (2015). "Hidden curriculum as one of current issue of curriculum." *Journal of Education and Practice* **6**(33).
[73] Pichon, A. (2023). "How many roads must a woman walk down?" *Nature Chemistry* **15**, 443–445. https://doi.org/10.1038/s41557-023-01161-w

After completing university, Nicholas found himself lacking the necessary skills and knowledge to navigate the job application process. With no professional career or university experience within his family, he felt the absence of social capital that he now recognises his soon-to-be colleagues had access to. It took him some time to secure his first career jobs, but eventually, he found success working in Parliament for fourteen years, ultimately as a senior policy specialist for the environmental and audit committee. In this role, Nicholas managed parliamentary inquiries and provided advice to Members of Parliament on scrutinising the Government's environmental and climate policies.

Having personally experienced the challenges of being a first-generation student with limited guidance and social capital, Nicholas felt a strong desire to give back and provide support to others facing similar struggles. When approached by Queen Mary's mentoring project to be a mentor, he saw it as an opportunity to help students who may be encountering the same difficulties he faced after leaving university.

Nicholas emphasised the importance of diversity in parliament, not just in terms of race, but also in terms of class and educational background. He understood the value of having mentors who can relate to and understand the unique challenges faced by individuals from underrepresented communities. He acknowledged, "I think it's essential because we're trying to address a real problem of underrepresentation."

Recognising that many individuals are the first in their families to attend university, Nicholas saw the need for mentorship to provide guidance and support in navigating higher education and career opportunities. He participated in a mentoring programme and mentored two individuals – a working-class young woman and a first-generation Polish student – studying at Queen Mary's. Nicholas provided them with guidance on writing applications and exploring post-university opportunities.

Nicholas shared a powerful moment when he received a text message from the Polish student thanking him for his help, as it led to her securing a job with the Metropolitan Police. This experience reinforced his belief in the impact and importance of mentoring, stating, "To get a text message like that, you realise that your support has actually changed someone's life."

Through his personal journey and experiences, Nicholas has become a passionate advocate for mentoring and giving back. He understands the barriers faced by individuals from underrepresented backgrounds and the power of mentorship in providing them with the guidance, support and social capital they may lack. Nicholas expressed, "I didn't have any guidance or a mentor when I was younger. I didn't ask for help, but now I realise how much it would have benefited me. If I'd had a mentor at the same stage, I wonder where I could have got to. I probably would've got a lot further a lot faster."

One of the main strategies to achieve equity in the workplace is finding role models and mentors from that background who are happy to share their experiences and help others to achieve similar progress in their careers. But don't only rely on people who look like you or who have a similar background. There may be few of those people in leadership positions and if they spend all their time mentoring, they can't do their work, which can, in turn, inhibit their career success. We share an example of this in Chapter 15. Also, while there are benefits to having people with similar backgrounds on your mentoring team, it is imperative that you diversify your mentoring team so that the guidance you receive is not in an echo chamber.

A strong motivator can be a very individual one, and that's a sense of personal fulfilment. We get a lot of pleasure from helping other people and seeing them succeed, particularly if we know that we have played a part in their success. In her TEDx talk, Dr Deborah Heiser, the CEO and cofounder of The Mentor Project, explains that our greatest natural resource is not oil or gas, it is people.

A quarter of a century of aging research shows that, as we age we search for meaning, values and joy. Mentorship is a profound way to bring about a sense of purpose and happiness.[74] Coined by psychologist Erik Erikson, this idea of wanting to give back and help the next generation is called 'generativity'.[75] We are built to give back, and mentorship is the perfect vehicle to make it happen.[76,77] While we may think it is the most seasoned of our workforce who want to give back, leading mentoring thought leader Kathy Kram's research has shown that a midcareer professional may find that entering into a mentoring relationship with someone more junior offers an opportunity at midlife to redirect one's focus into actions that are productive and creative.[78]

---

[74] Dr Deborah Heiser TEDx talk: **https://www.ted.com/talks/deborah_heiser_rethinking_aging_mentoring_a_new_generation?utm_campaign=tedspread&utm_medium=referral&utm_source=tedcomshare**
[75] Erikson, E.H. (1979-1974). *Dimensions of a New Identity*. W.W. Norton.
[76] Barnett, S.K. (1984). "The mentor role: A task of generativity." *Journal of Human Behavior and Learning* **1**: 15-18.
[77] Levinson, D.J., et al. (1978). *The Seasons of a Man's Life*. New York, Ballentine.
[78] Kram, K. (1983). "Phases of the mentor relationship." *Academy of Management Journal* **26**(4): 608-625.

Nobel Prize winner Dr Robert (Bob) Lefkowitz shares that if he is going to successfully support one of his mentees, two things need to happen. The mentee needs to be excited about the project they are working on, and Bob needs to be excited about it as well. When they are both excited, they are both invested in its potential and together will work hard to see it through.[79]

The purest reason to support someone else, and the one most likely to be sustainable and impactful, is your belief in the individual you are going to mentor and what they are setting out to achieve. You have a chemistry and rapport with them, believe in their potential and want to help them to fulfil it.

If we fully buy into somebody else's mission, we get pleasure from helping them to achieve it in a way beyond the joy we get from reaching our own objectives. Helping others to achieve their goals can bring huge satisfaction and be a very powerful motivator to mentor those people.

Organisational objectives

Many mentors are approached by HR departments, senior management teams or networks within organisations to help towards a key organisational goal. Mentoring others may be within your job description; more often it's likely to be a request for extra-curricular activity, but towards an objective you are bought into.

Forward planning is often the key driver for organisations to introduce mentoring programmes, with new directors being mentored as part of the Board's succession planning and mentoring support providing a key element within a 'rising leaders' programme designed to nurture the future leadership of the organisation.

Matthew Lewis led a global talent development programme from the CEO's office at GlaxoSmithKline (GSK). The goal of the programme was to accelerate the development of emerging leaders, and drive alignment and simplification across GSK by getting key talent from across the business working together.

As part of the GSK programme, participants got support from a number of people, including their own manager, a full-time performance coach and a mentor.

---

[79] Lefkowitz, R. and Hall, R. (2021). *A Funny Thing Happened on the Way to Stockholm: The Adrenaline-fueled Adventures of An Accidental Scientist*. New York, Pegasus Books.

The mentors were drawn from previous participants in the programme and met with their mentee every two weeks to discuss a range of mentee-led topics, which could range from limiting beliefs to support with living in a major city.

Matthew told us that the role of the mentor was key. "Having participated in the programme before, the mentors could share their own experiences and reinforce the behaviours needed to get the most out of the programme. It was also important that they were able to share their knowledge of navigating the organisation to make sure that the projects the mentees were working on were successful.

"The involvement of the mentors reassured participants when they most needed it and made sure that they could get the maximum benefit from their involvement, whether for their project, personal development or finding their next role."

As we've covered elsewhere in this book, mentoring doesn't just follow one trajectory. Successful organisations ensure that information, ideas, experience and expertise circulate between departments, divisions and the hierarchy, thereby knocking down silos. The best insights don't always flow down from the most senior tiers, and reverse mentoring is a great tool to ensure that new ideas and technologies best understood by younger generations are embraced by those who aren't as naturally inclined to adapt.[80]

It pays organisations to invest in and encourage effective mentoring. Not only do they benefit from the rewards mentioned above but good mentoring creates the sense of a better place to work. A 2019 Gallup study showed that only 15% of people are engaged at work, and that was before the pandemic.[81,82]

This is a significant problem as those who are engaged at work are more productive and innovative, not just happier. People are more likely to commit more of their futures to an employer who they feel cares about what that future

---

[80] Marcinkus Murphy, W. (2012). "Reverse mentoring at work: Fostering cross-generational learning and developing millennial leaders." *Human Resources Management* **51**: 549–573. https://doi.org/10.1002/hrm.21489

[81] Gallup (2017). "State of the global workplace." Canada. https://fundacionprolongar.org/wp-content/uploads/2019/07/State-of-the-Global-Workplace_Gallup-Report.pdf Retrieved 15 November 2022.

[82] Zhang, T., Wang, D.J. and Galinsky, A.D. (2023). "Learning down to train up: mentors are more effective when they value insights from below." *Academy of Management Journal* **66**(2): 604–637.

looks like and wants to help them achieve their full potential. Mentoring can also lead to increased engagement at work while working as the perfect retention tool.[83]

Meanwhile, if you can build the reputation of a caring employer who invests in their staff, more and higher calibre candidates will be attracted to apply for future roles, meaning that the quality of the workforce continues to develop externally through recruitment as well as internally through mentoring.

External objectives

When discussing personal objectives, we reflected on the importance of giving a hand up to people from underrepresented groups, as we have done when talking about the minority tax elsewhere in this book. Increased representation of certain demographics at senior levels of industry and commerce, or just within that industry, is not just a personal or organisational goal but often driven by industry bodies and governments too. There are many mentoring schemes developed by public bodies and charities to help to achieve these goals.

Vanessa Vallely OBE, Founder of We Are the City, told us, "In the last five years we have seen a massive increase in mentoring programmes and a recognition of their importance. There are many more government funded programmes across the UK for mentoring groups to support underrepresented communities.

"There is also a big increase in mentoring programmes being funded in schools, with government encouragement and corporate involvement.

"Whether or not they are being done in the right way, with the right support, funding and follow up to measure the results and impact is another story. There's still something missing when it comes to providing the same support for sponsorship for women to get to senior roles, for example. We can't just get there with mentoring alone, advocacy is a key part of the puzzle too, in order to bring opportunity to the mentees and propel women in industry."

In 2012 Chelsey Baker was one of the lead mentors with the UK's Start Up Loans finance scheme alongside the late Lord David Young. The government-funded programme invested millions of pounds into start-up businesses, providing

---

[83] Allen, T., et al. (2004). "Career benefits associated with mentoring for protegee: A meta analysis." *Journal of Applied Psychology* 89(1): 127.

them with mentoring support as part of the package. Lord Young said at the time, "The mentor is far more important than the money."

Chelsey's involvement with that start-up programme led to her recognising that there was so much support needed for small businesses that wasn't being leveraged. As a result, she launched National Mentoring Day,[84] now recognised as the largest celebration of mentoring in the world, designed to amplify all forms of mentoring to make it as accessible to as many people as possible, putting it at the forefront of business, education and society. Companies of all sizes now participate on 27th October every year, with a global goal of everybody involved mentoring at least one person on that day.

Chelsey told us, "The four founding pillars of National Mentoring Day are to celebrate, educate, connect and support mentors, mentees and mentoring programmes. The celebrate element is so important, we're celebrating the transformational power of mentorship. By sharing the success stories, we're inspiring even more people to take up mentoring."

Who should you mentor?

In Chapter 12 we will look at how organisations can effectively match mentors and mentees, but don't wait to be asked. Once you have made the decision that mentoring is for you, be proactive about taking the first step and finding a mentee who fits the bill for the objectives you have set yourself.

Those objectives outlined should provide a good guide to identifying whom you want to mentor. Sometimes those mentees will be obvious because of the objective, DEI-driven goals as an obvious example.

Speak to HR and the employee resource groups (ERGs) within your organisation who are running mentoring programmes and discuss the mentees they are seeking to match. Don't simply volunteer to be a mentor but share your objectives as a mentor with the person running the programme and work with them to find the best fit.

Have similar conversations with fellow leaders about who on their teams might benefit from your support. Perhaps offer to swap mentoring support, so that

---

[84] "National Mentoring Day." Retrieved 1 December 2023, from **http://www.nationalmentoringday.org**

you work with people on their team and they with someone on yours, giving those mentees some support outside the direct line of management and a different perspective to help with their development. Just make sure that your agreement with fellow leaders respects the confidentiality of the people you both agree to mentor.

You do, however, need to avoid falling into the 'Mini-Me Trap'[85] or succumbing to transference. It's natural to look for people to whom you relate, people whom you see a version of yourself in, to mentor. Similarly, it's easy to recognise or be attracted to qualities you see in somebody that remind you of someone else with whom you have worked previously and mentor on that basis.

There are some advantages to recognising yourself and others in people you mentor. You are far more likely to understand their thought processes and the challenges they face if your mentee has followed a very similar journey to your own or with which you are already familiar.

There is danger in mentoring a Mini-Me or clone of others though. We can create and perpetuate echo chambers, with the same ideas and approaches resonating through the generations. And the lack of cross-pollination of different ideas and objectives is not likely to serve the diversity of the workforce and the organisation as a whole.

We also need to take into account the different context faced by your new mentee, as well as their different personality, perspective or ambitions. It's too easy to just replicate what went before, without adapting to different circumstances.

We have to bear in mind that the underrepresented groups we've talked a lot about will, by their very nature, have fewer potential mentors who are 'like them'. Statistically, there are simply fewer of them in the C-Suite and other parts of management. Studies have shown that white men don't feel comfortable reaching out to women to offer mentoring, but will do so if there is a formal mentoring programme in place.[86]

---

[85] Woolston, C. (2019). "A message for mentors from dissatisfied graduate students." *Nature* 575(7783): 551–552. doi: 10.1038/d41586-019-03535-y. PMID: 31748721.

[86] Thomas, D.A. (1989). "Mentoring and irrationality: The role of racial taboos." *Human Resources Management* 28: 279–290. https://doi.org/10.1002/hrm.3930280213

So, while there are attractions to finding mentors from those underrepresented demographics, we also need mentors from the majority groups to step forward and support people who don't have their advantages. Furthermore, looking only for mentees who are from identical backgrounds will ensure that you continue to give and receive guidance in an echo chamber. We are not arguing that you don't get mentees who look like you, rather, that everyone is encouraged to diversify their mentors and build a mentoring team with a variety of people, backgrounds and experiences who can offer additional perspectives.

CHAPTER 6
RESPONSIBILITIES OF A MENTOR

In the early 2000s, Ruth mentored a young college student through a summer programme she ran. The programme was for promising underrepresented students who were contemplating becoming physician-scientists.[87] Odi Ehie was considering this career path but ultimately decided to focus on the MD degree. Over the years, Ruth and Odi kept in touch on and off. One day, an email came from Odi. She was finishing medical school and disenchanted with the career ahead. She began to contemplate if her lifelong ambition to become a physician was the right career choice. Many sleepless nights later, she emailed Ruth to ask for her help thinking through her healthcare career choice.

Ruth responded to the email, like she usually does. That led to a phone conversation, an introduction to someone in Ruth's network, which ultimately led to a research position. Dr Ehie fell in love with medicine again and went on to complete a residency and fellowship.

Today, she is a paediatric anaesthesiologist and the vice-chair of her department at the University of California, San Francisco. Over a decade after that fateful email, Odi revealed to Ruth that the email was a Hail Mary. It was her one final attempt at trying to find her purpose in healthcare. Responding to the email was meaningless to Ruth. It was part of her daily tasks. To Odi, it was meaningful and in this case, life-changing.

Mentoring is powerful and can change someone's life. But let's start with what mentoring is not. By no means is it solving your mentee's problems. You do, however, help them solve their own problems by offering perspective, enthusiasm and a safety net. Your advice can impact the career trajectory and chances of success of the people you support.

---

[87] Gotian, R., Raymore, J.C., Rhooms, S.K., Liberman, L. and Andersen, O.S. (2017). "Gateways to the laboratory: How an MD-PhD program increased the number of minority physician-scientists." *Academic Medicine* **92**(5): 628–634. doi: 10.1097/ACM.0000000000001478. PMID: 28441673.

As a mentor, you are the bridge between what they are doing and what they didn't even know is possible. You clear murky waters so that your mentee can make informed decisions. While the ultimate burden of their choices should lie with the mentee, that doesn't diminish the importance of the alternatives you suggest and the options for which you advocate.

That responsibility begins with the selection of your mentee, or your agreement to a request to be their mentor. Do you feel qualified to provide the support and insights that the mentee is looking for? Are you on board with what they want to achieve and do you believe in them – in their potential to reach their objectives? Do you have the time and inclination to commit to the mentoring process?

Unless you believe that you can help and support your mentee, and that the path they have their heart set upon is one worth exploring, you shouldn't take on the task. You may not agree it's the right one but that wouldn't necessarily exclude you from mentoring them if you can both be open-minded and explore the possibilities. You have to be all in and committed to this mentoring relationship if it is going to work.

Don't worry if you are not the world's expert on whatever topic they need help with. You just need to be the expert in the room, the one with patience, a listening ear and a willingness to share your perspective.

Statistically, you are not always going to share the same race, ethnicity, gender, religion, culture and upbringing as your mentee. That's fine, but there is one issue you should never compromise on – your values. Are your values aligned with your mentee's? You might have different beliefs about which pathway is right, what actions to take or which steps to prioritise. Those differences are fine; you can debate and agree to disagree on the final step. But values are far more important. If your fundamental beliefs conflict, then you will have a real challenge and the mentoring relationship may sour.

One of Andy's mentees, Chloe Petrovna Nwankwo, was the victim of racist bullying and came to him for support in developing an anti-bullying campaign. That campaign quickly evolved into one that embraced not just anti-bullying and anti-racism but a range of social issues that Andy felt very comfortable supporting.

Andy felt less comfortable, however, when Chloe began to include Bible quotes on the front page of the newsletter that lay at the centre of her campaign. Andy expressed concerns that the inclusion of Bible quotations would pigeonhole the newsletter as a niche religious publication and restrict the audience for an important message.

They both discussed their views and reasons behind them at length, and Andy suggested that Chloe reflect on her choices rather than make a snap decision. She came back and said that her religious beliefs were too important to her and that she would not be true to herself if she removed the quotes.

Andy reflected too and decided to continue with the mentoring, despite the disagreement. Although their beliefs on the role of religion within the campaign differed, their values didn't. Both Andy and Chloe felt strongly about the importance of making sure that victims of bullying were supported and didn't feel alone, as well as giving a voice to other social issues.

In this case, the mentoring relationship still felt right; Andy felt that his advice had been seriously considered and not ignored. But not every possible mentee will be a fit for you and you need to be brave enough to say 'no' if that's the case. Don't just turn them away though, offer an alternative option: someone from your network who is a better fit or better positioned to give them the support they need.

Understand your limitations

When you take on a mentee, it doesn't mean that you are expected to know all the answers or take the full burden of guidance on yourself. In fact, the best mentors say, "I don't know, but I can figure out who to ask." You can serve your mentee best by bringing your wider network into play and helping them to build their 'mentoring team'.[88] This doesn't replace your own ideas and experience; rather it serves as an enhancement.

If you are the mentor in a traditional-hierarchical mentoring relationship, the chances are that you will be far better connected than your mentee. We develop our networks over the course of our career. If we are mindful of maintaining and nurturing key connections, our people resource, or social capital, grows with us. Part of taking on a mentee is making that network, and the resources it offers, available to our mentees.

As you discuss challenges and next steps, always consider who you know who might shine a different light on a key discussion and give a more relevant or

---

[88] Gotian, R. (2020). "How to develop a mentoring team." *Forbes*.

insightful perspective than you can manage. You can't expect the other people in your network to volunteer their support, but you can ask the question and make the introduction if they are happy for you to do so.

> **Consider this script:**
>
> *"Sally, I know you have deep expertise in X. My mentee, Roger, is working on a project and has run into a challenge which would benefit greatly from your insight. Do you have some time where he can run his thinking by you and perhaps see what he is missing?"*

Andy's mentee mentioned above decided to start a podcast as part of her anti-bullying and social justice campaign. Despite having a relatively successful podcast of his own, Andy wouldn't call himself an expert in launching podcasts. But he knows people who are. Andy asked one of the people in his network if she would be willing to chat with his mentee about successfully starting a podcast. Not only did she do so, she took it a step further and started mentoring her regularly on developing the podcast and growing its reach.

Meanwhile, another of Andy's network, who has developed a membership programme packed with resources for podcast hosts, provided free access to Andy's mentee.

It is up to the mentee to decide to what extent they want to leverage the support offered to them. If they are honest and don't ask for an introduction they don't intend to follow up with, as well as reliable and respectful in the way they correspond and value the support offered to them, that should be good enough.

But let's be clear, when a mentor is sharing part of their network with a mentee, that is their political and social capital they are tapping into. Stress to the mentee that you can only tap into this network if they will hold up their part and make them proud. They can do so by being professional, curious, hardworking and clear in their communication.

As the original mentor, we would suggest checking in with both parties and satisfying yourself that both are happy with the introduction. If you want to build on those introductions, you can review the advice given and action taken in your own mentoring conversations.

Keep your mentee on track

If you're going to invest valuable time and experience in a mentee, you want to make sure that it's valued and respected. You can play a role in ensuring that happens by setting clear objectives and milestones from the beginning and holding your mentee accountable throughout the relationship. You don't necessarily need a structured agenda, but advance notice of key topics to be discussed will help both parties make efficient use of the time allotted and allow for any pre-work needed by either member.

If you have a good rapport with your mentee, it can be very easy for your mentoring sessions to descend into friendly, relaxed catch-ups with no real progress being made. Of course, small-talk is important; it helps you to get to know your mentee in a more rounded way and breaks down any perceived barriers. If you can create a genuine connection, encouraging your mentee to remove their metaphorical mask, then they are going to be more likely to open up to you, share more honestly and allow you to dig deeper and resolve real issues.

But too much small talk and too little focus can be a problem. Challenge your mentee from day one to establish what they want to achieve from working with you and how they will know if the relationship is beneficial. Consider phrases such as:

- *What are you looking to achieve?*
- *How will you know if this is working?*
- *How will you know when you achieve this goal?*
- *What is your timeline for achieving this goal?*
- *How much do you want me to push you?*
- *Are you looking for someone to keep you accountable or just a listening ear?*

Plans can change and you should be able to adapt, but you need a direction to set out towards in the first place.

Once your mentee has shared their initial objective, work with them to clarify and refine it and come up with an initial plan to get there. Understand what is standing in the way of them achieving their objective and how you can help them to navigate those hurdles.

Be in the room

Whether you are mentoring people online or together in the same room, you should be mindful and present for your conversation.

The chances are that your own role will provide you with any number of potential distractions and when your mentoring appointment comes around, you will have countless deadlines or challenges that need your attention. But they need to be set to one side and not prey on your mind when you are mentoring. You owe your mentee your full attention for the time you have agreed to spend with them.

If you are together in the same room, step away from your computer. If you can move away from your desk, even into a neutral (albeit confidential) space, that is ideal. Great mentoring conversations have occurred in hallways, conference rooms and coffee shops. But at the very least, ensure that your computer and any mobile devices are off and you are not to be disturbed.

If that is not a possibility, consider silencing your notifications (do you really need to be alerted every time you get a text message or someone likes your social media post?). This will also help with focus outside of your mentoring work. Obviously, if you are mentoring online, you are likely to be on your computer. Consider turning on the "Do Not Disturb" function which will silence alerts for the duration of your mentoring meeting.

If you are not in a position to give your full attention to your mentee, you cannot support them to the best of your ability. You need to be able to listen and reflect without distraction if you are to offer the best advice. Your mentoring meeting is not your time, it is your gift to your mentee. So, focus wholly on them.

It is better to reschedule a mentoring meeting to a time when you are less distracted than to try to wedge a meeting in when you are not truly focused.

In confidence

To make a genuine impact on your mentee's journey, you need them to be completely honest, vulnerable and transparent with you. For that to happen, they need to be confident that they can share openly with you without worrying about who else might hear about your conversations. The trust factor must be unwavering.

This is hopefully obvious advice but it's surprisingly easy to let confidences slip out when you're in related conversations. Maintaining confidence isn't just about not gossiping around the office or sharing your mentee's secrets on social media; there will be times in meetings when something shared by your mentee will be pertinent to the conversation, but it would be inappropriate to share it without their permission. Your first loyalty in such situations is to your mentee and you need to respect that. Breaking that seal of confidentiality is the ultimate loss of trust.

A fear of indiscretion is probably one of the biggest factors that will prevent a mentee from truly opening up and letting you help them. It will already feel natural to them to look strong and in control in front of you, particularly if you are senior to them in the same organisation. And that alone will inhibit open sharing. If they have to worry about what others think, as well as you, they will clam up. But if you can win their trust, you can enjoy some truly powerful, and empowering, conversations.

ICE CREAM

A mentor has many roles ranging from career development and emotional empowerment to network enhancement. These varying responsibilities and opportunities of a mentor can be summarised by the mnemonic ICE CREAM (Figure 6.1).

Introduce: One of the critical roles of a mentor is to introduce the mentee to new ideas, perspectives and people. Get them to think outside of their comfort zone of what could be, not just what is. Who are the people who can help them expand or showcase their ideas and projects?

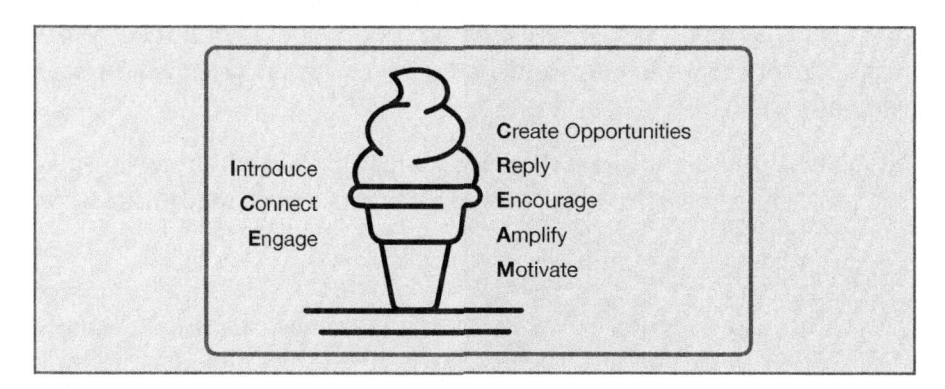

Introduce
Connect
Engage
Create Opportunities
Reply
Encourage
Amplify
Motivate

Figure 6.1 Responsibilities of a mentor

Connect: Innovation is the connection of two points other people don't yet see. Taxis and hotels are not new concepts but Uber and Airbnb turned the industry on its head. Help your mentee reframe problems,[89] think critically and take strategic risks, so that they start making connections which are not obvious to others.

Engage: Mentoring is a two-way relationship. The mentor cannot stand there and deliver a monologue and the mentee should not be passive either. It is a give and take, Ying and Yang, ebb and flow. The conversations and interactions should be engaging as they peel away layers of frustration, inhibition and vulnerability to get to the truth of the matter.

Create opportunities: Let's start with a basic premise that we don't know what we don't know. We aren't aware of what is possible and beyond the horizon. To expand outside our comfort zone, a mentee needs to take on stretch assignments. It is the mentor who can and should create those opportunities for the mentee by giving them new projects or recommending them to others who could use their expertise.

Reply: When a mentee is in the thick of things, they lack perspective and every problem seems like an insurmountable mountain. The longer they stew on a problem, the more disastrous the ramifications play out in their mind.

A mentor has perspective and can pull a mentee from their catastrophic thinking and offer sound guidance. For that to happen, a mentor needs to be able to respond to a mentee's questions and concerns in real time. A quick response can be just the reassurance a mentee needs.

Encourage: Not every day is rainbows and puppy dogs. Some days are just plain bad. Nothing is working, stress is mounting, and people are unresponsive. Maybe the mentee received unexpected bad news, or perhaps they didn't get a promotion they were after. All hope should not be lost, and a mentor can offer encouraging words, a shoulder to cry on, or a much-needed listening ear.

The mentor needs to encourage the mentee and help them put things into perspective. Get them back to their 'why', what is called in adult learning 'your

---

[89] Wedell-Wedellsborg, T. (2020). *What's Your Problem?* Boston, MA, Harvard Business Review Press.

intrinsic motivation'.[90,91] It answers the questions of why they are pursuing this path. When you recalibrate with your 'why', you will be intrinsically motivated to continue, despite setbacks.

Amplify: The extension of mentorship is sponsorship, the act of speaking about your mentee in the most positive light, usually when they are not in the room. By amplifying their work and good name, as a mentor, you are throwing your good name and reputation in support of your mentee. Consider talking about them in meetings, giving them a shout out on social media, letting others know when they did a good job or achieved something. It might be meaning*less* to you as a mentor, but meaning*ful* to your mentee to know that someone is singing their praises.

Motivate: There are days when sometimes, we just can't. We can't answer another email, have another whining conversation, deal with another crisis, or solve someone else's problem created by their disorganisation. Similar to the *encourage* trait, we need to motivate our mentees. Sometimes, it is more extrinsic[92] with the promise of a bonus, certificate or opportunity.

Just be careful not to do these too often, as extrinsic motivation is when others judge you. That is challenging to maintain and often short lived. It may work for the short term, but what is most durable is to help the mentee tap into their intrinsic motivation. Tapping into that source will help the mentee overcome repeated challenges, stay the course, and see every mistake and failure as a learning opportunity.

The bigger picture

While your primary responsibility is to your mentee, if your involvement is part of an internal programme or request, you can't ignore your wider responsibility to the organisation which employs you.

---

[90] Knowles, M.S. (1970). *The Modern Practice of Adult Education*. New York, New York, Association Press.
[91] Gotian, R. (2022). *The Success Factor: Developing the Mindset and Skillset for Peak Business Performance*. New York, NY, Kogan Page.
[92] Knowles, M.S. (1984). *The Adult Learner: A Neglected Species*. Houston, Gulf.

In Chapter 5 we explored why organisations need to introduce and encourage mentoring support, and it's important that you are aware of these objectives and keep them in mind in your discussions with your mentee. Reflect on those objectives as you go through your mentoring discussions.

If the organisation introduces mentoring programmes to engage with and develop its next generation of leaders, then that internal career progression should be part of the objectives set by your mentee and on the agenda for your discussions. Don't wait for the mentee to raise it and ignore it if they don't, bring it up and ensure that it's covered. That doesn't mean forcing an agenda that the mentee doesn't welcome. They should be aware of the purpose of the programme they are part of.

Tell them that the organisation sees their potential and is invested in their future within the organisation. They want to help them rise through the ranks and have a long career within the institution. Who doesn't want to hear that their good work is noticed?

If you spot someone with real potential, go beyond mentoring and become their sponsor. Advocate on their behalf, encourage them to apply for opportunities that will help them to reach their potential and amplify their brand. By supporting your mentee in raising their profile, you'll be supporting your organisation too by helping them to recognise the talent lying within its ranks.

Of course, the interests of the mentee and those of the organisation that has set up the mentoring relationship don't always perfectly align. The next ideal step for your mentee may, for example, be away from their current employer or role. How do you balance that conflict?

It's quite simple: you put your mentee first. Discuss with them both sides of the argument, including the reasons to stay where they are, of course. But if they need to move forward by moving on, support them in that direction. Who knows, your mentoring might be enough to convince them to stay but, if it doesn't, they are more likely to leave on a positive note and be an advocate for the organisation from the outside, telling future potential employees, clients or suppliers what a great and supportive culture it offers. It is also not inconceivable that they may return to the organisation after having acquired new skills elsewhere.

You may also experience conflict where the mentee's objectives or challenges directly impact the work you are doing in your day-to-day role. If this is the case, be open about it and recuse yourself if necessary. If you are comfortable that you can be objective in your mentoring, let the mentee and the organisation decide the best route forward.

Similarly, if you have a poor relationship with someone who plays an important role in the mentee's journey, challenge yourself on whether you can be objective and, if not, recuse yourself from that particular conversation and recommend an alternative way forward.

CHAPTER 7
THE INGREDIENTS OF AN EFFECTIVE MENTORING RELATIONSHIP

Who do you feel has had the biggest impact on your career?

Assuming you have been mentored in the past, we'd like you to take a few minutes to reflect on the mentors who have had the biggest influence on your journey.

Why did those particular mentors spring to mind?

What did they say or do and how did it affect your journey to where you are now?

Was there anything about the way they engaged with you and showed an interest in your success that inspired you to take action?

What did you feel like after speaking with them? Were you energised and motivated or depleted?

What would you say if you were to sit down and write a letter to thank them for their support? *We fully recommend that you do this. Your former or current mentor likely is not aware of the impact they had on your career. You can seriously make their day! Email them to us as well at* **authors@mentoring-guide.com**, *we'd love to see them and share some of your experiences (anonymously or not – it's up to you!).*

If you want to become the best mentor you could possibly be, a good place to start would be to understand the qualities you most value in the mentors who have supported you. Recognise the traits that you most want to emulate as well as the behaviour you don't.

Couple your own personal observations with the advice we share in this chapter to help you to create the best, most impactful, possible relationship with anybody you mentor.

Write your letter to your former mentor here.

Dear _____

Mentoring agility

What worked for one mentee may not be appropriate for another. Adults take in and process information differently, and they also value different things with varying levels of importance. Knowing how to reach each mentee where they are is critical. Some mentees might need to be told what to do while others want to weigh options and make the decision for themselves.[93,94] One is not better than the other, they are just different. We are not the same; it is always beneficial to have options at your disposal.

Experiential learning theorist David Kolb developed a learning style inventory to distinguish the variances in how people consume and process information.[95] For example, some might take in or process information by reading while others might need to talk it out; some might work better in groups while others prefer the isolation. As adults, we can all learn new things, but we all do it differently.

Understanding this variation will help you be nimble in your mentoring as you communicate in a manner in which your mentee will understand and offer resources which best align with the way they take in and process information. Not everything needs to be a conversation. Sometimes a podcast or article might do the trick.

As we've already stressed elsewhere in this book, successful mentoring relationships are founded on clear objectives and expectations. These are ideally set by the mentee, but not in isolation. Mentor and mentee should work together from their first conversation to set those objectives, understanding exactly to what purpose they are working together and what each party is looking for.

That doesn't mean that those goals are set in stone. The one thing you can be certain of is that change will come. Throughout the programme, conversations should be responsive to changes in circumstance and to new challenges that arise. You should always be reflecting back on the agreed outcomes and reviewing whether you are on track, the objectives have changed or if you need to find your way back to the path.

---

[93] Drago-Severson, E. (2009). *Leading Adult Learning*. Thousand Oaks, CA, SAGE.
[94] Drago-Severson, E. (2009). "How do you 'know'." *Yes!*. **Fall 2009**.
[95] Kolb, D. (1984). *Experiential Learning: Experience as the Source for Learning and Development*. Englewood Cliffs, NJ, Prentice Hall.

Good mentors are both flexible and adaptable.[96,97] While the two terms are often used interchangeably, there are some nuances. Flexibility refers to changes that are often made in real time, often met with compromise, such as meeting someone halfway. Flexibility often has us changing our tactical processes to fit the current situation. Your ability to remain flexible means you can determine a change of course as a situation unfolds, always with the end goal in mind. Often under the pressure of time, flexibility means you are able to modify plans and processes when necessary. You remain nimble as circumstances evolve.

Adaptability is more long term, requires an open mind, and is often met with a required change of cognition, behaviour and emotional regulation in novel situations of change and uncertainty.[98] Adaptability refers to "an individual's ability, skill, disposition, willingness, and/or motivation to change or fit different task, social, or environmental features."[99] Being adaptable implies that you are willing to learn, grow and develop new skills or perspectives to meet changing demands or circumstances. While flexibility occurs in real time, adaptability takes place over a length of time.

A firm foundation, coupled with the right balance of flexibility and adaptability, allows you to take a more strategic overview – finding balance to short-term imperatives while keeping on track towards long-term goals. This agility allows you to shift direction to accommodate for small changes in circumstance, while remaining open to major shifts in approach if needed.

However collaborative you are in having these conversations, ultimately the mentee drives the direction of these discussions. It's their journey after all, not the mentor's, and as previously discussed, you should not try to have the

---

[96] Broza, O., Kadury-Slezak, M., Biberman-Shalev, L. and Patkin, D. (2022). "Agility and flexibility: Key aspects for pedagogical mentoring in the age of COVID-19 crisis." *International Journal for Cross-Disciplinary Subjects in Education* **13**: 4631–4634. 10.20533/ijcdse.2042.6364.2022.0569.

[97] Cho, C.S., Ramanan, R.A. and Feldman M.D. (2011). "Defining the ideal qualities of mentorship: a qualitative analysis of the characteristics of outstanding mentors." *American Journal of Medicine* **124**(5):453–458. doi: 10.1016/j.amjmed.2010.12.007. PMID: 21531235.

[98] Zhou, M. and Lin, W. (2016). "Adaptability and life satisfaction: The moderating role of social support." *Frontiers in Psychology* **7**: 1134. **https://doi.org/10.3389/fsyg.2016.00134**.

[99] Ployhart R.E. and Bliese, P.D. (2006). "Individual adaptability (I-ADAPT) theory: conceptualizing the antecedents, consequences, and measurement of individual differences in adaptability," in *Understanding Adaptability: A Prerequisite for Effective Performance Within Complex Environments*, Vol. 6, eds Burke, C.S., Pierce, L.G., Salas, E., St. Louis, MO, Elsevier Science, 3–39.

mentee emulate your career and journey. As a mentor, offer advice and guidance, challenge and question the direction the mentee wants to follow, but once you are comfortable that they have weighed their options and come to a thoughtful conclusion, support your mentee and help them follow the path they have chosen for themselves.

Developing rapport

Mentoring relationships are naturally going to be more effective if there is a good rapport between mentor and mentee, mutual respect and a solid level of trust.

There is a fine line between getting along with your mentee and inviting them to your home for a weekly dinner and regular socialisation. Being friends, or as discussed earlier, 'friendtors', is fine, but be acutely aware that friendships can easily become counter-productive as you may settle too easily into a comfort zone; the mentee may not fully open up and the mentor may not push as hard.[100] Recognise the blind spots and plan accordingly.

You may not even particularly like each other. That's not to suggest that you *dislike* each other, which would make a mentoring relationship tough.

Rapport, however, can make a big difference. You want your mentee to feel relatively at ease in your company and that you can understand and empathise with each other. You should be excited, not depleted, when you see or hear each other.

It may feel superfluous to carry out your duties of providing advice and guidance, but small talk plays a key role in successful mentoring. Both mentors and mentees are humans with regular demands on their personal lives; mortgage, child or elder care, or family drama. This is referred to as a *cognitive load*.[101] These pressures weigh on us and take up valuable real estate in our brain. They impact our working memory storage and processing of information.[102]

---

[100] Gotian, R. (2022). *The Success Factor: Developing the mindset and skillset for peak business performance*. New York, NY, Kogan Page.
[101] Sweller, J. (1988). "Cognitive load during problem solving: Effects on learning." *Cognitive Science* **12**: 257–285.
[102] Schnotz, W. and Kürschner, C. (2007). "A reconsideration of cognitive load theory." *Educational Psychology Review* **19**: 469–508. **https://doi.org/10.1007/s10648-007-9053-4**

Through small talk, you get to know someone better as well as finding out what interests and challenges you share in common. Interests or experiences in common help to develop that rapport and empathy, knowing that, on some level, you understand each other. If you start your conversation with an agenda item, your meetings will become transactional and void of personality, the one ingredient that drives professional relationships.

Our lives are like a Venn diagram: we have overlap of interest or experiences; we just haven't figured out where that overlap is yet. Conversations are the perfect catalyst for this discovery.

Italian leadership strategist Luca Signoretti has an exercise in his talks on networking, where he asks people to pair up and talk about their interests until they find something they both share in common. In his experience, there is always something. Luca said, "If you are intentional in finding something in common with another person, you can always find it in a few minutes just by asking a few questions.

"It is important to be intentional when we build professional relationships. As much as we'd like the relationship to be based on some spontaneous, natural factor, the reality is that if you are serious about connecting with someone you need to go step-by-step in increasing the connection with the other person."

Of course, this shouldn't be a forced exercise and you shouldn't be spending your entire time together trying to find commonalities. Depending on personality type, some people will be more open to small talk than others, and you need to be conscious of not making your mentee feel as though they are being interrogated.

Your conversations should be natural but that doesn't mean that you can't encourage your mentee to open up by sharing your curiosity. If you are senior in the organisation compared to your mentee, showing your interest in them can put your mentee at ease and demonstrate that it is OK for them to open up and share with you. A small investment of curiosity at this early stage of the relationship, and at the beginning of each mentoring session, can pay off as you want to explore more deeply and enjoy more meaningful conversation.

Vulnerability – on both sides

Building that rapport and finding those shared interests can be a major factor in encouraging mentees to be vulnerable with you. As Bob Burg famously recognised, people open up to and like to work with those they know, like and trust.[103]

It is important that both parties in the relationship feel comfortable being both open and transparent. The mentor needs to be aware that their mentee may well look up to them. That could create a barrier to them truly opening up; if they are worried about looking bad in the eyes of someone they admire, they are likely to be less honest and vulnerable. So a mentor needs to bridge that gap and create a trusted connection, reassurance that you are there to support, not to judge.

This isn't a battle of egos, and mentors can succumb to the temptation of putting on their best front and 'looking good' in just the same way mentees can. If you are going to create a space where your mentee feels comfortable being fully honest with you, they need to feel that they can expect the same from you.

Megan Reitz, the co-author of *Speak Up*, insists a mentor can't just tell their mentee that they have a safe space to share in; they need to create the right environment.[104] In other words, you have to walk the talk.

Much of mentoring is mirroring. The mentee will respond to your cues; your curiosity, mood and persona. Megan explained, "If you are distracted, impatient, frustrated, bored or judgemental you will silence the other person and so creating an open environment is less about trying to fix the person who is remaining silent, telling them to be braver, and more about creating an environment where they don't have to be so brave in the first place."

Megan outlines two habits that affect mentors' abilities to show up well and put the other at ease, including 'advantage blindness' and 'superiority illusion'.

Advantage blindness[105] refers to the tendency to underestimate how power differences affect speaking and listening up. We all apply titles and labels to ourselves and one another – hierarchy, gender, expertise, ethnicity and numerous others, including of course 'mentor' and 'mentee'. These titles and labels construct relative status and authority and that in turn drives what gets said and who gets heard. When we have high-status labels (and 'mentor' is often regarded as higher status) we often underestimate the impact the labels have on others'

---

[103] Burg, B. (1994). "All things being equal, people do business with, and refer business to people they know, like and trust." *Endless Referrals*. McGraw Hill.
[104] Reitz, M. and Higgins, J. (2019). *Speak Up*. United Kingdom, Pearson.
[105] Fuchs, B., Reitz, M. and Higgins, J. (2018). "Do you have advantage blindness?" *Harvard Business Review* 10 April.

ability to speak up. That in turn means we don't do the work necessary to put the other person at ease.

Superiority illusion[106] refers to our habit of rating ourselves highly on listening. In her ongoing survey,[107] currently standing at over 17,000 employees globally, Megan has found that respondents invariably think they are good listeners – far better than their colleagues! "This is because we rate ourselves on our intent, and others on their behaviour," she explained. "It matters because, if we think we are already good listeners and approachable, we are, again, unlikely to put in the extra work required to help the other person to really say what they want and need to say."

Megan suggests that we should be aware of these habits and refers to three traps (Figure 7.1)[108] we should look out for:

Creating a Safe Space for Mentees

The three traps that mentors can fall into that make mentees less comfortable sharing with them:

1. We underestimate how scary we can be: Don't assume that your mentee is comfortable opening up to you, particularly if you are more senior to them.

2. We don't recognise the echo chamber around us: Are we repeating the same advice and opinions shared by other people just like us? Challenge yourself before challenging your mentee.

3. We are sending 'Shut Up' rather than 'Speak Up' signals: Ensure that your mentee feels listened to, heard and valued.

Figure 7.1 Creating a safe space for mentees
Source: Megan Reitz

Not all failures are bad. Some, in fact, are needed. In her book *Right Kind of Wrong*, Harvard Business School professor Amy Edmondson talks about

---

[106] Reitz, M. "You're not as good a listener as you think you are." **meganreitz.com**
[107] Reitz, M., Higgins, J. and Day Duro, E. (2021). "The do's and don'ts of employee activism: How organizations respond to voices of difference," Hult Research.
[108] Reitz, M. "How your power silences truth," Tedx Hult Ashridge.

intelligent failures which pave the road to success.[109] She advocates for normalising these intelligent failures, which are based on trying something new, not being lazy or sloppy.

In *Just Ask*, Andy shared a Harvard Business School study that further demonstrates why it's so important for mentors to park their egos and be open about their own mistakes and challenges with their mentees. One of the study authors, Alison Wood Brooks, told Andy, "People tend to hide their failures from others as they're happening and talk to very few people about them after they've happened. If we can get over the initial reluctance to reveal failures, there are surprising benefits.

"Doing so decreases *malicious envy* (defined as when we want somebody else to fail). It increases *benign envy*: respect and admiration from others. It also motivates other people to do better themselves.

"Given that we're naturally inclined to share successes, we would recommend taking advantage of these already occurring situations and coupling the sharing of success with sharing failures. This strategy is especially inspiring for leaders, whose achievements and successes are self-evident but the struggles they overcame to succeed are unobservable unless they share them with their employees."[110]

While everyone is fascinated with the success seen as the tip of the iceberg, people don't see, and therefore don't understand, what lies below the water line – the road paved with failure, rejection, failed attempts and frustration, overlaid with grit, resilience and persistence.

Respect and trust

Mentor and mentee may not particularly like each other but it is important that you respect and trust each other. The mentor needs to respect the work of the mentee and believe that they have the capacity to succeed, while the mentee should want to listen and consider the advice of their mentor because they believe that it will make them stronger and more successful. They each must fundamentally believe that the other has their best interest at heart.

Both need to trust the other's judgement, transparency and honesty.

---

[109] Edmondson, A.C. (2023). *The Right Kind of Wrong*. New York, NY, Atria Books.
[110] Lopata, A. (2020). *Just Ask: Why Seeking Support Is Your Greatest Strength*. Panoma Press.

Trusting someone in the office isn't as simple as looking just at the person. There are three levels of trust in a professional environment you need to be aware of (Figure 7.2).

Trust in the **person**
Trust in the **role they represent**
Trust in the **organisation they work for**

Figure 7.2 Three types of trust

Your mentee can trust you as a person implicitly but if they have been let down previously by someone in a similar role, or have a toxic relationship with the organisation as a whole, that will influence how they perceive you and your advice. It will always be taken with a dose of doubt and possible disdain. They will wonder if you are out for yourself or if you have an ulterior motive. If you are struggling to get through to them and create a connection, consider all three levels of trust. It genuinely might not be personal.

As well as trusting your judgement, your mentee will want to trust your discretion. Will what they share remain confidential? There will be times when they are happy for you to share the details of your conversations, but never assume and always check with them.

It's not just the content of the discussions about which you might need to remain discreet. Some mentees may not want to publicise their relationship with you. Have a conversation with them at the outset of the relationship and find out what they are comfortable with.

Vanessa Hall, author of *The Truth About Trust in Business*,[111] told us, "Trust cannot and should not be assumed.

---

[111] Hall, V. et al. (2009) *The Truth About Trust in Business*. Emerald Book Co.

"One of the dangers in mentoring is assuming a level of trust based on competence, based on doing the hard yards, on earning your stripes, on your credibility. Many trust models will say that trust is based on credibility. The issue is that trust is not always given, regardless of credibility, competence, integrity or transparency.

"Some mentees may have an issue with authority. Some may be highly creative and truly believe their untested ideas trump your sound advice. Some may have had poor mentorship in the past, or been given some bad advice and may begin to project that experience onto this new mentoring relationship.

"And remember that trust can take time to build, but can break in an instant, so honour the trust, respect it, guard it, nurture it, and it will hold the relationship together."

What to think about when mentoring someone from a different generation

As we've mentioned elsewhere, this is the most generationally diverse workplace in history, with an increased chance of mentoring others from a different generation, with the divergence in outlook, values and behaviour that accompany such differences. Just as we should think about how cultural assumptions and nuances in language can impact how our message is received when we mentor someone from another country, we need to be aware of similar distinctions in generational communication.

It is important, however, to not overthink those differences and treat someone based on general theories about how their generation thinks and acts. The multigenerational workplace expert Lindsey Pollak, author of *The Remix: How to Lead and Succeed in the Multigenerational Workplace*,[112] stressed, "We are more aligned in our mentoring needs than we are different."

Lindsey believes that the key to mentoring across different generations lies more in open communication than in a set of rules. "When you mentor somebody of a different generation, check your assumptions about what you think is kind, appropriate or effective. Have an open conversation about your style and your mentee's preferences. How you like to be mentored may not be how your mentee wants to be mentored.

---

[112] Pollak, L. (2019) *The Remix: How to Lead and Succeed in the Multigenerational Workplace*. Harper Business.

"At the beginning of your mentoring relationship ask questions. 'Do you like a lot of praise? Do you like me to give you positive feedback before negative? Do you like me to ask you a lot of questions or pull back?'"

There has been a lot of press coverage and conversation about how younger generations, specifically Millennials and Generation Z, behave differently in the workplace. That might cause you to reflect on how you approach mentoring them.

Lindsey once again urges caution in overthinking. She told us, "I think we make tremendous assumptions based on articles in the press. I have so many Gen Zs who ask me to tell other generations that they do like human interaction because everyone thinks they spend all of their time on TikTok. That's not true.

"What you do need to think about is how young people have grown up in a global culture where their voices are listened to. 'Don't speak unless spoken to' is not really the case anymore, they have a desire for a relationship to be two-way. Because they are used to making videos and telling the world what they think, they are going to expect that their opinion will be asked for and listened to."

Neurodiversity and mentoring

As a mentor, you need to be thoughtful about how your mentee will respond to working with you, particularly if they are neurodivergent. One of Andy's mentees became very anxious during one session; he hadn't been aware previously that she has autism and he had to learn to adapt his style for future sessions.

Samantha Hiew, PhD, is a scientist and multi-award-winning social entrepreneur who founded ADHD Girls[113] and she herself identifies as an autistic, dyspraxic, ADHDer and having Tourette's. Samantha shared with us some simple steps for a mentor to consider if working with a neurodivergent mentee (Figure 7.3).

1 Understand their neurodivergence: Take the time to educate yourself about their specific neurodivergent condition or challenges. This will help you better understand their strengths, weaknesses and unique perspectives.
2 Tailor your mentoring strategies: Recognise that neurodivergents may have different learning and information processing styles and communication preferences. Be flexible and adapt your mentoring approach to accommodate their needs.

---

[113] ADHD Girls. Retrieved 15 August 2023, from http://adhdgirls.co.uk

Working with a Neurodivergent Mentee

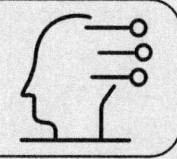

1. **Understand their neurodivergence:** Educate yourself about their specific neurodivergent condition or challenges.

2. **Tailor your mentoring strategies:** Be flexible and adapt your mentoring approach to accommodate their needs.

3. **Build trust and rapport:** Take the time to genuinely connect with your mentee, listen actively, and validate their experiences.

4. **Be patient and non-judgemental:** Neurodivergents may face difficulties in articulating their thoughts, feelings and needs. Create a safe and non-judgemental space for them to express themselves freely.

5. **Break down tasks and set achievable goals:** Don't overwhelm your mentee; break down tasks into smaller, manageable steps.

6. **Provide structure and clarity:** Clear communication and well-defined expectations are essential to help neurodivergents understand how they can succeed.

7. **Be a reflective listener:** Help them gain insights into their own thoughts and actions. Summarising and reflecting back their desires and needs can be beneficial.

8. **Offer support without being condescending:** Respect their autonomy and empower them in their journey.

9. **Remind them about the great things they do.** The compliment needs to be genuine.

10. **If your mentee shows signs of anxiety:** Take a pause, help them with breathing exercises and move onto a different topic or see if you can approach the challenge from a different perspective.

Figure 7.3 Working with a neurodivergent mentee
Source: Samantha Hiew: ADHD Girls

3   Build trust and rapport: Establishing a foundation of trust and rapport is crucial in any mentoring relationship, but particularly with neurodivergents. Take the time to genuinely connect with your mentee, listen actively and validate their experiences. This includes speaking face-to-face whenever you can, even if on videoconference calls. Hiew told us, "It is much more effective if you have that first conversation face-to-face. When we can see your

expressions, when you talk about something, it's a lot easier to decipher how you feel about certain things."

4. Be patient and non-judgemental: Neurodivergents may face difficulties in articulating their thoughts, feelings and needs. Practise patience, and create a safe and non-judgemental space for them to express themselves freely.

5. Break down tasks and set achievable goals: Don't overwhelm your mentee; help them to organise their thoughts and navigate overwhelming situations by breaking down tasks into smaller, manageable steps. Setting achievable goals can boost their confidence and motivation.

6. Provide structure and clarity: Clear communication and well-defined expectations are essential for neurodivergents. Provide structure, clarity and consistency in mentoring sessions to help them understand what is expected of them and how they can succeed.

7. Be a reflective listener: Neurodivergents often struggle with metacognition[114] and self-reflection. Act as a reflective listener and help them gain insights into their own thoughts and actions. Summarising and reflecting back their desires and needs can be beneficial.

8. Offer support without being condescending: Respect their autonomy and empower them in their journey.

9. Remind them about the great things they do. Samantha explained, "Many neurodivergents suffer from years of debilitating self-esteem due to receiving so much negative messaging about themselves. By the age of ten, a child with ADHD would have heard 20,000 negative messages.[115] The compliment needs to be genuine too, we're very good at sniffing out lies and dishonesty."

10. If your mentee shows signs of anxiety, take a pause, help them with breathing exercises and unless you've been discussing something that needs to be resolved urgently, either move onto a different topic or see if you can approach the challenge from a different perspective.

Remember, each neurodivergent is unique, so it's important to approach mentoring with an open mind, adaptability and a willingness to learn from them as well.

---

[114] https://www.psychologytoday.com/gb/blog/your-way-adhd/202202/adhd-and-self-awareness

[115] Jellinek, M.S. (2010). "Don't let ADHD crush children's self-esteem." *Clinical Psychiatry News*.

Getting your message across

One of the worst feelings as a mentor is knowing that you have given the right advice but seeing your mentee take a different route, and fail. Particularly if you know that they have ignored, or simply not heard, your advice, rather than weighed it up along with other options and then chosen a different path.

The question to ask yourself is whether they didn't follow your guidance, or didn't fully understand it. You need to ensure that your message lands clearly with your mentee, so that they can consider it properly. And you don't do that by talking *at* your mentee.

If you sit them down and give them a lecture on the steps they should take, the chances are that it will go in one ear and out the other. You have forced your mentee to be defensive and keep their guard up. It's hard to do that while listening and processing new information.

Although, as a mentor, you may have more to contribute to the conversation, it's still vital to listen to your mentee. Give them the space to speak and share before you suggest or solve. Dale Carnegie said, "A person's name is to that person the sweetest, most important sound in any language."[116] Mentors need to listen and engage in the conversation from that point, challenging and offering constructive criticism as well as positive reinforcement.

When you do advise, don't just tell your mentee what to do, but work through scenarios with them and bring your advice to life by sharing stories which are the foundation for your perspective. When have you found yourself in a similar spot, and how did you move forward? Rather than suggesting that they take the same approach, discuss how your experience relates to theirs and whether it provides ideas for what to do next.

Stories are incredibly powerful in bringing data and ideas to life. The Nobel Prize winning biochemist Dr Bob Lefkowitz found that his teaching of medical students went to another level when he told stories rather than simply presenting data. He said, "In both my clinical work and in my research, the art of telling stories, of putting data together in different ways, has been extraordinarily important.

---

[116] Carnegie, D. (1936). *How to Win Friends and Influence People*. Simon & Schuster.

"This was brought home to me in a professional setting, most acutely, for the first time when I was a third-year medical student at Columbia. I was doing my very first clinical clerkship; this was my first real clinical exposure after two intensive years of basic science and medical education. I had been sent to the Mount Sinai Hospital in New York City. And there, I was assigned to the clinical service of a wonderful attending physician named Dr Mortimer Bader.

"On the very first day of rounds, I was assigned to present the case, which I did. And then there was a discussion of the differential diagnosis. I thought I had done pretty well and that we would now move on to the next case. But instead, Dr Bader stopped me cold by saying, 'Okay, Mr Lefkowitz. Now, I would like you to present the case to me. You can't change any of the facts. But I want you to tell me a different story'.

"I was basically gobsmacked. I had no idea what he was talking about. I asked, 'How can I present a different story? I mean, the story is the story'. He said, 'Well, maybe not. You can't change any of the facts, but go ahead'.

"I couldn't do it. So, we went around the room, asking the students and then the more senior people, the interns, and nobody would take it on. So, he said, 'Well, let me demonstrate'.

"He then proceeded to tell a rather different story, again, using all the same facts, but putting the emphasis on some features, leaving out entirely other features. It was a rather different story and it led to a different differential diagnosis, which, as an aside, turned out to be the correct diagnosis, not the one that my story had taken us to.

"That was my first exposure in a clinical setting to how data, in this case clinical data, are not a story. The story is something you impose on the data with your own analytical abilities and your own creativity."

Bob elaborated on this in his book, *A Funny Thing Happened on the Way to Stockholm*,[117] when he explained, "As a scientist, I learned that data alone have little meaning until we impart it through narratives that are creatively constructed—based on the data—to yield some sort of conclusion or finding. As a mentor, I always take great interest in the stories of my trainees' lives, and often illustrate key points (both scientific and philosophical) by telling stories."

Using storytelling to bring your mentoring message to life is not just about sharing your own experiences but, as illustrated by Bob Lefkowitz, inviting your

---

[117] Lefkowitz, R. and Hall, R. *A Funny Thing Happened on the Way to Stockholm*. Pegasus Books.

mentee to interpret situations from different angles, creating conflicting stories using the information they have available to them and playing out different scenarios to help come up with a way forward together.

As the mentor you can coach them through this process and challenge them to continually reflect on their assumptions and find different possibilities. Ultimately, they need to take ownership of the answer but don't let your mentee settle for the first possibility they come across.

It's OK for you to disagree with your mentee and for them to disagree with you. A healthy discourse does no harm if you want to find the best route forward and for the mentee to really buy into it. If anything, it can lead to a better solution by revealing and accounting for blind spots. And you need to be robust in your feedback. Dame Katherine Grainger, the Chair of UK Sport, Olympic Gold Medal rower and six-time World Champion, told *The Times*, "You would rather your coach tell you genuinely what is needed and where your failings are and your strengths are, than sugar-coating it and keeping it positive all the time."[118]

If you don't feel that your message is landing, or you're not sure how to provide the best advice, remember that you are just one part of a potentially powerful mentoring team. Bring colleagues and connections with complementary expertise into the conversation and invite them to share their own experience and perspectives. Even if it matches with yours, it may make a big difference hearing it from somebody different, reinforcing your core message.

Never assume that what you share has landed as you intended. If your mentee doesn't seem to be on the same page, invite them to play back what they have heard as well as checking your own understanding of what they are looking for. Assumption is one of the biggest enemies of clear communication.

Accountability and feedback

Ruth once had a mentee who wanted to get into medical school. Not just any medical school but a very specific one, and only that particular school. Sadly, the components of her application were far below what that school wanted. Ruth recommended a long list of ideas how her mentee could strengthen her application and become more competitive, based on Ruth's two decades of experience reading admissions applications.

---

[118] Syed, M. (2017). "Why leaders must be encouraged to speak their mind." *The Times*, 27 September.

The mentee dug her heels in and insisted that she didn't need to change a thing. In her mind, it was the medical school that was in the wrong. She applied, and was rejected, applied again, and was rejected.

This went on several times without a change in outcome. Why would there be a different outcome, when nothing changed in the application? The more stubborn the mentee became, the more exasperated Ruth became.

"Why do I bother?" Ruth thought to herself repeatedly. Whenever an email hit Ruth's inbox from the mentee, Ruth would sigh and brace herself as she felt she was hitting her head against the wall. The mentee didn't want guidance, she wanted to whine and pass blame.

Eventually, Ruth severed the mentoring relationship feeling she could not help someone who wouldn't listen.

There is absolutely no point in engaging in solution-rich mentoring conversations if action is not taken. It is frustrating to the mentor and the mentee, who will always question why they are not meeting their goals. Mentors can support mentees by holding them accountable for taking action, or justifying the decision not to, and checking in on their progress.

Do you know what the difference is between dreamers and doers? Dreamers talk about all the things they will do one day, while doers make today day one. Dreamers talk in abstract terms without a deadline and doers talk about immediate steps within a specific time frame.[119] A mentor can help a dreamer become a doer.

In a formal mentoring relationship, it helps if somebody keeps a record of the key takeaways and commitments from each session. We are going to discuss this in more detail in Chapter 8.

The point of note taking is to remember what you promised to do and by when and to track your progress. Often, when we get frustrated at our lack of progress, it's because we are looking for a tangible marker to say, "You made it!" We don't often look back at the journey and everything that was achieved to get to this point. The notes offer a trail of breadcrumbs that are proof of what was already accomplished.

---

[119] Gotian, R. (2021). "6 Reasons Why Some People Dream And Others Achieve." *Forbes*.

At the very least, the mentee should capture their key learning points and commitments as bullet points and share them with their mentor by 48 hours after their conversation, while everything is still relatively fresh in their mind.

Doing so proves that the mentee is serious about the guidance they received and offers enough time for them to explain how they will execute the plan and/or do their due diligence. It puts them in the driver's seat of their career.

Capturing the information after the conversation encourages the mentee to reflect on what has been discussed and take the time to decide exactly what they are comfortable committing to, rather than writing down ideas as they come up and forgetting them as the conversation moves forward.

It is very helpful if the mentor has the chance to read through those notes ahead of the following meeting, providing an aide memoire and enabling them to frame some key questions and hold their mentee accountable more effectively.

When discussing action taken, the mentor should be objective and non-judgemental. Remember, you are there to support and develop, not to rate and criticise. As already stated, that doesn't mean that you can't question and challenge, quite the opposite, you should! But you should do so in a constructive way that helps to move the conversation forward while teaching your mentee critical thinking skills. Build up your mentee rather than knocking them down.

The praise sandwich

Many people favour 'the praise sandwich' approach to delivering feedback. It is designed to ensure that people can receive feedback in a positive way and not be discouraged by it, with any criticism wrapped in positive comments. Certainly, it helps to soften tough insights but it's often poorly delivered, with very faint or meaningless compliments used to envelope the all-important improvements that can be discussed. People are so used to the praise sandwich that it is expected and often followed by an internal carefully hidden sigh or eye roll.

Alternatives have been suggested, such as Disney Pixar's 'plussing' approach,[120] based on the improvisational technique of 'Yes, and...'. In Pixar, if somebody

---

[120] Burkus, D. (2018). "No one wants to eat your compliment sandwich," *Psychology Today*, 22 August.

has a criticism to make, they have to add (or 'plus') a suggestion to fix the issue they have identified. This approach helps ideas grow and develop. It also removes the power dynamic as anyone can add to share another perspective.

By definition, feedback is based on past actions or behaviours. We cannot change the past so bringing it up makes the person being addressed become defensive. Instead, says Dr Marshall Goldsmith, the #1 ranked executive coach in the world,[121] we should focus on the infinite possibilities of the future. This approach destigmatises the feedback and changes the perception from criticism to possibilities.[122]

In this model, the person receiving the feedback remains open minded and listens carefully to the ideas for the future. They are not to be argumentative or respond with anything more than 'thank you.' This allows them to take the ideas without it feeling like a personal attack. It also is based on the idea that the person receiving the feedback is capable of making positive changes in the future.

Instead of depleting, this form of feedback becomes energising, and filled with hope and optimism. The focus is on a plan of action for the future so that the mentee can meet their goals.

Ultimately, if you have set the foundations of your relationship with your mentee and developed strong rapport and trust, you should be able to deliver constructive feedback that helps them to move forward without trying to soften it every time. That's a big 'if' and as Megan Reitz pointed out earlier in this chapter, you shouldn't assume that the relationship is where you think it is. So, check in regularly and make sure that your mentee is taking on board your guidance in a constructive and positive way.

Planning the perfect mentoring meeting

Prepare for your meetings in advance and ensure you cover the following areas, maintain the momentum in your mentoring relationship and keep moving forward (Figure 7.4).

---

[121] Thinkers50. *Marshall Goldsmith*. Retrieved 1 August 2023, from **https://thinkers50.com/biographies/marshall-goldsmith/**

[122] Goldsmith, M. (2003). "Try feedforward instead of feedback." *Journal for Quality and Participation* **2003**: 38–40.

Before the meeting

- Remind yourself of what was discussed in your last meeting and what progress you want to hear about.
- Ask your mentee to let you know in advance what particular challenges they would like to discuss.
- If you're speaking to others who work with or around your mentee, be aware of any challenges you might want to raise if they don't.
- Think about how you can raise any challenging topics in a way most likely to lead to a positive, constructive conversation.

During the meeting

- Check in with your mentee about how they are in general, in and out of work, before focusing on your agenda.
- Review progress made since the last meeting. What have they put into practice, what worked and what didn't? Treat missed objectives as a learning opportunity and not as failure.
- Celebrate and explore wins as well as addressing challenges.
- Review their objectives for the programme and explore whether anything has changed.
- Ensure you are both clear about next steps – ask your mentee to repeat back to you key takeaways and commitments so that you don't assume you're on the same page.
- Set a date for your next meeting. It can move if absolutely necessary but it's important to get something in the diary.

After the meeting

- Encourage your mentee to keep a journal, noting key challenges, wins or notable conversations they want to discuss *when they happen*, rather than relying on their memory when you get together.
- Send your mentee blogs, videos, podcasts or introductions that build on your previous conversations.
- Check in with your mentee if you know they have a landmark meeting or feedback scheduled.
- Remind your mentee to reach out if they have any issue they need some support with that can't wait until you next meet.

Figure 7.4 Mentoring meeting planning

The mentoring environment

We've talked a lot in previous chapters about how the environment in which you conduct your mentoring conversations can impact the results you achieve. Ensuring that your conversations are discreet and private, balancing the convenience of online conversations with the relationship and rapport-building power of meeting in person, and minimising distractions and interruptions all need to be taken into account.

Asynchronous mentoring

If everything is an emergency, then nothing can really be an emergency. Prioritising is critical and recognising that not everything needs an immediate response will help decrease stress and anxiety. Let's move away for a moment from the assumption that all mentoring needs to take place in real time. There's a place for asynchronous mentoring too, where the question or challenge is sent by the mentee without the expectation of an immediate response.

Email and texting are effective approaches to dealing with quick questions, where a full meeting is not necessarily appropriate, reviewing materials or just giving some quick feedback on a new idea or suggested route forward. It can also give the mentor time to reflect on their response or pull in ideas from elsewhere before replying.

If you have a mentoring team, some members of that team may play more of this role, there when you need a quick response, perhaps by email or your internal communications channels, rather than in real-time conversation. But it's not an either/or choice. Even in a formal mentoring relationship, giving your mentee the option to send a quick email between meetings adds value, keeps you connected and enhances the level of support you can offer without adding too much of a burden on you as a mentor.

Asynchronous communication methods can be effective for mentoring relationships, allowing both mentor and mentee to communicate on their own schedules. Figure 7.10 shows ten asynchronous ways to communicate with your mentee.

Ten asynchronous ways to communicate with your mentee

1. Email: Don't assume that your mentee is comfortable opening up to you, particularly if you are senior to them.

2. Messaging Apps: Use platforms like WhatsApp, Slack or Microsoft Teams to exchange messages, share resources and answer questions asynchronously.

3. Video Messages: Record short video messages using tools like Loom, and send them to your mentee to provide personalised feedback or insights.

4. Voice Messages: Send voice messages through apps like WhatsApp for a more personal touch when explaining complex topics or giving feedback.

5. Mentoring Platforms: Many mentoring platforms offer built-in messaging systems that facilitate asynchronous communication while keeping all mentoring-related discussions organised in one place.

6. Online Discussion Forums: Create a private discussion board or forum on platforms like Slack, Discourse, or even a dedicated website where you and your mentee can post questions, share resources and have ongoing conversations.

7. Shared Document Collaboration: Use tools like Google Docs, Microsoft OneDrive, or Dropbox to collaborate on documents, share feedback and track progress on shared projects.

8. Blogging or Journalling: Encourage your mentee to maintain a blog or journal where they can reflect on their progress, challenges and insights. You can provide feedback or comments asynchronously.

9. Scheduled Check-Ins: Set up regular asynchronous check-in times using scheduling tools like Doodle or Calendly. Your mentee can select a time slot that works for them to discuss their progress or ask questions.

10. Task Management Tools: Tools like Trello can be used to create and assign tasks, track progress and communicate asynchronously about project-related matters.

Figure 7.5 Asynchronous mentoring

Remember that the key to successful asynchronous communication in mentoring is to establish clear expectations, response times and guidelines for using these methods to ensure effective and meaningful exchanges.

Back to the future

Every few months, Ruth gets a phone call, text or email from a former mentee, some whom she mentored over twenty years ago. Something happened in their life that triggered a memory of a mentoring conversation they had together. Out of the blue, they would reach out and share the memory. Sometimes it was a memory of them having imposter syndrome and Ruth guiding them through overcoming it, or other times, they shared that Ruth made them feel seen and that they didn't need to hide any part of who they are.

Dr Odi Ehie, whom you met in Chapter 6, shared that being connected to someone in Ruth's network caused her to stay in medicine at a time when she was doubting her place in healthcare. Often, Ruth has no recollection of having said what was, for the mentee, incredibly potent.

We began this chapter by asking you to think back to the mentors who have really impacted you over the years. We asked what you would say to them if you were to write a letter thanking them for their advice and influence on your journey.

Now we want you to look into the future. Think about the people you are mentoring now, or just about to. What do you want to be known for? What would you like them to write to you in five or ten years' time? How would you like them to see your influence and impact on their career? Not just feedback on how you had an impact on what they have achieved but how you went about that task.

If they go on to be mentors, what would you like them to say they have learned from how you mentored them?

Get a picture of the mentor you want to be and the impact you wish to have. Remember, the way you approach this relationship impacts not just your mentees but the people they themselves work with and mentor in the future. You have the ability to cast a stone and create a mentoring ripple effect.

Write a letter from your current mentees to you in five years' time:

Dear _____

CHAPTER 8
HOW TO DELIVER THE BEST VALUE

Can one person do it all? In Chapter 3 we looked at the different forms of intervention and outlined the differences between mentoring and coaching, sponsoring and others. We were clear that these approaches are not mutually exclusive; in fact the best mentors will fulfil whatever role is most appropriate in any given situation. It is the ultimate form of agility.

A good mentor gives directive advice when needed but we have seen how important it is to help your mentee take ownership of their choices. Active listening techniques such as maintaining eye contact, avoiding interrupting, listening without judging or imposing opinions, asking clarifying questions and paraphrasing will encourage the mentee to talk and the mentor to listen more. It will catalyse creative and critical thinking; a crucial life skill.[123,124] It can be tempting to feel that you know the answer very early in a conversation, yet by modelling curiosity, exploring together and seeking a solution through questioning, you can reach a much more suitable, tailored and satisfying approach.

We have stressed the importance of opening your network to your mentee several times and frankly, cannot emphasise this enough. You won't know all of the answers, but your connections may well do. You'll know people who have relevant expertise and experiences and who are better suited to going deeper with your mentee than you might be. As adults, we learn from our experiences,[125] and we each have unique journeys. Those in our network can help solve problems you may not even recognise yet.

---

[123] Brookfield, S. (1987). *Developing Critical Thinkers: Challenging Adults to Explore Alternative Ways of Thinking and Acting*. San Francisco, Jossey-Bass.
[124] Brookfield, S. (2012). *Teaching for Critical Thinking: Tools and Techniques to Help Students Question Their Assumptions*. San Francisco, CA, Jossey-Bass.
[125] Kolb, D. (1984). "Structural foundations of the learning process." *Experiential Learning: Experience as the Source of Learning and Development*. Engelwood Cliffs, NJ, Prentice Hall. Chapter 3.

Open doors for your mentee, including those doors that they need to open but aren't aware exist yet. Allow your mentee to enrich their network through your support. Don't just show them how things are done, instead, show them what is possible.

And, like it or not, you are a role model for your mentee. It can't be a case of 'do as I say, not as I do', particularly if you work in the same organisation. They will be watching you and your actions need to be consistent with your advice and guidance. If they are not, you will be viewed as inauthentic and untrustworthy.

Have you ever looked at any organisation's mission statement? We mean really looked at it. There was likely a committee that diligently worked to craft the mission statement down to its core and argued over the placement of every comma. But if the actions of the organisation don't align with the words, then the organisation cannot be trusted.[126] For example, if a company says they value work-life balance and schedule meetings for after hours and retreats on weekends, are they living up to their espoused values?

Values should be established in your conversations with your mentee and your actions need to align with the values you've expressed in those exchanges, as well as with those of the organisation you represent. Values drive behaviour.[127] People will respond more to what you do than what you say, and those actions will live longer in their memory. Your mentee wants to feel pride in working with you. Are you acting in a way that will benefit them by that association?

The best mentoring conversations

Whatever your mentoring style, you are likely to make your biggest impact on your mentee during the focused meetings you arrange to explore their challenges and goals. If you can ensure that your conversations flow naturally, with plenty of structured advice, breakthroughs on challenges and clear actions for them to implement, you'll be moving in the right direction.

---

[126] Carucci, R. (2021). *To Be Honest: Leading with the Power of Truth, Justice, and Purpose.* Kogan Page.

[127] Sullivan, W., Sullivan, R. and Buffton, B. (2001). "Aligning individual and organisational values to support change." *Journal of Change Management* 2(3): 247-254, DOI: 10.1080/738552750.

That said, sometimes, silence is golden. People need time to reflect and process what they have just heard or learned.[128,129] Give them the space to do so without peppering them with more questions or ideas. Give pause for their questions and comments.

Establishing connection

It starts with how you get the conversation flowing. Remember the importance of that rapport-building small talk; it shouldn't necessarily be a case of getting straight down to business. Look for those commonalities we discussed in Chapter 7. It doesn't have to be personal; you can reference a talk they delivered recently, a post made on the company's internal network or on LinkedIn or experience you know they had such as a recent ski trip or conference they attended.

Tell them how what they said resonated with you and ask for some more background to their thinking. If you begin a conversation by showing a genuine interest in your mentee, they will feel more at ease and less intimidated. It makes the conversation less transactional and therefore builds a solid and fruitful relationship.

Don't be frightened to enjoy yourselves too, it's OK to laugh and have fun in sessions with your mentee. Laughter will help you both to relax and establish rapport and we all look forward more to meetings that we know we will enjoy.

In his book *A Funny Thing Happened on the Way to Stockholm*, Dr Bob Lefkowitz encourages readers to have fun with their mentees. "Humour is a great prod to creativity," he said. "In my experience, the more people are laughing, the more creative they become. This may be due to the fact that humour requires seeing unusual connections between things. 'Getting' a joke is like making a little discovery: you have a flash of insight and suddenly see a funny connection that you didn't previously see."

---

[128] Alerby, A. and Elidottir, J. (2003). "The sounds of silence: Some remarks on the value of silence in the process of reflection in relation to teaching and learning." *Reflective Practice* 4(1) 41–51, DOI: 10.1080/1462394032000053503.

[129] Ollin, R. (2008). "Silent pedagogy and rethinking classroom practice: structuring teaching through silence rather than talk." *Cambridge Journal of Education* 38(2): 265–280, DOI: 10.1080/03057640802063528.

Listen for, not to

Then let your mentee speak. As mentioned above, one of the best ways you can deliver value is to listen. Don't rush to judgement, seek to learn instead. Listen 'for' your mentee, rather than 'to' them: seek to understand and look for clues and information in what they are telling you and what they are omitting, which might point to a wider or underlying issue, or suggest a natural solution that they are overlooking.

In *Seven Habits of Highly Effective People*,[130] Stephen Covey discussed the now well-known concept of active listening, first introduced by psychologists Carl Rogers and Richard Farson in 1957.[131] Habit 5 is to "Seek first to understand, then to be understood," yet, Covey explained, "Most people listen with the intent to reply, not to understand. You listen to yourself as you prepare in your mind what you are going to say, the questions you are going to ask, etc. . . . Consequently, you decide prematurely what the other person means before they finish communicating."

Many mentors are guilty of this behaviour. As soon as our mentee begins to outline their challenge, we think we know exactly how they should respond. Instead of listening further and asking questions in order to better understand the challenge, we leap forward with our ideas. It's a natural thing to do, particularly if you are one of life's 'fixers'; our enthusiasm to help others can get the better of us.

Daniela Landherr, a former Head of Talent Engagement at Google, asked a pertinent question when guesting on Andy's *Connected Leadership Podcast*. She asked, "How can we move away from trying to be the smartest in the room to how can we be the most open to learning?"[132] Mentors can add so much value to their mentees by seeking to learn first; the more you understand, the better the advice you can give. And that means listening.

---

[130] Covey, S.R. (1989). *The Seven Habits of Highly Effective People: Restoring the character ethic*. New York, Simon and Schuster.
[131] Rogers, C. and Farson, R.E. (1957). "Active listening." *Journal of Consulting Psychology* **21**(5): 376–380.
[132] Landherr, D. (2023). "Fail fast, Learn fast," *The Connected Leadership Podcast*.

Adult learning professor Dr Stephen Brookfield teaches educators and mentors how to leverage discussion as a way of teaching and mentoring. Some of his most popular techniques include:[133]

- In group discussions, let the most junior person speak first.
- Give people an uninterrupted two minutes to speak, and reserve all questions to the end.
- You can only make a comment if you build on what someone else says.
- Ask open-ended questions and avoid those that require a yes/no response.

They all seem so simple, but they can be remarkably difficult to execute.

When you do offer advice, bring it to life by telling stories, as discussed in Chapter 7, and make it a conversation. Ask your mentee how they feel about your suggestions and to reflect them back to you in their own words, how they see themselves moving forward. Don't simply assume that your ideas have landed; listen to how they sound when presented by your mentee and make sure nothing has been missed. Are they excited by your ideas and the direction they are now taking?

This is where body language is telling. When someone is excited their entire demeanour changes. Their shoulders lower away from their ears; stress seems to melt away as their face becomes illuminated. You can tell instantly that they are excited about the topic. As a result, you become more interested.

Parking your ego

Humility is a hallmark of a great mentor. It can be very flattering to be approached to mentor somebody but it's important to keep reminding yourself who the relationship is really about. It's not about impressing your mentee with your achievements; in fact, they will probably learn more from your failures than from your successes.

Tailor your guidance to your mentee's individual needs and be open to seeing your ideas adapted to suit their situation or personal preference. It doesn't make

---

[133] Brookfield, S. and Preskill, S. (2005). *Discussion as a Way of Teaching*. San Francisco, CA, Jossey-Bass.

it a reflection on you or your advice if they choose to go in a slightly different direction. So don't take it personally. In fact, using your advice as a launchpad is a sign of independent thinking and a higher order of adult development.[134]

When asked how a mentor measures their success, the best accounting is by measuring their mentee's success. Dr Bob Lefkowitz waited a lifetime to win science's biggest prize. Usually, the Nobel Prize for Chemistry is shared with one or two other scientists. When Bob got that pre-sunrise life changing phone call in 2012, one of his first questions was "Who am I sharing it with?"

He learned that his co-recipient was none other than Dr Brian Kobilka, his former mentee. When Ruth asked Bob if it felt odd to share his field's biggest award with a mentee, he quickly responded. "Are you kidding? There is no greater honour than seeing your mentee succeed. Their success is how I measure my success." Pulling others up and shining a light on them is a sign of an all-star mentor.[135]

Rather than impress your mentee with your achievements, let your mentee's achievements shine and allow yourself to bask in their reflected glory. Show real belief in and enthusiasm for their project and goals; celebrate and enjoy their success the same way you would your own. With their permission, amplify their achievements by letting others know. Mention it to key people and post about it on social media.[136] If your mentee sees that you are fully invested in what they are striving to achieve, they will be more motivated to ensure that they push on and succeed.

When you achieve something, share it with your mentee at that time. Involve them in the experience and help them to understand what went into reaching your own goal. Be transparent about the struggles and how you overcame them along with the questions and unanticipated consequences which arose. Seeing and understanding your decision-making process is some of the best mentoring you can do. It's not about what you achieved but how you achieved it.

Recognise when your mentoring sessions with them have helped you by giving you some inspiration or motivation and acknowledge that, both to them and publicly.

---

[134] Drago-Severson, E. and Blum-DeStefano, J. (2017). *Tell Me so I Can Hear You: A Developmental Approach to Feedback for Educators*. Harvard Education Press.
[135] Gotian, R. (2022). *The Success Factor: Developing the Mindset and Skillset for Peak Business Performance*. Kogan Page.
[136] Gotian, R. (2020). "How to amplify the voice of your mentees." *Forbes*.

Accountability and empowerment

Most people want to achieve but fail to take action. They have a plan but never put it into place. Progress starts with the first step. We've talked a lot about goal setting and holding your mentee accountable. This can't be stressed enough; when you are busy, it can be very tempting to treat each mentoring meeting as a standalone conversation. If you do so, you will miss the opportunity to ensure progression and great ideas will be forgotten and left behind.

Build in time to reflect on key actions moving forward and to look back on what worked, what didn't and how you need to respond. Track progress (we will talk about ways to capture this information shortly); you want to be able to look back at various points throughout your relationship and reflect on how effective the mentoring has been. You should be able to do so by looking at tangible information, not just based on how each party feels about the relationship.

We often don't recognise just how much we have truly accomplished until we start to list it all. A running list helps keep the motivation high. A parallel list on challenges overcome might also prove useful as you and your mentee can be reminded just how long the journey is to become an overnight success.

Capturing challenges and accomplishments to review

As you travel through your journey with your mentee, capture the challenges they are facing and what they have achieved in addressing them and what is still left to achieve (Figure 8.1).

Challenges	Accomplishments	What's next?

Figure 8.1 Challenges and accomplishments capture grid

Empower your mentee and make sure that they take final ownership of the decisions you reach. As we've already stated, it's their career and you don't support them if you don't allow them to stand on their own two feet. Advise and recommend but, ultimately, stand behind whatever decisions they make for themselves.

Providing a helicopter view

Your mentee is going to be immersed in their role. An important part of your job as their mentor is to provide the helicopter view of their career and performance. You can help them to see the full perspective, not just the blinkered view inhibited by the immediate challenge facing them. Help them to see their blind spots, enabling them to make better decisions.

One of the times you can make a huge impact on your mentee and help them to see the bigger picture is when things go wrong. It's a human instinct to recoil from a task when faced with a failure, perceived or real. But failure is merely data; it provides you with feedback to help you do better next time. That's exactly why every professional athlete records their workouts and games, and watches not for what they did right, but how to improve on what they did wrong. "It's the small details that differentiate between being good and outstanding," shares two-time NBA champion Zaza Pachulia.[137]

Roberto Forzoni, a performance psychologist who has worked with a number of leading sports teams and high-performing sports stars like tennis player Andy Murray, explained that we tend to assess our performance based on either ego orientation or task orientation. When we are ego-oriented, we focus more on what people think about us or what we think about ourselves, rather than how well we perform the task itself. And that impacts our view of what constitutes success or failure.

Roberto told us, "If you're an athlete, you might want to define what that failure is, so you know when you failed or when you didn't. It gives you feedback on where you are now and where you can get to. In sport, maybe you don't achieve a certain level of performance, but your performance is improving all the time. Is that failure? You might say, 'Yes, because I'm not winning', but you're improving all the time."

In May 2023, NBA basketball player Giannis Antetokounmpo was asked in a press conference whether he viewed the most recent season as a failure. His

---

[137] Gotian, R. (2023). "Agility in basketball: An interview with 2x NBA champion Zaza Pachulia." *Forbes*.

response was insightful and went viral. Antetokounmpo asked the reporter whether he got a promotion in his job every year. The reporter said no, to which Giannis responded, "So every year your work is a failure? No? Every year you work, you work towards a goal. It's not a failure, it's steps to success."[138]

You can help your mentee to change their attitude to any perceived failure and see the experience as part of a wider picture. Make sense of it with them and identify what needs to happen next as a result of lessons learned. Do they need to change their objectives or intentions? Are there new areas for development which you need to focus on together to help them move forward?

A mentor has a dual role of simultaneously being knowledgeable and therefore asking sophisticated questions, yet maintains some distance from outside groups, and therefore those same queries might seem barbaric to others. In adult learning, this dual role is termed a *sophisticated barbarian*.[139] Provide your mentee with an objective view and help them make sense of their experience with a calm mind and a focus on moving forward.

Analogue or digital?

Your mentoring conversations should ideally feel natural and light but there can be a danger of being too informal. As we touched on in Chapter 7, one of the decisions you will need to make with your mentee is how important it is for both of you to capture, at the very least, key commitments, takeaways and progress. It helps keep both of you accountable.

A lot of this will be down to personality type, engagement style and preference, both yours and theirs. Some people naturally take down and refer back to pages of notes from any meeting. Others have to be forced to record anything. There is no one right way.

Who takes the notes and when will depend a lot on learning style. The most important thing for both parties is to be able to listen and engage fully in the conversation. If note-taking gets in the way, keep it to a minimum.

---

[138] Bleacher Report (2023). "Giannis calls out reporter in heated response: 'There's no failure in sports.'." from **https://www.youtube.com/watch?v=n2QCiJC06y4**
[139] Yorks, L., O Neil, J., Marsick, V. J., Nilson, G. E. and Kolodny, R. (1996). "Boundary management in action reflection learning research: Taking the role of a sophisticated barbarian." *Human Resource Development Quarterly* 7(4): 313–329.

Date of meeting	Area of discussion	Takeaway	Commitment

Figure 8.2 Mentor meeting summary

As a mentor, you can capture key discussion points, takeaways and commitments for yourself so that you have something to reflect back on before your next session or if you want to check in. But you need to find the right balance between writing and fully listening when your mentee is speaking, particularly if you can't carve out the time to write notes immediately after your mentoring meeting (Figure 8.2).

Andy has used various platforms to encourage his mentees to capture, track and share takeaways and progress, from bespoke platforms such as CoachAccountable[140] to collaboration and project management tools such as Microsoft Teams, Trello and Slack. Even speech to text platforms such as Otter.ai are useful for capturing notes of the conversation.

The challenge has always been encouraging mentees to use them. Busy people often don't find the time to capture notes and share them, particularly if they are writing them down for themselves with pen and paper.

There are now a number of AI tools which allow you to upload a recording of your session and not only get a pretty reliable transcription but then interrogate the platform for key takeaways, commitments and reminders. Given the rate of explosion of AI at the time of writing, we feel that it would date this book tremendously if we started to list our current favourite tools! As just one example, this functionality was integrated into Zoom in late 2023, with meeting summaries available just after a meeting ends and AI interrogation available live.

When it comes to writing articles with her mentees (the life blood of any academic), Ruth prefers the analogue approach. In her office, there is a board that

---

[140] Coach Accountable. Retrieved 1 July 2023, from **https://www.coachaccountable.com**

captures the different stages of the academic writing process. Each stage of the process gets one column. The name of each article, the authors and anticipated journal name are all listed on an orange Post-It note. As progress ensues, and the article moves through the writing and submission process, the Post-It note is moved one column to the right.

This allows Ruth and the mentee to see if there is a bottleneck, and to anticipate when she can work on a new project. The visceral response of getting closer to submission and then publication is the motivation Ruth and her mentee use to keep going.

When the article is finally accepted, the mentee is called to Ruth's office to move the Post-It note to the final 'Published' column. The short yet liberating and exciting task is captured on video and posted on social media. It's a real rite of passage which honours the journey while holding the mentor and mentee accountable. The social media posts show that as a mentor, Ruth realises the journey is as important as the accomplishment.

Delivering value beyond the mentoring meeting

Effective mentoring doesn't start and end in formal meetings or calls. If a mentor is fully invested in their mentee's success, that support and belief alone will likely motivate the mentee to perform better and take the action to which they've committed.

This doesn't mean that you, as a mentor, have to be looking over your mentee's shoulder all of the time, or have an open-door policy for them to approach you at any time. Regular check-ins can have a powerful cumulative effect through little touches to express your interest and demonstrate that you care. And your mentee shouldn't hold back from asking for your advice or insights when they really need it; they just need to know your boundaries.

In spacing your meetings and communication, seek to strike the right balance between maintaining momentum and focus on what the mentee is trying to achieve with giving them the time and space to take action and reflect. If you will be unavailable for a while due to vacation or your own workload, simply be transparent and no one will expect to hear back from you as you try to get off the grid.

Be proactive in your support between meetings. If you read a book, listen to a podcast or plan to attend or give a talk or event that will be helpful to your mentee, let them know. These in between quick messages send a signal to your mentee that you are thinking of them. If you haven't forgotten about them, how can they ignore doing what they promised? And as we've already stressed, make key introductions to other people who can help them on their journey.

Throughout your relationship, encourage your mentee. Give praise and recognition, both direct to them in confidence but also externally to other stakeholders if appropriate. Acknowledge the progress they have made and work done.

You are there to be a critical friend but sometimes it's easier to focus on one element of that equation and not both. If you truly want to deliver value to your mentee through your relationship with them, provide the challenge and encouragement that they need and be there for them at all times.

CHAPTER 9
HOW DO YOU KNOW AND WHAT SHOULD YOU DO IF THE RELATIONSHIP IS NOT WORKING?

Not all mentoring relationships run smoothly and not all mentors and mentees naturally sync. Just because you like or respect each other in your day-to-day interactions, it doesn't automatically mean that the mentoring chemistry will be right or fruitful.

Even when the chemistry does work, mentoring relationships can run their course. It does not mean anything is wrong with either party. You need to be able to find a way to be adult about recognising and discussing whether things aren't going according to plan and come up with the best route forward.

Remember, you don't need to be best friends for the mentoring relationship to work. We wouldn't suggest mentoring somebody you actively dislike, or vice versa, nor should you be upset if you're not being invited over for dinner or spending your weekends together.

We've discussed how helpful having a strong personal rapport can be in a mentoring relationship but actually a *learning rapport* is more helpful. According to researchers, "The importance of cultivating a positive relationship between student and teacher is recognised as important to student learning. Perhaps a way to further mutual understanding could be through the concept of building an 'alliance' between student and teacher.

"The key features of this alliance are mutual respect, shared responsibility for learning, effective communication and feedback, cooperation, willingness to negotiate conflict and a sense of security."[141]

---

[141] Tibeius, R., Sinal, J. and Flack, E. (January 2002). "The role of teacher-learner relationship in medical education". *International Handbook of Research in Medical Education.*

A great deal of adult learning happens through the four-step process of observation, namely attention, retention or memory, behaviour change and motivation.[142] But your mentee will have a challenging time getting out of the starting blocks without what adult learning social-cognitive theorist Dr Albert Bandura called self-efficacy.[143] This is our own estimate of how competent we believe we are likely to be in a specific environment.[144] This self-belief influences how effective we are in our interactions with others and with our environment.

Dealing with a lack of engagement

If your mentee isn't engaging with you, don't judge them and write them off. Instead, take a step back and try to understand what is going on. One size doesn't fit all when it comes to mentoring. Mentees will have divergent learning styles. It can be easy to become frustrated when one mentee doesn't respond in the positive way another did, but it might be that they don't take in and process information in the same way.[145] Just as we all learn differently, so must we all be mentored in a bespoke manner.

Once you have understood what makes your mentee tick, you can adjust your approach to get a more positive response.

Dr Ellie Drago-Severson teaches that people have different ways of knowing. One is not better than the other and unlike child development, in adult development you are who you are. There are no stages you need to go through. In fact, they are not stages at all; they are all variations of normal.

Dr Drago-Severson outlines four main ways of knowing which helps us to understand what is important and drives the mentees' learning.[146,147] Understanding the nuances will help you develop bespoke mentoring plans and elevate the effectiveness of your mentoring (Figure 9.1).

---

[142] Hergenhahn, B.R. and Olson, M.H. (2005). *An Introduction to Theories of Learning* (7th ed.). Englewood Cliffs, NJ, Prentice Hall.
[143] Bandura, A. (1986). *Social Foundations of Thought and Action: A Social Cognitive Theory*. Englewood Cliffs, NJ, Prentice-Hall.
[144] Lefrancois, G.R. (1999). *The Lifespan* (6th ed.). Belmont, CA: Wadsworth Publishing.
[145] Kolb, D. (1984). *Experiential Learning: Experience as the Source for Learning and Development*. Englewood Cliffs, NJ, Prentice Hall.
[146] Drago-Severson, E. (2009). "How do you 'know'." *Yes!*. Fall 2009.
[147] Drago-Severson, E. (2004a). *Becoming Adult Learners: Principles and Practices for Effective Development*. New York, Teachers College Press.

How Do You 'Know'?

Each of us has a 'Way of Knowing' that filters our experience of ourselves, others, and our relationships. This chart offers a framework based on Robert Kegan's constructive-developmental theory to understand how each of us, depending on our way of knowing, develops during adulthood. It also includes ideas about how we can challenge ourselves and support each other's growth. Use the top part of the chart to identify which 'way of knowing' best describes you. The bottom part shows some ways you can further your development to incorporate other ways of knowing.

Ellie Drago-Severson writes, consults, and teaches about adult educational leadership at Teachers College Columbia University.

	Instrumental Knower	Socialised Knower	Self-Authoring Knower	Self-Transforming Knower
Stages:	I am rule-based	I am other-focused	I am reflective	I am interconnecting
The most important thing is:	Fulfilling my own needs, interests, and desires.	Meeting expectations and getting approval.	Staying true to my values, which I generate.	Reflecting on my identity, being open to others' views and to changing myself.
Concerns:	Rules. Clear definition of right and wrong. Immediate self-interest. Other people are either helpful or obstacles. Abstract thinking has no meaning.	Authority figures set goals. Self-image comes from others' judgement. Responsible for others' feelings and vice versa. Criticism and conflict are threatening.	Set goals based on own values and standards. Self-image based on my evaluation of my competencies and integrity. Contradictory feelings and conflict are ways to learn.	Set goals in collaboration. Share power. Find common ground, even with seeming opposites. Open to exploration, conflict, complexity, and others' perspectives.
Guiding questions:	"Will I get punished?" "What's in it for me?"	"Will you like/value me?" "Will you think I am a good person?"	"Am I staying true to my own personal integrity, standards, and values?"	"How can other people's thinking help me to develop and grow?"

Tasks at your 'growing edge':	Be open to possibility of new 'right' solutions. Take on tasks that demand abstract thinking.	Generate own values and standards. Accept conflicting viewpoints without seeing them as a threat to relationships.	Open up to diverse and opposing views. Accept and learn from diverse problem-solving approaches.	Accept that some differences cannot be resolved. Avoid insisting on absolutely flat, nonhierarchal approaches.
Learning exercises to try:	Dialogues that offer multiple perspectives and go beyond 'right' and 'wrong.'	Dialogue that helps to generate and clarify one's own values. Share perspectives in pairs or triads before sharing with larger groups and authority figures.	Facilitate dialogue, especially when perspectives are diametrically opposed.	Affiliate with an authority or an impersonal system. Commit to a project without a clear purpose. Appreciate the time it takes to reach a conclusion when others may not move at the same pace.
Ways to support the growth of these folks:	Set clear goals and expectations, agree on step-by-step procedures and specific due dates. Offer concrete advice, specific skills.	Invite to leadership roles. Demonstrate ways to confirm, acknowledge and accept others' beliefs. Model disagreement without threat to relationships.	Offer opportunities to promote, analyse and critique one's goals and ideas. Encourage consideration of conflicting or discordant ideas.	Encourage refraining from taking over and rushing a process. Model sensitivity to those who do not have the same capacity (e.g., for conflict).

Figure 9.1 Ways of knowing. Image courtesy of *Yes! Magazine* **www.yesmagazine.org**, based on the work of Ellie Drago-Severson

Source: Adapted from Drago-Severson, E., *Leading Adult Learning; Supporting Adult Development in our Schools*. Thousand Oaks: Corwin/Sage Publications, (2010). **www.yesmagazine.org/51facts** for additional citations.

The *Instrumental* Knower is rule-based with an immediate self-interest. The most important thing for them is fulfilling their own needs, interests and desires. Other people are either helpful or obstacles. These mentees are concrete thinkers and need rules to function.

The *Socialised* Knower is other-focused and always working to meet expectations and obtain approval. Their self-image comes from others' judgement. To them, criticism and conflict are threatening to relationships. Just think of those people who are constantly checking how many and who liked their posts on social media.

The *Self-Authoring* Knower is reflective and stays true to their values. They set goals based on their own values and standards. Their self-image is based on their evaluation of their values and competencies. To them, contradictory feelings and conflict are a passageway to learn; it offers them data.

The *Self-Transforming* Knower is consistently open to others' points of view, reflecting on their own words and actions. They seek common ground even with those who seem to have polar opposite viewpoints. These mentees are open to exploration and conflict. They are open to sharing their power.

Your mentoring technique should be aligned with the mentee's way of knowing. For example, if your mentee is an instrumental knower, help them meet their concrete needs and goals by offering detailed and step-by-step instructions. Over time, help them grow by encouraging them to see outside what they see as the right and only way. This can be done by engaging in open-ended discussions about others and introducing more abstract goals.[148]

A *Socialised* Knower, on the other hand, will require having their ideas acknowledged by their mentor. This support will allow them to take bigger learning risks. These mentees can grow by learning to outwardly speak about their own perspectives before gathering the opinions of others. Mentors can teach these mentees to not get fixated on their own ideology.[149]

Mentors need to understand that each mentee will need a different level of support and challenges through which they can grow and learn effectively.

---

[148] Drago-Severson, E. (2008). "4 Practices Serve As Pillars for Adult Learning." *National Staff Development Council*, Cahn Fellows Program. **29**: 60–63.

[149] Drago-Severson, E. (2009). "*Leading Adult Learning: Practices for Building Schools and School Systems as Learning Centers.*" Thousand Oaks, CA: Corwin Press.

As well as understanding how your mentee learns best, understand what else is happening around them and how it might be impacting their ability to fully prioritise their work with you. Are they getting support from their colleagues and line manager? Are internal politics coming into play and are they getting pushback when they take time out of their daily responsibilities to meet with you or take the action to which they have committed?

Are other priorities winning the battle for their attention? It's easy to be enthusiastic when a mentoring programme begins but deadlines and targets have the habit of monopolising people's attention. Before long, one meeting gets cancelled, followed by another. Then you can't remember the last time you met. It's hard to focus on the medium- and long-term when short-term priorities are pressing insistently.

Intrinsic motivation is your 'why'.[150] It is the reason for pushing you through hard times and gets you excited to move forward. It's the reason for bouncing out of bed in the morning and why you can't quiet your mind at night. It's your reason for being.

Returning to your 'why' is critical and reignites the metaphorical fire in your belly. Revisit your communication with your mentee and refocus on why they want mentoring support. Shine a light on their objectives from the programme and the impact of achieving those objectives on their career or role. Help them to balance their priorities and decide what is most important for them.

This is where being a nimble mentor is so effective. You have to change the focus of your conversation and help them to manage short-term priorities first, to enable them to make space for the longer-term work you'd like to do. Can you support them in navigating pushback on their team if that is the case? Not by intervening on their behalf but by assisting them in coming up with a strategy to get their colleagues on board.

Ultimately, if nothing changes, you may need to address the elephant in the room. Are they really committed to this mentoring relationship or are they in the programme because they have been put forward for it or because it looks good on their CV? They need to be honest with you, as a lack of commitment means that they are wasting your time and theirs. Neither of you comes out of the relationship better off than when you went into it.

---

[150] Deci, E.L. and Ryan, R.M. (2000). "The 'what' and 'why' of goal pursuits: Human needs and the self-determination of behavior." *Psychological Inquiry* 11: 227–268.

The best outcome is to turn things around and to work with a fully engaged and committed mentee. The second best outcome is to agree to part ways and to invest your time and experience in someone who will value it and move forward as a result.

Dealing with pushback

As we've stressed throughout this book, your mentee is ultimately responsible for the decisions they make and the path they choose to follow. Your role is to provide advice, guidance and feedback, but they are under no obligation to follow it.

Don't take it personally if your mentee chooses a different approach to the one you've suggested. When someone challenges our ideas, it can feel like a personal attack, and we may react emotionally to protect ourselves. At the same time, our emotions can also cloud our judgement and make it harder to listen to the other person's perspective. This can lead to a cycle of escalating emotions and arguments that are unproductive and damaging to relationships.

It's important to recognise when that is happening and take steps to slow down our response, allowing our rational mind to step in and lead our contribution to the conversation. Emotional responses are probably the leading cause for disagreements escalating; just watch how people lose control of their contribution when they become emotionally driven in a debate.

It's OK to challenge your mentee on their decision and discuss the pros and cons of each option. This is the time to leverage your active listening skills.[151] Understand the reasons why they want to try a different way, paraphrase what you have heard and repeat it back to them to check that you have fully understood. Feel free to test their arguments by asking questions but do so in a spirit of enquiry, not competition. If you have to battle each other, make it a battle of ideas, not one of egos.

If you can fully understand how they have arrived at their decision, it becomes easier to assess the relevance and viability of their view and use it as a foundation for further discussion. Never tell them they are wrong, offer a different

---

[151] Gotian, R. (2023). "10 easy ways to elevate your active listening skills." *Psychology Today*.

perspective or food for thought. Consider phrases such as "I wonder what would happen if...," or "Let's reimagine."

Once you know that their mind is set, work with them to make sure that their chosen strategy works effectively for them. It's not a zero-sum game about who is right and who is wrong or winning the argument. You share the same goal, namely, the mentee's successful progression towards their objective.

The mentoring cycle

Even when mentoring relationships go well, there may come a time when they have run their course. Try to recognise the signs of a tired or complacent relationship; more small talk and less focus at meetings, less frequent meetings, more frequent postponements and short-term cancellations, less accountability and less action (Figure 9.2).

Don't give up on the relationship and assume that it has run its course just because you see these signs. Ask yourself whether the relationship is simply flagging and needs a boost. Sit down with your mentee and review their objectives, progress to date and the support they now need. Discuss whether you are still the best person to provide that support. If not, identify who within your network they should approach next.

If you have been meeting on a regular basis, you may just need to take a break. Build in a gap to allow your mentee to take stock, see where they are for themselves and understand whether they still value your regular input. Agree on a

Signs of a Tired or Complacent Mentoring Relationship

More small talk
Less focus at meetings
Less frequent meetings
More frequent postponements and short-term cancellations
Less accountability
Less action

Figure 9.2 Signs of a tired or complacent mentoring relationship

date for them to come back to you and either pick up the regular mentoring again or take the exit ramp and move onto the next stage of their career.

As we've previously discussed, you don't disappear from their lives, you just step back into a more informal role on their mentoring team.

Some people believe that there is a natural length of time for a mentoring relationship, but the research doesn't support that claim.[152] Mentoring relationships don't have a sell-by date; we can't give catch-all advice when there are so many factors to consider, including the objectives you're working towards, the relationship between the two of you and the frequency of your meetings.

If you do feel that it is time to move on, try to raise the topic in a positive and constructive way. You want to feel comfortable that you can suggest ending your formal role without your mentee taking offence or feeling rejected. Present it as a new opportunity for them and suggest the next step, whether recommending and introducing a new mentor or a different form of career development.

Offer to remain available as a resource to them and check in with them every now and again. It will mean that your mentee won't feel abandoned by you and will give you the satisfaction of knowing how your advice continues to positively impact their success.

Making sure your mentoring doesn't affect you

In Chapter 6, we asked whether you have the experience, expertise and time to commit to supporting your mentee. If you don't, you risk not just letting your mentee down but letting yourself down as well.

While you may have the bandwidth at the start, it may wane as other commitments and pressure points impact your life. Mentors are human with obligations and responsibilities which add cyclical and unpredictable stressors in our life. Just imagine, a sick child, lost day care, an ailing parent, a leaking roof or a pandemic.

---

[152] Kram, K. (1983). "Phases of the mentor relationship." *Academy of Management Journal* 26(4): 608–625.

At the start of the COVID pandemic, people all over the world were stranded in their homes. New York City was at the epicentre of the virus. Leaving the house required identification and could only be done for specific purposes such as picking up medication at the pharmacy or getting food.

People handled this lockdown in different ways, from frozen in fear to extremely productive. Part of what drove the variance in response was cognitive load, meaning, what was weighing on their mind. There was one particular situation which nearly caused a multi-year fruitful mentoring relationship to dissolve in the ugliest fashion.

For academics, many viewed the lockdown as a time to catch up on writing papers and grants, the life blood of those in academia. There is always much to do but a scarcity of time. Now there was no excuse. One mentor told her mentee in no uncertain terms, to start working on his grant and gave him a significant to do list. The mentee was single, living alone, and the mentor assumed he needed something productive to do, instead of watching the endless loop of the devastating news programmes.

The mentee went on a rage, documented for eternity on Twitter. He was outraged that the mentor did not consider his sense of panic. His parents were frontline workers, and he feared for their safety every second of every day. He couldn't think straight and was far from productive. Yes, he didn't have children to feed or home school, but that did not mean he was thinking clearly.

The mentor was equally panicked over the safety and well-being of her elderly parents, but her approach to dealing with it was vastly different. It wasn't safe for the mentor to visit her parents and at their advanced age, they couldn't figure out how to use any video technology so that she could see them. She worried every time they went to the grocery store or felt the slightest bit unwell. The only way she kept her sanity was to compartmentalise and keep busy. She gave herself a long to do list, and one by one, she started tackling the tasks.

The problem is that the mentor incorrectly assumed that her mentee would benefit from the same tactical approach. Yes, they were both in New York City facing the same pandemic, both had a significant cognitive load filled with worry and dread, but the key difference is that they were able to deal with it differently.

The Twitter rage and ensuing disintegration of the mentoring relationship could have been avoided if the mentor and mentee had a transparent and vulnerable conversation about their worries and how each worked best under that level of stress to address those concerns. One could have helped the other instead of believing their coping mechanism was universal.

We all need to find the right balance in the commitments we make. While it's important to pay it forward, supporting other people beyond our standard responsibilities, we need to do so in a way that doesn't adversely impact our core responsibilities or our own well-being. There are still only 24 hours in the day, not all of them need to be spent on work.

When your mentee is under pressure, facing seemingly insurmountable challenges or really struggling, that can impact you too; their pain becomes your pain. A good mentor will find it hard to completely divorce themselves emotionally from their mentee's journey. After all, we are personally invested in their progress.

Being a mentor is no doubt a rewarding and fulfilling experience, but it can also come with its own set of emotional challenges. You want your mentee to succeed; after all, their success is your success. But not every day is going to be perfect or productive and it's important to recognise the potential emotional burden that working with a mentee can bring. We've developed some strategies for handling that strain so that you can engage fully with the mentoring process without letting it overwhelm you (Figure 9.3).

Handling the strain as a mentor

1. Set boundaries
2. Practice active listening
3. Seek support
4. Practice self-care
5. Focus on the positive
6. Set realistic goals
7. Be empathic
8. Be honest and transparent
9. Give yourself breaks
10. Reflect creatively

Figure 9.3 Handling the strain as a mentor

1. Set boundaries and adhere to them: It's important to establish clear boundaries with your mentee from the outset. Consider articulating time, frequency of meetings, expectations, deadlines and communication preferences. This will help you manage your time and emotional energy better and not always feel as if you are 'on call'.

2. Practice active listening: Sometimes the best mentoring is not saying anything at all. Instead, it is listening. Show that you are actively listening to your mentee by reiterating main points of what they are saying with phrases such as "So what I am hearing is. . . " or "Would you say your pain concern is. . . ". By doing so, you are in a better position to understand their needs and feelings, which can help you respond to them more effectively.

3. Seek support: Mentors are human, which means they have feelings and react to stress. It's important for a mentor to have their own support system, such as friends, family or other mentors. This can help you manage any stress or emotions that arise from your mentoring relationship. It's a lifesaver to ask other experienced mentors for guidance on "how would you handle this situation. . . ".

4. Practice self-care: If you are tired, hungry or as they say in the United States hangry (that feeling when you are angry when hungry), that is of little use to you and your mentee. Make sure to take care of yourself physically, emotionally and mentally. Take breaks, get enough sleep (remember, sleep is not a weakness) and eat a nutritious meal.

5. Focus on the positive: Who doesn't love a pity party? Recognising mistakes and failures is important as they pave the road to success. But dwelling on them serves little purpose. While it's important to acknowledge and address any negative emotions that come up, it can also be helpful to focus on the positive aspects of your mentoring relationship, such as the progress your mentee is making.

6. Set realistic goals: What is easy for you may be a challenge for someone else. Make the goals relatable and achievable. They should have the right balance where it is a bit of a challenge, so that it is exciting, but not so much that it is overwhelming. Make sure, as a mentor, to be their safety net.[153,154]

---

[153] Drago-Severson, E. (2009). "How do you 'know'." *Yes!* Fall 2009.
[154] Drago-Severson, E. (2009). *Leading Adult Learning.* Thousand Oaks, CA, SAGE.

7 Be empathic: Try to put yourself in your mentee's situation and consider what they might be feeling or questioning. This can help you respond in a way that is supportive and compassionate and avoid sounding tactical.

8 Be honest and transparent: You cannot do it all. It's important to be honest with your mentee about what you can and cannot provide in terms of support. If you are having an unusually stressful week or deadlines coming up, let your mentee know that you will not be as available as usual. This can help you avoid being misunderstood or taking on too much emotional burden.

9 Give yourself breaks: If you find yourself feeling overwhelmed or emotionally drained, it's okay to press pause and take a break from your mentoring relationship. This can help you recharge and come back with renewed energy and focus. Just let your mentee know that you will be incommunicative for a specific period of time (give dates), but look forward to resuming when you return.

10 Reflect creatively: Reflection, and taking action on said reflection, is a critical part of growth in adults. Look for creative outlets to reflect on your experiences. Journalling, talking to others and creative arts are all well-documented strategies.[155,156,157]

Taking on a mentee means taking on responsibility to the person you're supporting, to the organisation who brought you together and to yourself. These responsibilities need to be taken seriously when considering requests to mentor, but we hope that they won't deter you from lending your expertise, experience and insights to those who can benefit from them. You have a lot to offer, and your mentee can and will benefit from your insights.

---

[155] Mezirow, J. (1991). *Transformative Dimensions of Adult Learning.* San Francisco, Jossey-Bass.
[156] Cranton, P. (2006). *Understanding and Promoting Transformative Learning: A Guide for Educators of Adults.* San Francisco, CA, Jossey-Bass.
[157] Hoggan, C., Simpson, E. and Stuckey, P. (2010). *Creative Expression in Transformative Learning: Tools and Techniques for Educators of Adults.* Jossey-Bass.

CHAPTER 10
WHY DO MENTORING RELATIONSHIPS GO WRONG?

Not every mentoring relationship has a happy ending.

There are no guarantees that your mentoring relationship will work out perfectly for both parties. Despite best efforts, sometimes it just doesn't work out.

Of course, there is a great deal you can do to make the relationship work. And by 'you', we mean all parties: the mentor, the mentee and the organisation you work for. Many mentoring relationships will fail purely because one or more parties haven't given enough consideration to what needs to happen to make it succeed.

A match made in heaven . . . or hell?

Within a formal programme, it all begins with the matching process. Who decides who mentors whom? In an ideal world, mentees will recognise the people who they feel will give them the support and advice they need to progress their career and approach them directly. But many people don't know how to start looking for a mentor for themselves (we'll address this in Chapter 15), so the organisation needs to support their search and provide a matchmaking service.

There are so many ways in which matching processes can, and often do, come tumbling down. It all begins with an assumption – looking to match people with something in common, whether it be race, gender, background, role, school or something else. We have discussed elsewhere in this book the upside of people from underrepresented demographic groups mentoring other people with the same background or underrepresented status. But it doesn't always work and has some serious limitations.

Just because somebody has the same background, doesn't automatically mean that they will be a perfect match. While it can be a positive indicator, it's equally, if not more, important to look at whether the experience of the mentor is a match for the mentee's goals, and whether values are aligned. Then of course, the personalities must complement each other.

Always seeking to partner people from the same background or who have similar experiences can also restrict both organisational and individual growth by stifling the flow of new ideas. Organisations should strive to encourage cognitive diversity – bringing different perspectives and backgrounds into the same conversations stimulates fresh thinking and innovation and decreases the risk of being in an echo chamber of ideas. In an arena like mentoring, which is heavily focused on problem-solving, such an approach can pay huge dividends.

In Chapter 12 we will share some of the different factors you may want to consider when trying to create the perfect partnership.

Even if you can tick all of the boxes we will discuss, the matching process shouldn't be left either to technology or to somebody sitting apart from the eventual mentoring relationship. Mentor and mentee both need a say in whether they feel there is a fit. Create opportunities for prospective participants to meet and talk to each other, such as an initial 'speed mentoring' session where the panel of mentors and the mentees in the programme can have conversations with each other and begin to identify with whom they would like to work or organise social gatherings with structured ice breakers that offer opportunities for people to meet each other.

It's ok to say "no" . . . and it's ok to be told "no"

Nobody should feel obligated or pressured in any way either to mentor or to be mentored by somebody else. Both parties should be positive and, dare we say, excited at the idea of working together. (We were going to say both parties should be 'comfortable' about the prospect, but it should ideally be much more than that. If you're excited to get started, you have a much better chance of both doing what it takes to get the most from the relationship.)

If either party doesn't see the fit, it should be made easy and acceptable for them to decline an invitation, without any adverse implications. Open, constructive and honest communication is welcome if it is going to be supportive and useful for the person who is being vetoed.

A mentee needs to feel secure about declining the offer of support from a mentor who is more senior to them in an organisation. It will be easier if the recommended mentor is in a different line of delivery in the organisation, so that there are no direct feared consequences. But that doesn't mean that it will feel easy for the mentee to do.

The mentee may fear that questions might be asked about their ambition or attitude, their reputation will be damaged across the senior levels or that they will find it difficult if they have to interact with that spurned mentor in the future.

They need to be reassured that the process is managed thoughtfully.

If you are a mentor whose offer of support is turned down, don't take it personally. There may be many reasons why a mentee wants to go in a different direction; don't let your ego and pride take over. If appropriate, ask for feedback. If you have skills or experience that the mentee wasn't aware of and would, in fact, be a better fit for them than they thought, it's a good opportunity to have that conversation.

But don't worry about it. There is no shortage of mentees in need of good mentors and the number of outstanding mentors is in short supply. So, if you don't get one, you will certainly get others in the not-too-distant future.

When one door closes, another opens. You can leverage this moment. Managed effectively and positively, it's also a great opportunity to get some real feedback and understand how you are perceived across the organisation.

Be the leader you are and reassure the mentee, who may well be struggling with the concerns mentioned above, that no offence is taken. And, if you are happy to, offer your services as an informal mentor as and when the need arises.

The blind leading the blind

In our experience, there seems to be more training for mentees than for mentors in organisations. The little training that exists is limited. Mentors are expected to be successful in the role purely on the basis of their career success to date. But just because they have succeeded in a role (quite possibly a technical one) doesn't mean that they will be suited to share the right advice and insights with a mentee.[158] There are nuances related to communication, motivation and empathy that don't come naturally to many.

---

[158] Gotian, R. (2016). "Mentoring the mentors: Just because you have the title doesn't mean you know what you are doing." *College Student Journal* 1(4): 1–4.

Organisations can't rely on mentors to simply share their experience without training in how to do so effectively. If the only experience they have to share is what they have learned on their journey, it doesn't necessarily follow that replicating their travels will be relevant for their mentee, who may face different challenges.

The mentor will bring their own biases with them based on how they have been supported and how they like to be taught. They need to understand how to mentor people from different backgrounds, with different learning styles and from different demographic groups. That doesn't come naturally to many people. It will pay for an organisation to invest in upskilling their mentors to enable them to be far more effective in the role.

Invest in your mentors and you invest in your staff in turn. They will get the support and advice they need to produce better results. And better mentoring will lead to increased retention, better-equipped future leaders and more positive word of mouth about the organisation as a great place to work.[159,160]

Introduce training for new mentors to equip them for the post before they start working with colleagues, and then support them on their journey. Host resources to support them on your internal network or learning management system and perhaps also have an experienced mentor to offer them ongoing support, mentoring the mentors, or create an in-house mentors' community for them to share challenges and ask for advice, discreetly and confidentially, of course.

No one knows all the answers or has experience with every situation, so allowing for a learning community where mentors can learn from each other helps the mentors grow while developing their mentees.

The team overseeing the mentoring programme should also check in at intervals during the programme with each party to make sure that they are happy and everything is on track.

---

[159] Eby, L.T., Allen, T.D., Evan, S.C., Ng, T. and DuBois, D. (2008). "Does mentoring matter? A multidisciplinary meta-analysis comparing mentored and non-mentored individuals." *Journal of Vocational Behaviour* 72(2): 254–267.

[160] Allen, T., Eby, L., Poteet, M., Lentz, E. and Lima, L. (2004). "Career benefits associated with mentoring for proteges: A meta analysis." *Journal of Applied Psychology* 89(1): 127.

Being on the ball

Attending a self-development programme several years ago, Andy and his fellow participants were told that it was important to 'be on the field and not in the stands' if the programme was to be successful. The same applies to a mentoring relationship; both parties, as we have stressed throughout the book, have to be committed to the process and play their role to ensure that it works.

If either decides to be a spectator instead, hoping that it will work just by having the appointments on their calendar, the relationship is going to fall a long way short of its potential. Mentoring doesn't work if it is passive. It must be purposeful and with intent.

Much of what we will share here has been covered already from the perspective of what is needed to make a mentoring partnership successful. It naturally follows that, if you don't take those key actions, your relationship is more than likely to fail. So, here is a reminder of the simple oversights that could dampen the outcomes of any mentoring relationship:

Poor planning

Being part of the game means keeping your eye on the ball. In mentoring terms, that means maintaining the momentum of the relationship. Keep meetings scheduled and respected, not bumped constantly because something more important has come up. Treat mentoring appointments as you would an engagement with a key client. If your career is important, act like it.

Allow sufficient time for those meetings, not just for the conversation itself but to prepare for it, reflect on it afterwards and to take the action you need in order to ensure that your conversation has real meaning. Paraphrase and review next action steps.

Unclear communication

We've talked at length about agreeing to objectives from the programme. These need to be understood clearly by both parties, as well as the expectations each has of the other. Know what you're working towards and understand just what each party is expected to bring to the table in order to reach those objectives and the limits of those expectations (discussed below). These are foundational steps, and the mentoring relationship can crumble without this initial alignment.

Adults learn from their experiences, so it is important to reflect on them.[161] Talk about your takeaways and learning, and ensure that both parties know what has landed and what the mentee (or, in some cases, the mentor) is going to act upon. Is it next steps on a critical project, submitting a paper, giving a presentation or making an introduction? So many things are promised during a meeting that, without a summary at the end, things can fall through the cracks. Have a clear mutual understanding of what you will revisit in your next meeting and for what you will hold the other accountable.

Yes, mentees can and should hold their mentors accountable as well. Mentoring is, after all, a two-way street.

Be open with each other; mentees need to be able to share where they are struggling, which relationships with colleagues are not working and what concerns they have without fear of repercussions. In short, they need psychological safety.[162] Mentors need to set boundaries, explain the limits of their ability to help, be honest when they don't have an answer (but commit to helping to find one) and share their own failures, as discussed in Chapter 7.

Don't pretend that everything is perfect. Mentoring relationships aren't designed for mutual back-slapping. Progress will be impeded if false platitudes are freely distributed. The more open your communication, the more open the road ahead to achieve something memorable.

Not managing expectations

A mentor is there to support their mentee, but the work has to be done by the mentee, and their achievements are theirs. We've already stressed how mentors need to advise and guide their mentees, and to respect that the ultimate decisions are their own.

Similarly, mentees need to be respectful of their mentor's time and energy. A mentor has their own, usually demanding and high-pressure, job to do and

---

[161] Knowles, M.S. (1984). *The Adult Learner: A Neglected Species* (3rd ed.). Houston, Gulf.
[162] Edmondson, A.C. (2018). *The Fearless Organization: Creating Psychological Safety in the Workplace for Learning, Innovation, and Growth*. John Wiley & Sons.

they don't get recognition for their work with their mentee. They are judged more on billable hours, organisational performance or other day-to-day responsibilities, not on what their mentee achieves.

For every minute they spend with you, there is something pressing waiting for their attention. So, respect that and manage what you ask from your mentor and when you ask it or by when you expect a response.

Mentors need to be aware of their own time and energy too, ensuring that they don't burn out.[163] If you're struggling to commit because of pressure from elsewhere, be open and honest about it and explore alternative approaches with your mentee and with the team supporting the mentoring programme.

On the flip side, when a mentor gets very engaged in and excited about a mentee's progress, their enthusiasm can often get the better of them. Don't overwhelm your mentee and don't take over their job on top of yours! Ensure that your mentee feels supported, rather than suffocated.

Let down by the culture

The mentoring culture is defined not by the words people say but by the actions people take. Mentors and mentees can be perfectly matched, trained up and committed to the process. But if mentoring is not valued and elevated across the organisation, the lack of support they get can have a huge negative impact on their chances of success.

How is mentoring spoken about within your organisation? Is it embedded in your culture, not just in words, such as in your mission statement, but reflected in actions at every level? Do people talk about it in day-to-day conversation, raising consciousness not just of the power of mentoring but of access to mentoring support for those who need it?

Do people understand who your mentoring programmes are for, how they can access them or aspire to be invited to participate and what is in the programmes for them?

Are the photos of mentors and mentees seen anywhere? Are the successes of their mentoring shared publicly?

---

[163] Gotian, R., et al. (2022). "Don't let mentoring burn you out." *Harvard Business Review*.

Senior leadership and line management have a responsibility to role model the power of mentoring and support those being mentored, as we will explore in the next chapter.

Mentoring needs to be so valued in your culture that it's seen as an integral part of a mentor or mentee's role and not as an add-on, if you have the time, or a distraction. Mentoring cannot and should not be done in remnants of time. We talked earlier in this chapter about treating mentoring meetings as you would a meeting with a key client; mentoring really does need to be valued that highly and, if it is, it can have a massive positive impact across the organisation.

Companies are sometimes concerned that people who aren't selected for a mentoring programme will feel resentful at being left out and driven by a fear of a backlash, they choose the perceived easier route of scaling back the offering. That's the wrong approach. Empower those who aren't invited into a mentoring programme to organically seek their own mentoring relationship or inspire them to demonstrate why they should not have been overlooked.

Make it something to aspire to, a recognition of achievement, drive and potential and ensure that your recruitment process accounts for possible unconscious bias that leads to high-potential candidates being ignored.[164]

It's important that mentoring is available to everyone. It's the next natural step in the career journey for those who have proven they have the potential to shine, whether in their current role or further up the ladder. The next layer may be group mentoring facilitated by a master mentor, or access to high-level people within the organisation.

And it should be a recognition of achievement for mentors too. To be invited to mentor someone else is acknowledgement of the respect you have earned for your work and achievements to date and something to be proud of. You have proven that you can guide the next generation of leaders.

In many organisations, giving back to others is not recognised or rewarded in the way it should be. Remuneration and bonus programmes focus on who is responsible for a final outcome, not all of the people who played a part in the journey. And that stops people stepping forward for roles like mentoring.

---

[164] Rivera, L.A. (2015). *How Elite Students Get Elite Jobs*. Princeton University Press.

We like an approach that Microsoft takes (Figure 10.1).[165] During the appraisal process, people are asked to reflect on:

- What impact they have made personally on their team, the organisation or customers.
- What impact they have made using other people's ideas and contributions.
- How they have helped other people to make an impact.

This takes the focus away from just paper targets and objectives but looks at the role everyone plays within the organisation, helping others to be their best. Mentoring should lie at the very core of that philosophy.

Put mentoring at the heart of your values, make people proud to be involved either as a mentor or mentee and ensure everybody values the mentoring process. Then you'll have every chance of a successful and vibrant mentoring programme.

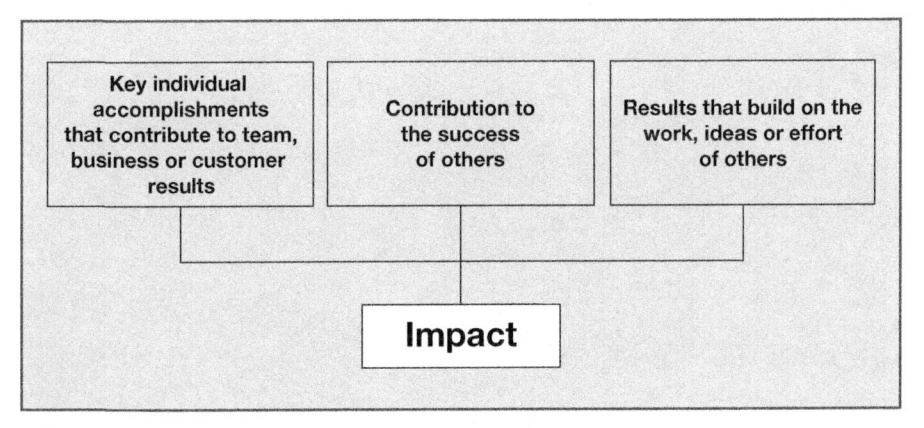

```
┌─────────────────────────────────────────────────────────────────────┐
│  ┌──────────────────┐   ┌──────────────────┐   ┌──────────────────┐ │
│  │ Key individual   │   │                  │   │ Results that     │ │
│  │ accomplishments  │   │ Contribution to  │   │ build on the     │ │
│  │ that contribute  │   │ the success      │   │ work, ideas or   │ │
│  │ to team,         │   │ of others        │   │ effort           │ │
│  │ business or      │   │                  │   │ of others        │ │
│  │ customer results │   │                  │   │                  │ │
│  └────────┬─────────┘   └────────┬─────────┘   └────────┬─────────┘ │
│           └──────────────────────┼──────────────────────┘           │
│                          ┌───────┴────────┐                         │
│                          │     Impact     │                         │
│                          └────────────────┘                         │
└─────────────────────────────────────────────────────────────────────┘
```

Figure 10.1 Microsoft's impact conversations

---

[165] https://www.linkedin.com/business/talent/blog/talent-engagement/steps-microsoft-took-to-renovate-culture

PART 3
SUPPORTING MENTORING AS AN ORGANISATION

CHAPTER 11
WHO IS RESPONSIBLE FOR LEADING THE PROGRAMME AND WHO NEEDS TO SUPPORT IT?

Sometimes there are best-kept secrets. But certain things should not be available only to those who 'need to know.' A mentoring programme is of no use to anyone if people aren't aware of it. We have come across many organisations that officially have a formal mentoring programme in place, but the programme lies dog-eared, unloved and unused on a shelf. That's a pity as the potential for success is enormous and there are pernicious consequences to not having a robust and popular mentoring programme.

Programmes need to be owned, promoted, supported and tracked. Everybody who could potentially access the programme needs to be aware of its existence, their personal suitability to apply for the programme, what would be expected of them if they participated and what they can look forward to in return. The process should be streamlined and not needlessly cumbersome. That is always a turn off. To maximise its potential, it needs to be easy to apply and be supported by line management.

Advocacy should come from above – as we discussed in Chapter 3, the senior leadership team need to be role models for, and visible supporters and sponsors of, the programme – and from below. Participation in the programme needs to be embraced by colleagues and direct reports as well as senior managers. In short, there needs to be a top-down and bottom-up support system for the mentoring programme.

Who runs the mentoring programme?

We usually see mentoring programmes being owned by one of three functions within an organisation. Two of those functions take responsibility as part of their day-to-day responsibilities; the third is more likely to see a volunteer lead mentoring over and above their regular role.

The most obvious home for mentoring programmes is either the Human Resources department or the Learning and Development team. In some organisations, L&D responsibilities as a whole fall under the remit of HR.

It makes sense for the HR or L&D teams to oversee mentoring availability within their organisation. These teams are responsible respectively for employee welfare and for staff and leadership professional development strategy and delivery. They are also able to take a firm-wide view, curating mentees with mentors who are in different teams or divisions but who are best placed to provide what the mentee needs while ultimately being of benefit to the mentor as well.

The challenge comes when the HR or L&D team is overloaded with other priorities. We have seen mentoring treated as a 'nice to have' or easy to discard option far too often; the perceived value needs a long view and patience and is often not strong enough for it to be prioritised over and above other delivery targets or those with immediate results.

Often, when this happens, it is Employee Resource Groups who pick up the slack. ERGs are employee-led groups with similar challenges, backgrounds or interests, such as women's networks, ethnic networks and LGBT+ networks. A key part of the mission of many ERGs is to uplift groups that are often seen to have been disadvantaged. They will often see mentoring as a key way to deliver the support that will help their members overcome discrimination and boost their careers.

This is a double-edged sword. Having to work to solve the underrepresentation which you did not create is emotionally exhausting. We've already discussed the 'minority tax' on a couple of occasions in this book. There is an implicit or explicit expectation to represent your 'otherness'. You are often asked to lead diversity efforts when sadly they are non-promotable tasks, and you do this in addition to your other responsibilities. As a result, you spend a longer time in lower ranks and are less likely to hold leadership positions.

While these ERGs are a fantastic support system, because of their nature, they can often run the risk of turning into an echo chamber. Disparate voices, perspectives, experiences and access can provide opportunities and open doors most mentees didn't know existed.

Whoever runs the mentoring programme, it's not simply a case of providing a list of people willing to mentor those who subscribe to the programme. They need to be able to think about appropriate recruitment and training of each group, track the success of the programme and ensure that the mentoring is as broadly accessible as possible. And they need to have both the resources and time to do so.

The role of senior management and line managers

Earlier on in this chapter we suggested that senior and line management both need to support any mentoring programme. Without their buy-in, the path ahead is hard for any mentoring programme to establish itself and be sustainable.

Senior management

In any organisation, people look to senior managers to get a hint about what steps will help them to climb the ladder or be successful in other ways. Programmes that are referenced in Town Halls, on social media and in other internal communications will be taken far more seriously than those where leaders barely seem aware of their existence. The mentoring programme needs to be inculcated into the vernacular and culture of the organisation.

Ideally, you want senior leaders to step up as mentors and engage actively in the programme. Even if they can't commit to that, you want them to stress the importance of mentoring, share their own experiences and encourage people to sign up. They should show an interest in the mentoring programme, not just giving the nod at a board meeting to setting up the programme in the first place but asking to see how it is progressing and what results it's achieving. By sharing their own stories, it sets an example that mentoring is leveraged at every level of the hierarchy and has led to individual, team and organisational success.

After all, this is a core channel through which your organisation will be nurturing the senior leaders of its future.

If you want mentoring to become part of the culture of the organisation, senior leadership need to set the tone of the conversation and help to embed its importance in everyday exchanges at all levels. They need to do this through their words and actions. One without the other is meaningless.

Line management

Line managers have a similar responsibility to encourage people to treat mentoring programmes seriously and to see them as a positive opportunity for career progression. If you're not careful, they can have a strong adverse effect on the success of your programme.

If they don't buy into the value of mentoring for their team, they can make it difficult for a mentee to engage, not allowing them time to fully partake in the process, pressuring them to cancel meetings if there are other priorities or making them feel guilty about taking time out of their day-to-day role.

It sends a signal that "I am being pressured to allow you to do this, but I don't really want you to engage." There can be many reasons for this. Most glaringly, if the mentoring is successful, the mentee may get promoted, which means their manager needs to find a replacement. Until they find and train a successor, it is the manager who may need to roll up their sleeves and do additional work alongside their regular responsibilities. As crazy as it sounds, they might subconsciously want the mentoring to *not* work out.[166]

Just as senior management sets the tone of the conversation about mentoring for the organisation, line managers set the tone for their team. Rather than viewing mentoring as a distraction from team performance and achieving targets, and reflecting that view to their team, you need to ensure that your line managers understand the benefits to everyone under their wing if one or two bring back new perspectives, ideas and skills as a result of their mentoring meetings.

Take the direct route as well; line management is not just about hitting team targets, it's about nurturing the people you are responsible for. Ensure that support for staff development is reflected in annual appraisals for managers and

---

[166] Gotian, R. (2020). "Why your boss shouldn't be your mentor." *Forbes*.

that they are held accountable for their team members' commitment to and ability to engage in mentoring relationships.

Line managers should be encouraging their reports to apply for mentee roles when suitable, not making it harder for them to do so. It is especially helpful if the line managers themselves participated in the mentoring programme as either a mentor or mentee.

Beyond your own walls

Throughout this chapter, we have focused on who runs mentoring programmes within an organisation and what needs to happen to make them successful. We believe, however, that there is a tremendous opportunity that a lot of organisations miss out on, which is collaborating on mentoring programmes with one or more organisations beyond your own walls.

There are a host of benefits to sharing ideas and cross pollinating with other organisations in your sector, or even beyond. Bringing together mentors and mentees from different worlds can increase the range of ideas brought to challenges, so many entities create their own 'way of doing things', a perceived wisdom that becomes so ingrained that it is rarely challenged. It is just accepted.

Let people challenge those ideas, whether they are accepted wisdom in your organisation alone or across your industry or sector. Bring in mentors from public service to work with private industry mentees, and vice versa.

While this is something you can do yourself, with a little bit of research, networking and outreach, there are companies who specialise in putting these programmes together for you, particularly in specific sectors.

In 2016 Max Fellows, a sales director for a mid-sized events agency, and Mel Noakes, who was Global Head of Events for Sony Mobile, got together over dinner and created Elevate, a free mentoring programme and community for the events industry, who we mentioned in Chapter 3. Max and Mel realised there was a gap in the industry when it came to people supporting each other and accessing structured mentoring and a significant lack of structured training and learning, which created huge voids in both confidence and expected capabilities.

Max explained, "A mid-tier manager progresses through the ranks up to directorship within three years. They will have likely had no additional training, so they find themselves with the complexities of a senior job role with people management, staff wellness, leadership nuances, client crisis management and more challenges they haven't previously had to address. This has led to a huge lack of confidence."

They noticed that individuals were seeking development and connection, but there was no proper framework in place. People were hesitant to approach their managers for mentoring because they feared it would reflect negatively on their ability to do their job and companies also struggled to provide effective mentoring because they lacked the trust and resources to do so.

When they founded Elevate, mentoring programmes in the industry were limited and specific, targeting only certain demographics or roles. Mel told us, "We were in the middle of our careers and there was nothing for people like us to go to. We weren't junior enough to be deemed to need it, nor were we senior enough to have the coaching and support from board members that you typically get. It left us wondering where the support was for people like us."

According to Max and Mel, a cross-sector mentoring programme provides a unique opportunity for individuals in the creative event industry to learn from each other. By bringing together individuals from different sectors within the industry, Elevate allows for a diverse range of perspectives and experiences to be shared. Mel told us, "By going outside your organisation, you gain trust and confidence that you can be honest, that your reality isn't going to lead to challenges internally. Additionally, we find that internal mentoring within the same organisation can become very tactical and transactional."

Additionally, a sector-wide scheme provides access to mentoring for smaller organisations, which might have been difficult to offer otherwise, due to a lack of relevant experience within their ranks and an enhanced risk of conflict of interest.

Max and Mel chose to run their programme specifically for the events sector because of the common challenges faced by people working within the industry. Mel explained, "There are some natural challenges that come in specific industries. If you talk to people in the creative event space, they will understand the complexity, the challenges, the stress, the realities of client demands, the time pressures and much more. We share a common language.

"You have a common map and a common playing field that means you understand each other because you're in the same world."

Without the appropriate support and resources, a mentoring programme will not be able to achieve its intended effect. Mentoring works well, but it cannot be something one person does for an entire organisation. That is simply not realistic. Mentoring programmes can be housed in a variety of different groups within an organisation. Each has their pros and cons. As long as you are aware of the drawbacks and work to fill the gaps, the benefits should far outweigh any deficits.

CHAPTER 12
HOW DO YOU IDENTIFY AND MATCH MENTORS AND MENTEES?

The 'secret sauce' of any mentoring programme is the ability to get the right people working together. If mentor and mentee find the right chemistry, work together towards a common goal and are committed to a successful outcome, the rest will naturally follow. If, on the other hand, there's a mismatch, it will be hard to achieve the results you're looking for.

When looking at the matching process in this chapter, we are going to assume, where relevant, that you are forming a programme based on a traditional-hierarchical model, with a senior mentor supporting up-and-coming talent. That doesn't mean that many of the observations made aren't equally applicable to reverse, peer-to-peer or to other mentoring models.

And, of course, while seeking to match mentees with specific mentors, you should still encourage them to think of their wider Mentoring Team, not relying purely on these formal arrangements.

Who should be in the programme?

The first step to effective matching is to make sure that you have the right people to choose from in the first place. When setting up your mentoring programme, be clear about eligibility criteria and the qualities you are looking for in both mentors and mentees. You don't just want warm bodies as mentors. You are looking for people who want to give back, and believe in generativity – paying their wisdom forward to the next generation so that the knowledge lives on.

Just because somebody has been successful in their career, doesn't mean they will be a good mentor.[167] And simply because someone has expressed a desire to move forward in their career, it doesn't mean they are ready to be mentored.

If you are clear about the broader remit, the right people should be much easier to identify.

Who among your senior leadership team and more senior employees is best placed to help mentees achieve success as defined by the remit of the programme? And which employees are best placed to benefit from participation?

The former seems to be a pied piper of sorts, always helping and seeing the potential in others. The latter are likely those characterised as high potentials. They are already on your radar but would benefit from some guidance so that they may turbo boost their productivity, effectiveness and career. They are also consistently seeking to listen and learn, rather than be the loudest voice in the room or last to speak.

If your programme targets developing future leaders, people who have progressed rapidly through the organisation themselves may make excellent mentors, while those who are earmarked as having high potential, qualified for a graduate or accelerated promotion programme or who have been nominated by their managers as high performers would be standout mentees.

Alternatively, for mentoring programmes that form part of a DEI initiative, you might work closely with relevant ERGs or the HR department to identify the right candidate for each role.

You also want to ensure that both mentor and mentee understand what you are trying to achieve. While the primary focus for participants is making sure that their individual relationship thrives, they have a responsibility to do so within the remit of the programme as a whole. It's important that they recognise how their success impacts the perception of mentoring across the organisation and the likelihood of more support for future similar interventions. If this is to succeed, thrive and scale, all parties need to be invested in its outcomes and reach.

All participants should be committed to their role in the programme and both able and willing to invest the time needed to contribute effectively.

---

[167] Gotian, R. (2016). "Mentoring the mentors: Just because you have the title doesn't mean you know what you are doing." *College Student Journal* **50**(1): 1–4.

Streamlining the process

It's important to make it as easy as possible for people to find their partner in your mentoring programme. The approach needs to be simple, easy to understand and not time-consuming to engage with. If the process becomes too bureaucratic, people will become confused and disengage from the process. Your programme, as a result, will have a less positive impact and start to disintegrate.

The obvious place to start any matching process is by listing mentors and mentees on the programme, together with the key topics they can or want to talk about. Mentors should be listed with a summary of their experience, expertise and areas of particular strength. Mentees should share their desired outcomes from the programme and areas for development that have been identified during their appraisals and other discussions with their managers.

Many programmes will start and stop at that point, but those who work in the mentoring space strongly believe that there are other, less obvious, considerations that can have a huge impact on the success of a mentoring relationship.[168] Figure 12.1 shows the factors that your matchmaking process should take the following into account.

Is there a conflict of interest?

Mentors should not be in the direct line of reporting of the mentee, nor should they have a stake in any projects the mentee is working on.[169]

Will they connect on a human level?

Let participants know something about the person they could be working with, not just their achievements or needs. Ask each participant to write a personal profile, sharing some fun facts about themselves, what their hobbies and pastimes are or listing their favourite films and books. While these might seem frivolous, they will humanise people, help potential partners to recognise areas of commonality and identify people they might more easily bond with.

---

[168] Johnson, B., et al. (2020). "Why your mentorship program isn't working." *Harvard Business Review*.

[169] Gotian, R. (2020). "Why your boss shouldn't be your mentor." *Forbes*.

Making the Perfect Mentoring Match

1. Match need with ability to support: Ask mentees to list the support they are looking for and mentors to list their experience and expertise. Look for matches.

2. Ensure no conflict of interest: Can the mentor give objective advice or are they involved in the projects, relationships or decisions under discussion?

3. Seek compatibility: Will mentor and mentee connect on a human level? Ask everyone in the programme to share something about themselves personally.

4. Lived experience: Does the mentor understand from their own experiences what the mentee is going through? Can they be culturally sensitive if needed?

5. Compatible learning and communication styles: Will mentor and mentee engage positively or will different styles lead to a clash?

6. Shared values: Opinions may differ but opposite values may lead to trouble.

7. Cognitive diversity: Will the different experiences and background of a mentor help to spark new ideas for the mentee and provide challenge to their comfortable worldview?

Figure 12.1 Matching mentors and mentees

If this seems stiff or difficult to some, consider doing a video interview with the mentors where their personality can shine through.

Managing cultural challenges

Ask your mentee if there are any cultural or other concerns their mentor needs to recognise and be able to consider when working with them. While we have talked about the importance of cognitive diversity elsewhere in the book, it's still critical to be sensitive to potential challenges when mentors work with people who come from a different culture or religion or who have a different gender or sexuality to them.

Allow the mentee to express a preference if they'd prefer to work with someone who already understands these areas and their importance to, and impact on, them. If they are open to working with mentors from a different background, ensure that you give the mentor the training and support they need to allow them to anticipate any potential challenges, avoid causing offence and respond when something comes up that they do not have the knowledge or background to manage.

Are their communication styles and learning preferences compatible?

We talked in Chapter 8 about how important it is to ensure that communication styles and learning preferences align. Some mentors make use of personality profiling tools to understand their mentee's style and how to best work with them. If used thoughtfully, they can be useful tools as a general guide to understanding a mentee, or to help participants gain insights into their own reactions and approach. But there are challenges too, as they are not scientifically developed and could lead to some pigeonholing. We certainly wouldn't recommend them as a core part of the matching process, but they can play a key role if used as a very light guide to ensure that completely incompatible personalities aren't put together.

Do their values align?

While opinions might differ without harming the relationship, if the worldview and moral compass of the mentor and mentee are poles apart, it's likely to impact how they value their conversations and respect each other.

Will their backgrounds and experiences be different enough to breathe new ideas into the conversation and challenge thinking?

We have already discussed the dangers of surrounding yourself with people like you. Matching mentors and mentees who share different backgrounds, experiences and perspectives can lead to more challenging conversations and an increased chance of innovative approaches and outcomes.

Technical support

The challenge of matching mentors and mentees has been such a compelling issue that there has been a growth in technology designed to get around it.

Of course, any conversation about the role of technology in mentoring in the modern era is incomplete without a look at how artificial intelligence might change the goalposts. As we mentioned earlier, the development of AI is moving so quickly that we would be amazed if new advances have not reached the market by the time we publish, let alone by now if you are reading this sometime later.

Peter Brown, PwC's Global Workforce Leader, sees a number of uses for Generative AI in the matching process, as well as for mentoring generally. He told us that AI's ability to analyse and manipulate large amounts of data about mentors and mentees more efficiently than humans can lead to more precise and compatible matches. With AI, organisations can develop algorithms to consider various criteria such as skills, experience and personality traits to identify the best mentor–mentee matches. AI can also continuously learn and improve the matching process based on feedback and success metrics.

Peter is keen, however, to stress that AI will complement and not replace mentors. He told us, "The use of Generative AI in a mentor–mentee relationship is a classic case of where technology can be used to augment, but not replace human beings. As brilliant as it is, AI is unable to provide, for example, the emotional connection, empathy and nuanced advice – all these innate, human qualities can't be replaced by it. So, I think it's to be used in concert."

Getting mentors and mentees together

For all of your planning, and whatever algorithms you put together, nothing beats the ability to find out who you like by meeting face to face. Move beyond solely using paper or technology to match people, let them have real conversations and find rapport and connection for themselves. Once we have met someone in person or, to a lesser degree, online, it's much easier to instinctively recognise whether or not we can see ourselves working with them and respecting their advice.

Many organisations put on 'speed mentoring' events. Ideally, these take place in person. They can, of course, be hosted on platforms like Zoom or Teams, but we believe that physical events are far more effective, if they are practical and accessible.

Speed mentoring is based on the more commonly recognised speed dating events that became popular in the mid-late 1990s. Typically, people will move along a line of potential partners and enjoy a short conversation with each one. After each interaction, participants on both sides are invited to tick a box on their list of partners if they want to 'match' with someone.

Only if two parties 'match' are introductions made.

This can work well with mentoring too; only if mentor and mentee select each other will they be invited to take the next step and discuss a mentoring relationship. This manages the challenge of one being seen to turn down the invitation from the other and gives the match a much stronger foundation from which to build.

The exit ramp

Despite best efforts, the mentoring relationships might sour or not be useful.[170] Bad mentoring is worse than no mentoring, as once a mentee feels burned, they no longer trust the mentoring process.[171] As we know mentoring has so many personal and professional benefits,[172] we need to ensure that we don't lose mentees due to bad mentors.

While the mentoring match is a clear first step, it is imperative to ensure that we consider the full picture of where mentoring relationships can go wrong, as discussed in Chapter 10, and make sure that there are guardrails and an exit ramp if it is becoming stagnant or toxic.

---

[170] Chopra, V., Edelson, D.P. and Saint S. (2016). "Mentorship malpractice." *JAMA* **315**(14): 1453–1454. doi:10.1001/jama.2015.18884.

[171] Ragins, B. and Miller, J. (2000). "Marginal mentoring: The effects of type of mentor, quality of relationship, and program design on work and career attitudes." *Academy of Management Journal* **43**: 10.2307/1556344.

[172] Kammeyer-Mueller, J.D., and Judge, T.A. (2008). "A quantitative review of mentoring research: Test of a model." *Journal of Vocational Behavior* **72**(3): 269–283.

CHAPTER 13
HOW WILL YOU MEASURE SUCCESS?

In a 2022 Enterprise Nation survey on the state of mentoring in the UK, 76% of businesses responding said that mentoring has been important to their business growth. Respondents reported receiving support in areas such as personal growth and development, specific expertise such as marketing, strategy, finding new markets and leadership.[173] Every new study reinforces previous academic research that mentoring benefits all parties involved – mentor, mentee and the organisation.

We've already argued strongly in this book that mentoring adds huge value to a business, both on an individual and an organisational level. That doesn't mean that you can just take that success for granted. If you are going to invest time and resources into a mentoring programme, you need to measure your return on investment. Having clear results from your programme will be essential when creating the business case to continue or expand the activity as well as to engage with more mentors and mentees in the future.

A one size fits all approach is far from likely to work effectively for mentoring (or anything else for that matter). The individual nature of a mentoring relationship means that success of a programme cannot simply be measured against generic institutional objectives. Yes, you would want to factor the organisation's goals into mentoring programmes, such as increased diversity at senior levels and bringing through the leaders of the future, but these shouldn't be the only metrics.

Much of the value to mentees cannot be measured easily. There are many intangible benefits to be gained from a programme, ranging from small nuggets of advice or information to ideas on how to change approach, key introductions and increased confidence; value that can't be seen on a balance sheet.

---

[173] Mentoring Matters Report, Enterprise Nation, Newable, Association of Business Mentors. (2022).

Any approach to gauging the success of a programme needs to balance what is measurable with what is simply observable or can be reported by the mentee. Start with what is tangible, such as improved performance, achieving career milestones, taking the lead on more presentations, or winning more business.

Identify the right goals

At the start of the programme review the mentee's goals and ask them how they will know they have been successful.

What would be observable if goals have been achieved?

What would they be doing or seeing more of if they want more confidence in a particular area?

How could you determine that relationships have improved if there has been a lack of support from colleagues in another part of the organisation?

Write these down as you will refer to them later. More often than not, mentees have a laundry list of goals they would like to achieve but have not given any thought to what it looks like when those aspirations become a reality. As such, they often incorrectly believe they have never met the goals, or miss the opportunity to celebrate when they do.

Don't completely build your measurements around the objectives set at the beginning of the programme. We will talk about unintended consequences shortly. New ideas and perspectives introduced through effective mentoring will often lead to revised goals and a new journey being plotted for the mentee. Any measurement of the impact of a programme should allow for changes of course and the benefits accrued as a result.

Measuring success

Measurement of success of a mentoring programme or the relationships within can't just be taken at the point of completion. The fact that mentoring is designed to lead to career-long benefits for the mentee means that, ideally, you will track the progress of mentees over the course of time, as long as you remain connected.

If you are running an internal programme for an organisation, this doesn't mean that you stop tracking someone's progress when they leave. Your data will be far more meaningful if it takes a comprehensive, long-term view, wherever people end up.

The challenge is that most people are looking to report instant results. There is nothing immediate about mentoring; it is a slow burn where advice marinates over time. Depending on the situation, some success measures won't be seen for a long time.

What can you measure?

Depending on the objectives of the mentee and individual circumstances, there are a number of areas you can explore when seeking to measure the success of individual mentoring relationships (Figure 13.1).

What Can You Measure?

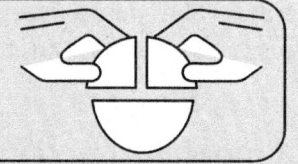

The relationship between the mentor and mentee after professional network growth.

- Skills development
- Promotion and career progression
- Performance in role
- Competency and knowledge
- Self-confidence and self-efficacy
- Professional network growth
- How much participants valued the programme and support

Figure 13.1 What can you measure?

Skills development

Has the mentee (or mentees across the programme) targeted specific technical or soft/power skills that they want to improve?

How will you test their progress? What signs can you look for to indicate positive improvement?

Promotion and career progression

A tangible measurement, what new jobs has the mentee landed? What proportion of mentees on the programme have progressed within a certain timeframe or achieved a stated level?

On an organisational level, you can also look to measure retention among the mentee group compared to their peers.

Performance in role

Measured by comparing appraisals and other assessments as well as through direct conversations with line managers and colleagues.

Competency and knowledge

Has their understanding of their role, other functions that interact with theirs and of the wider industry improved and how has that impacted their performance?

Self-confidence and self-efficacy

Has the mentee (or their mentor, their line manager and their colleagues) seen a clear improvement in areas in which previously they struggled with self-belief, such as giving presentations or attending external meetings?

Do they have a greater level of belief when approaching new tasks or opportunities that previously they would have shied away from? Would they now be more likely to step forward for something unknown?

Professional network growth

How has the mentoring programme impacted the visibility of the mentee and their reputation, both inside the organisation and with key external stakeholders?

Is their name mentioned more frequently when they are not in the room, and for the right things?

Are opportunities coming to them and are they being put forward when recommendations for tasks or roles are made?

Do they know to whom to turn for support and advice beyond their direct mentor and is that help forthcoming? Do other teams internally support their projects more willingly than previously?

The relationship between the mentor and mentee

How strong has the connection between mentor(s) and mentee(s) become, particularly if they didn't know each other before the programme began?

Are they collaborating with each other? Has the mentor also become a sponsor for the mentee and are they proactively speaking about them in relevant conversations?

Has the mentee become an advocate of the programme or of their mentor?

How much did participants value the programme and the support they received?

This should apply to all parties, and for mentoring programmes to be sustainable and scalable, you need to attract more mentors and mentees on an ongoing basis. This becomes much easier if previous participants speak highly of their experience.

It can impact how the programme is perceived across the organisation and feed the company culture going forward.

The Net Promoter Score question of 'how likely are you to recommend this programme to a colleague?' would be a good indicator of how well it has been received.

If you were to then ask what about the programme makes it referable, or otherwise, you will have more meaningful data.

Getting feedback

Your ability to effectively measure the success of your programme is dependent on the data you collect from people who have participated in it. This is complicated by the workloads of the types of people who are involved, as senior and rising executives tend to be short of time for additional tasks, not least of which are questionnaires and surveys!

Any request for feedback needs to be quick to understand, easy to follow and simple to respond to. Understand precisely what key information you are looking for and how you can collect it in the most practical and efficient way possible. It's not just the participants who will appreciate this; unless you love immersing yourself in data, you'll be more likely to process and take action on concise responses as opposed to pages of feedback.

Andy asks all mentees to complete a short questionnaire at the end of a professional relationships mentoring programme, to help understand how they have benefited and where he has made an impact. He asks the following questions about the programme itself (Figure 13.2):

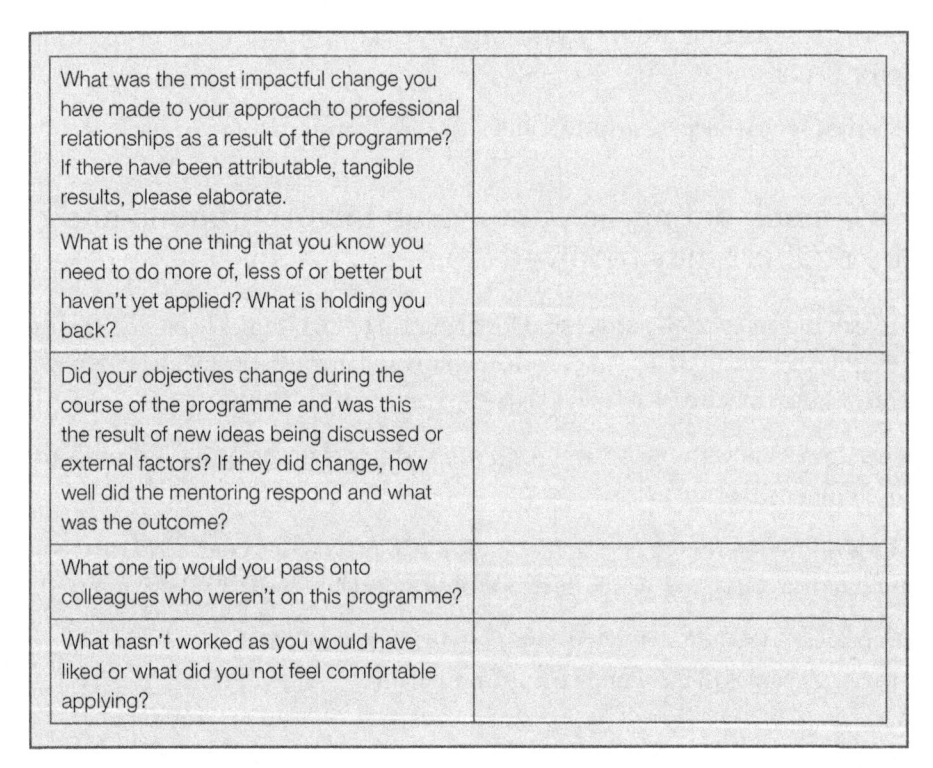

What was the most impactful change you have made to your approach to professional relationships as a result of the programme? If there have been attributable, tangible results, please elaborate.	
What is the one thing that you know you need to do more of, less of or better but haven't yet applied? What is holding you back?	
Did your objectives change during the course of the programme and was this the result of new ideas being discussed or external factors? If they did change, how well did the mentoring respond and what was the outcome?	
What one tip would you pass onto colleagues who weren't on this programme?	
What hasn't worked as you would have liked or what did you not feel comfortable applying?	

Figure 13.2 Mentee feedback survey

The goal of these questions is to encourage the mentee to reflect on their progress through the relationship and to identify exactly what has changed for them, as well as what they need to do more of. Responses provide a good indicator of how much the programme has resonated and progress made.

Andy then follows up with a small number of key questions about the format of the programme itself (length of sessions, whether people prefer meeting online or in person) and their experience of working with him personally. He uses this data to consider tweaks to the process or his approach to help to continually improve the experience and outcomes for mentees.

Ruth does something similar utilising a Critical Incident Questionnaire, conceived by Dr Stephen Brookfield.[174] This is a tool to understand which methods and delivery systems are working and which are not meeting their intended result. It delineates between what empowers the mentee and what keeps them at a distance.

As each person consumes and processes information differently, what works for one mentee might not work for another. It's not that one is better than another, it's just a comfort and preference, which leads to optimised learning.[175]

You don't need to just rely on feedback at the end of a programme. You can also check in with mentee's managers halfway through a programme, if relevant, to make sure progress is being seen, and in the areas they want. In addition, look for rolling feedback throughout a mentoring programme with email check-ins, hallway conversations and other touchpoints. These can be with the mentor and/or mentee, but also with their managers and colleagues and other participants across the programme.

Very often you'll learn more through these casual conversations than when you ask for formal feedback.

---

[174] Brookfield, S. (2014). "Critical incident questionnaire." Retrieved 2 October 2014, from https://static1.squarespace.com/static/5738a0ccd51cd47f81977fe8/t/5750e567f699bbceac6e97f5/1464919400130/CIQ.pdf

[175] Gilstrap, D. L. and Dupree, J. (2008). "Assessing learning, critical reflection, and quality educational outcomes: The critical incident questionnaire." *College & Research Libraries* 69(5): 407–426.

PART 4
BEING MENTORED

CHAPTER 14
WHY IT'S NEVER TOO LATE TO BE MENTORED

Most of this book has focused on becoming the most effective mentor you can be, so that it benefits the mentor, mentee and the organisation. We have looked at the mentoring relationship broadly and specifically, while exploring the challenges facing those putting together mentoring programmes.

Now it's time to focus on how to get the most out of the relationship as a mentee. In order to avoid duplicating previously shared content in this chapter, we want to focus on where being mentored will fit into your busy lives and how to approach and leverage the relationship.

You're never too successful to need a mentor

As a Primetime Emmy nominated director and producer, known for the *Oprah Master Class* series and the critically acclaimed feature film *Still: A Michael J. Fox Story*, among others, Annetta Marion can be considered to be successful and close to the top of her profession by any standards. But she still swears by the support she gets from a team of mentors.

In fact, she was already established before she benefited from working with mentors. As a result, Annetta tries to be the mentor she missed earlier in her journey when she works with her mentees now.

Annetta told us, "I'm thrilled with the professional guidance and support for my work as a director on network and streaming platforms. Mentors have ripped apart my reel and given me great but tough feedback on improving it, made introductions to decision-makers, helped me hone my personal pitch for meetings and also helped me on the creative side, suggesting movies to watch for research and sharing important filmmaking seminar information. This is amazing and so much fun for me since I didn't have the opportunity to go to film school."

Most of Annetta's mentors come from the Directors Guild of America, with a formal mentor through the DGA Episodic Television Mentoring Program, backed up by a whole support team of experienced directors and producers. She doesn't just value their guidance and individual support but stresses that the community as a whole provides a huge ongoing benefit as she moves onto new challenges and opportunities.

It's easy to fall into the trap of viewing mentoring as something for early-rung leaders, those on the way up and needing the support to get there. The traditional-hierarchical view of mentoring reinforces this image – the sage and experienced older leader sharing their experience and expertise with those following in their footsteps.

But that doesn't necessarily need to be the case. It's often been stated that even the world's leading athletes benefit from the support of a coach, someone who can work with them to find the extra few percent to improve their performance and take them to gold. In *The Success Factor*, Ruth shared that all high achievers surround themselves with mentors even after their Olympic gold medals and Nobel Prizes. For leaders, whether in business, government or the non-for-profit and charitable sector, it's the same; you are never too senior to learn new ideas, benefit from a fresh perspective or to be challenged by someone you trust.

You don't face an either/or choice between mentoring or being mentored. Do both. Every person at every level should mentor someone and be mentored. While it may look different for every person, the need for mentoring does not diminish once you rise through the ranks; it just looks different.

Senior leaders, particularly (but not exclusively) those who are relatively new to their role, can't operate successfully in isolation. There are many times when you will benefit from the support and insights of those who have been there before, although they might not be as readily available within your organisation as you might like.

There is an historic organisational knowledge which isn't codified. It's filled with ideas of who is the expert in which domain, organisational culture, what has been tried in the past and failed (and why), and who you need to convince in advance before bringing up a new idea.

Many years ago, Andy delivered a presentation at the London headquarters of a major Australian bank. Before the attendees arrived, Andy was introduced to the European CEO of the bank and they discussed what Andy was going to be speaking about. The CEO walked over to a flipchart, picked up a pen and started drawing.

14 WHY IT'S NEVER TOO LATE TO BE MENTORED

"Are you going to talk about this?" he asked, as he drew a pyramid on the flipchart.

"When I joined the bank, there were a lot of people at the same level as me," he said, drawing a lot of small circles at the base of the pyramid. "I could turn to any number of people for advice and support, both at my level and above."

He then drew some more circles halfway up the flipchart, as he continued to explain, "As I moved up in the organisation, there were still people around me to turn to, but they became fewer in number."

He then drew one single circle at the very apex of the pyramid. "And now, it's just me. There is nobody else at my level or above me in the organisation to turn to for support, so I have to go elsewhere."

He then drew another pyramid alongside the first, with a similar lone circle at its apex and drew an arrow between the two.

When you reach the senior levels of your organisation, it can become much harder to find mentors within its walls who can be objective and avoid the conflicts of interest we have discussed previously. This does not mean that you have reached the end of your race and get awarded a medal for those who no longer need help. It means that you look elsewhere for that support. After all, there is always more to learn.

You still need support though. Leadership is tough and there are many areas where the insights and advice of others can make the difference. Sometimes they can help you see coming challenges that otherwise you'd remain oblivious to until too late, at other times you might look for a sounding board before making a big decision. We all need to weigh different options before making big decisions; an objective view can be invaluable, even essential, in many situations.

The challenge is that most people don't wish to disagree or offer opposing viewpoints to the senior leader. As such, they are walled off from the truth. This puts the leader in a sealed off echo chamber, void of the undercurrent of grief and concerns brewing at the edge of disaster.

As a senior leader, you have to juggle challenges such as dealing with a Board of Directors, particularly when you transition from being their peer to being their boss. How do you get the most out of people who are not only competing with each other but also with you, eyeing your role for themselves? You'll need to manage conflict on the board, referee disputes, keep those who miss out motivated and ensure that everybody pulls together as a team, irrespective of the outcome.

According to Brian Chernett, founder of The Academy for Chief Executives, Ella Forums and Wisdomwins, who has been mentoring business, charity and public sector leaders for thirty-five years, "The only challenge is people. How do you actually get your people to work with you, not against you and not against each other?"

Leaders often come from an inner circle of people where differences of opinion are common. Brian shared examples of charity Chief Executives, who have to balance the competing demands of trustees and board members, and leaders of growing family businesses, who may have been imposed by the founding family but not necessarily have the support of their fellow directors.

Brian told us, "It's easy for a Chief Executive to find themselves facing difficulties in gaining their senior leadership team's cooperation, in a position where their former colleagues challenge their decisions or authority. It's hard work and this highlights the importance of having a mentor who can provide guidance and help the new leader navigate these potential conflicts."

You'll find yourself having to deal with more external stakeholders as well, such as politicians, shareholders, unions and more. These key relationships may well be completely new to you as you reach senior levels. But they should be embraced as they can be pivotal. Until you get to understand people and know how to navigate key conversations, you'll need the insights of people who are already familiar with the landscape and the best way through it. Here, understanding company culture will make or break your leadership, so any insight you can get is immensely valuable.

Transition into senior leadership roles includes a shift from 'doing' to 'planning'. Strategic thinking becomes much more of a core part of your role and responsibilities. You will need to manage competing demands, such as: setting the path ahead for the organisation, introducing and managing change effectively, dealing with unforeseen events, steering the organisation through a crisis, communicating effectively, and maintaining organisational and staff confidence.

On a personal level, your next career move can become less obvious and choices more limited. There are much larger repercussions to the decisions you make about your future; you shouldn't make them without somebody advising who has your best interests at heart.

These are just a handful of the challenges facing people as they climb the career ladder and progress to roles with more responsibility. Thinking that you can approach these challenges without advice and support is questionable at best. Having somebody, even better a team of people, on hand who can be objective, challenging and who will push you to be your best can only benefit all parties.

What help could benefit you right now?

In Chapter 7 we asked you to think back to the mentor who made the biggest impression on you over the course of your career and write a letter to them, sharing the impact they made on you and outlining how their support benefited you.

What would you give for similar support with a similar impact at this stage of your career? Imagine having a guide by your side who didn't judge you and wanted only what is best for you. They will cheer you on when you are feeling the weight of the world and call you out when you are too focused on your own pity party.

Don't simply seek a mentor after being inspired by this chapter to do so. Remember our advice earlier in the book about the importance of having clear objectives in a mentoring relationship. How could a mentor best help you in your current role and at this stage of your career?

Look at your medium- to long-term objectives and identify the mentoring team who can help you get there. Set those goals and communicate them clearly, as well as identify how you'll measure your progress. At the same time, look to understand what support you need in the short term, whether from that mentoring team or from individuals best suited to provide specific input.

What are your top priorities right now, both personally and professionally? As your environment, role and circumstances change, so will the answer to this question. You should be continually reviewing your needs and the support around you. Once a month ask yourself what the biggest challenge you need to address is, how your mentoring team can help you to do so and who else you know who might be able to support you.

What are you working on at the moment that would benefit from another perspective? Hopefully, you are already discussing these projects with colleagues within the organisation. But who else could help? Someone who might be more objective, carry fewer assumptions and not be influenced by the personal consequences of your decisions.

Letting go

If you're in a leadership role and used to being the one to provide the answers and setting the lead, you might need to challenge that mindset when entering a mentoring relationship. Remember that you're there to learn and be challenged, not to tell or make excuses. The more you open your mind to learning, the greater the opportunity to grow.

That doesn't mean that you can simply dump everything on your mentor, they are there to support you and provide different perspectives, not to be at your beck and call. Just because you are now at a higher rank, does not mean that mentoring etiquette and best practices don't apply to you. Everything we've previously said about setting and communicating expectations, as well as being conscious of your mentor's cognitive load, stands. Don't overburden them but don't be afraid to ask for their help either.

And be good to yourself. Being a mentee can provide you with a mental oasis, particularly at times of high challenge and stress. As a leader, it is hard to let your guard down. This is one relationship in which you can be completely vulnerable. Allow yourself the time and space not to be the boss for a while and learn to be led once more, rather than always being the leader. You're now the mentee, not the mentor, so switch off the need to be in control.

CHAPTER 15
HOW DO YOU FIND THE RIGHT MENTOR FOR YOU?

Okay, you are convinced. No matter your place in the corporate hierarchy, having a mentor is beneficial. Having established that you would like to benefit from having a mentor yourself, there should be no surprise where we suggest you begin your search. The clearer your objectives and the support you need to achieve them, the easier it should be to identify the right mentor to help you on that journey.

With that objective in mind, you can look to identify people who have been there before, whether they have experienced similar challenges, navigated the route you're focused on or helped other people you know achieve a similar goal. A mentor who understands how to handle similar stakeholders and navigate institutional politics can be a game changer.

You may look for someone with specific expertise or qualities; a small business owner, for example, might look for a mentor with expertise in channel sales, while a new leader in a large organisation might want to work with somebody experienced in lobbying. You may choose somebody because you recognise that you need to be challenged and you are confident that they will ask tough questions and not settle for the first answer you give them.

Before you begin listing names, list the expertise and qualities you are looking for (Figure 15.1).

Objective	Experience and expertise needed	Mentor qualities	Potential mentors
Promotion to the Board.	Board level experience. Navigating the board recruitment process. Understanding the strategy and direction of the organisation	Challenging – will push me to be ready for the role. Honesty. Willing to be an advocate.	
Scaling a business and readying it for sale.	Experience of growing and selling a business. Maximising sales. Managing investor relationships.	Detail-oriented – will get into the numbers with me.	
Future talent – career development.	Young enough to be able to relate to challenges of the modern world. Experienced enough to push back and share the potential pitfalls ahead.	A good listener, willing to challenge and hold me accountable.	

Figure 15.1 Example mentor selection table.

Should your mentor look like you?

While many of the people we spoke to when writing this book have emphasised the importance of finding mentors who share similar backgrounds or experiences to you, particularly for people who come from traditionally underrepresented backgrounds, not everyone agrees entirely.

Professor Miranda Brawn, the Founder of the Miranda Brawn Diversity Leadership Foundation, recalls looking for a mentor when she was working at a top US investment bank in her twenties. She approached the first Black female Managing Director in Europe for help with her career goals and was provided with great advice and support from her on how to get promoted within the bank. However, she was also advised to find a second mentor who was working in the front office to help achieve her front office career aspirations.

Miranda explained, "I wanted to work in the front office on the trading floor and she explained that she didn't know anything about that role. She advised me that I needed a white male mentor who worked in the front office to help me because there were no potential mentors of colour on the trading floor at the time, and so I found five. Within six months, I was working on the trading floor in my desired front-office role.

"The moral of that story is to seek help from those who are performing and have the right experience in the role that you desire regardless of their background. Your mentor does not need to look like you and/or have a similar background.

"There's a belief that, if you're a woman in the workplace, you have to find another woman who is similar to you to mentor you. That's far from the truth, you need people who are actually doing what you want to be doing, in order for them to handhold you down that road."

Miranda emphasised the importance of seeking mentors who have specific knowledge and experience related to one's desired career path or goals. Mentorship should be based on the mentor's ability to provide guidance in the areas that are relevant to the mentee's objectives, rather than solely focusing on shared backgrounds.

That does not exclude the benefit of having support from people who understand the journey though. Miranda was able to develop a strong relationship with her first female mentor and turn to her for more general career support and sponsorship. This led to Miranda becoming one of the handful of Black vice presidents at the bank.

"We developed a really good relationship, which led to a friendship that still exists today. In return, I launched an in-house mentoring and professional development programme when I chaired their Black network group to help other employees get matched with mentors for their career aspirations."

Where to find the right mentors

There are a couple of additional things to remember as you embark on your search, both covered in detail already in this book. First of all, you shouldn't limit yourself to just one mentor. Yes, it's good to have a formal mentor who you meet on a regular basis, but they can be just one part of your mentoring team. Not everyone you identify will have the time or inclination to commit to a formal relationship, but they will be happy to answer questions or give you feedback as you need them. A single mentor only allows you to tap into one person's experience and perspective while having a broader reach of ideas is optimal.

Secondly, avoid conflict of interest. Quite often, line managers will put themselves forward as a mentor, seeing it as part of their role. Welcome their interest and support, certainly, but don't rely on them as your primary mentor and find a different relationship away from your reporting line where you can be more open and honest without fearing repercussions.[176] It's also a double-edged sword. If your boss is your mentor, and they do such a good job that you leave, they now need to replace you. Until they find your successor, your responsibilities may fall on them, and now suddenly they have more work.

As we discussed in Chapter 14, this might mean going outside your organisation, particularly as you reach more senior levels. That's fine, you just need to consider whether you want to stay within your sector or industry, which would give you the advantage of mentors who understand the landscape and the people but potentially still leaving conflicts of interest. Alternatively, you might go outside and benefit from a different perspective and way of working, but lack of understanding of the specific constraints of your industry. Retirees are great for this role as well as they are not beholden to an organisation and will be much more liberal with their comments, specifically as they relate to team players and office politics.

Of course, it's not an either/or question. If time allows, and you're building your mentoring team, why not find people from both groups to support you?

Whatever you choose, begin by looking within your network, to people you already know. If you already know, and are known by, potential mentors, there is a greater chance that they will be willing to help you (which we will explore shortly) and understand your strengths, weaknesses and potential. An established relationship will make it easier for you to hit the ground running.

You probably have more potential mentors within your network than you give yourself credit for. Repeated studies and theories calculating the average number of people in a network abound. The two most famous theories are Girard's

---

[176] Gotian, R. (2020). "Why your boss shouldn't be your mentor." *Forbes*.

Law,[177] which states that the average person knows 250 people, and Dunbar's Number,[178] which puts the number at 150.

There are plenty of issues with the use of these statistics. For a start, they are often used to make an argument (the average size of somebody's network) that wasn't the premise of the original studies. Correlation does not necessarily mean causation.

For example, Robin Dunbar's study explored how many people the average person could have a meaningful connection with and was based on his research exploring a connection between primate brain size and average group social size, and then the results were extrapolated for human beings. So, it's a bit of a stretch to then apply it to social networking theory in the manner it has been.

However, they provide a good reference as a starting point to understand that we have the potential for support among existing relationships. When you are put on the spot and asked to identify a mentor from people you know, you are likely to struggle. Your brain can't picture your entire network in one go, and you'll find your thinking limited to a small number of people who are front of mind.

To expand the scope of your thinking, start breaking your network into groups of people. Add labels to people based on how you know them. Think of friends, fellow students and professors from your college or university days, people you have worked with at different jobs, former clients or suppliers. Break your personal networks into groups as well, such as family members, contacts in religious or community organisations, parents of your children's friends or people you share interests and hobbies with.

Lastly, consider who your professional heroes are. Who do you look up to for always being innovative and taking a thoughtful approach? What is it about them that draws you to their way of thinking? As Ayse Birsel shares, what you admire in your heroes are qualities and characteristics you likely possess yourself.[179] These people can help draw those qualities out of you. There is a good chance that they are in your sphere of influence and therefore, you could approach them.

---

[177] Girard, J. and Brown, S.H. (1977). *How to Sell Anything to Anybody*. Touchstone.
[178] Dunbar, R.I.M. (1992). "Neocortex size as a constraint on group size in primates." *Journal of Human Evolution*. 22 (6): 469–493.
[179] Birsel, A. (2015). *Design the Life You Love*. New York, Ten Speed Press, an imprint of the Crown Publishing Group, a division of Penguin Random House LLC.

We would encourage you to be open to finding mentors from within those personal networks as well as your professional ones. We are often too quick to pigeonhole others by how we know them and forget that people have a life beyond the life they have with us. But in that life, they may have exactly the experience, expertise or outlook that we're looking for.

If you can create a clear and healthy divide between your mentoring relationship and personal friendship, there's no reason this can't work. Andy mentors somebody from the group he often hikes with. They have a simple rule, they keep small talk about hiking to a minimum on mentoring calls and they keep talk about mentoring to a minimum on hikes. They are separate worlds and rarely the twain will meet.

Mentoring by a friend has benefits as peer mentors offer empathy, know what you are dealing with and, most importantly, know you, your strengths and blind spots.

Looking outside your network

We have to accept that not everyone will be able to find a mentor from among their existing connections or might feel more comfortable working with someone with whom they have no previous relationship.

If you do want to identify someone new, go back to your Mentor Selection Table (Figure 15.1) and remind yourself of the expertise and qualities you are looking for. Who have you seen from a distance who ticks the right boxes? They may have been a speaker at a conference, a workshop leader, or a leader whose work you admire.

Even in today's virtual world, it is possible to find a mentor through various channels including hosting a virtual event with invited speakers you admire, connecting with fellow alumni from your college or looking at those who made interesting comments at some of the virtual events you've attended in the past.[180]

---

[180] Gotian, R. (2020). "How do you find a decent mentor when you're stuck at home?" *Harvard Business Review*.

Other people can help you in your search too. Referral is a great way to find and get in front of mentors. Even if you have identified the right person for yourself, we would always recommend finding a mutual contact (LinkedIn is a great place to do this research) and asking for an introduction. The next best thing to somebody knowing you, in terms of how open they will be to working with and supporting you, is their trust in the person who introduces you.

If you don't have anybody on your wish list, ask. Ask your network whom they would recommend and help them to make the right recommendation by sharing your objectives and the qualities you're looking for. As well as speaking to people you trust in person, post the question on sites like LinkedIn and Twitter.

This may feel uncomfortable, and we'll explain why you feel that way in a moment. But it shouldn't be. Cast your net wide and you'll get more suggestions; you are not duty-bound to accept every recommendation, but it can certainly pay to explore them.

Ask formal bodies for help as well, starting with your line managers and HR department in your organisation, even if you're looking for a mentor from outside. They may well know someone. If you are a member of a professional association, ask if they have a mentoring scheme or could recommend a senior member as a potential mentor for you. Look to sector-specific mentoring programmes, such as the PM Forum Mentor Match in professional services and Elevate in the hospitality industry.

There are also mentoring-specific organisations, such as the Association of Business Mentors, who will be happy to help you find a suitable mentor if you approach them.

Don't overthink this. You likely have your go-to person to whom you go for questions, to serve as your sounding board, or talk to when imposter syndrome starts to percolate. You may not have affixed the 'mentor' label to this person but if they are successfully executing all the common mentoring tasks, then with or without the title, they are your mentor.

If you are waiting for the perfect mentor to come along then you'll be waiting forever. Nobody is perfect, not even you. Also, no one will have the exact alignment of gender, race, culture and occupation you are looking for. In fact, finding someone who is exactly like you may reinforce the echo chamber instead of offering you new perspectives.

Why we don't like to ask for help

There's a large elephant in the room that we need to address right now. Everything written in this chapter so far makes an assumption, but it's a dangerous one. We have assumed that you are happy to ask people for help, whether it's direct advice and guidance or asking others to introduce you to or recommend potential mentors.

Why people don't ask for help

Most people are reluctant to ask for help. We fear the risk of rejection, uncertainty, perceived reduced status (what is known as *status threat*) or giving up authority.[181] Scientists have labelled this as social pain, which can feel just as real as physical pain. But we can't get ahead on our own. We need the assistance of others. It's as simple as that.

The key is that, if you understand human motivation, you will find people who are eager to help and the task of asking for guidance will feel significantly less challenging.[182] Typically, there are several things that hold us back from asking for guidance, all of which are quite likely to be in play when it comes to asking for support finding or being a mentor.

1. We don't want to be a burden

There tends to be a lot of awkwardness associated with asking for help. The person asking feels on the back foot, aware that they are seeking a favour and not sure whether the person they are asking will appreciate their request.[183]

This is despite the fact that decades of research has shown that we, and others, get pleasure from helping others.[184] If we are asking the right people for help

---

[181] Grant, H. (2018). "How to get the help you need." *Harvard Business Review* (May–June 2018): 142–145.
[182] Grant, H. (2018). *Reinforcements*. Boston, MA, Harvard Business Review Press.
[183] Zhao, X. and Epley, N. (2022). "Surprisingly happy to have helped: Underestimating prosociality creates a misplaced barrier to asking for help." *Psychological Science* 33(10): 1708–1731. **https://doi.org/10.1177/09567976221097615**
[184] DePaulo, B. (1983). "Perspectives on help-seeking." In B. DePaulo, A. Nadler and J. Fisher (Vol. Eds.), *Help Seeking. Vol. 2. New Directions in Helping* (pp. 3–12). New York: Academic Press.

15 HOW DO YOU FIND THE RIGHT MENTOR FOR YOU?

and making it easy for them to help us, why would we be a burden? This, of course, assumes that you are approaching people who are invested in their relationship with you, not complete strangers.

We are offering them the chance to delight in being a part of our success. People want to help, often they just don't know how. Tell them specifically what you need assistance with and watch them line up to help you.

Reframe how you see the act of seeking support. Instead of worrying about how people perceive the request, ensure that you frame it in a way they will respond to positively, seeing it as an ask they can meet without it being an additional obligation.

You can make it easy for people to help you by being clear and specific about your request. Avoid being vague, and make sure you are doing the work first, not leaving it to them to guess. Telling a potential mentor you need help planning your career is too vague. Where does one start? Telling them you need help seeking a stretch assignment or targeting a particular new role is clear, specific and achievable. There are clear start and end points, challenges you can identify and discuss on the journey, and you will be able to identify success when you've reached specific milestones.

Timing is everything. Approaching a potential mentor before they need to present to the board or are working toward a major deadline will likely not get you the result you are seeking. Ask at the right time. Not when the other person is busy, stressed or otherwise preoccupied. And don't sandwich your request quietly as an afterthought to a longer and deeper conversation about something else.

Make sure it's a pleasure to help you by giving feedback on your progress and displaying your gratitude. Expressions of gratitude don't have to be expensive gifts; a handwritten note or sincere phone call can often mean much more.

Just don't ignore the person who helped you once you have moved on, that includes the person who recommended or introduced you to your mentor, as well as the mentor themselves. Leaving them in the dark about your progress will make it feel as if you are a transactional human, always seeking self-gain. People will pick up on that quickly, and you will notice that people no longer wish to help you. In fact, they may go out of their way to avoid you.

2. We don't want to be seen as vulnerable

The feeling that others might think we don't know what we are doing or consider us incompetent is a leading cause of not asking for advice. This fear, however, is misplaced.[185] Perceived vulnerability is one of the biggest brakes on seeking support, as people fear they won't look smart. Research has shown that this fallacy is embedded in children from as early as seven years of age,[186] so it's no wonder we carry around those feelings as adults. Yet the fear of being seen as vulnerable comes from a simple misunderstanding.

People see vulnerability as a weakness.

Vulnerability isn't a weakness, it's a strength. It takes strength to tell other people that you don't have all the answers, that you're struggling with something, or that you need help. And the support you receive as a result of asking for help will often lead to your desired outcome, which surely makes you stronger. In fact, there is a body of research that shows that you are seen as *more* competent by the advice giver when asking for help.[187]

Asking for help is a strength, not a weakness.

You can, of course, look weak when asking for help. That has nothing to do with vulnerability, though; it's all about how you position your request. It's just as easy to ask from a position of strength . . .

"I feel that I've excelled in my current role and I'm ready for my next move. Would you work with me to help identify what that role should be and to prepare me for it so that I can hit the ground running?"

as it is to do so from one of weakness . . .

"I'm struggling in my role and nobody is happy with my performance. Can you help me work out what I'm doing wrong?"

---

[185] Brooks, A.W., Gino, F. and Schweitzer, M.E. (2015). "Smart people ask for (my) advice: Seeking advice boosts perceptions of competence." *Management Science* 61(6): 1421–1435.
[186] Good, K. and Shaw, A. (2022). "Being versus appearing smart: Children's developing intuitions about how reputational motives guide behavior." *Child Development* 93(2): 418–436. https://doi.org/10.1111/cdev.13711
[187] Brooks, A.W., Gino, F. and Schweitzer, M.E. (2015). "Smart people ask for (my) advice: Seeking advice boosts perceptions of competence." *Management Science* 61(6): 1421–1435.

Even when you do ask from a position of weakness, it takes strength to recognise the help you need and request it.

3. We make assumptions

Nobody likes to be turned down. It's a blow to the ego. For a variety of reasons, people might not want to help you, they might not be able to help you, they may be too busy to help you, or they might not know how to help you.

All of those are possibilities, but let those people decide that for themselves. Too often we don't ask for the help we need because we *assume* that we'll get a negative response, not because we *know* that we will.

If we do get a negative response, we view that as a rejection. And nobody likes to be rejected. So, we don't ask. It's safer that way, isn't it?

Stop assuming that people will say "no", and make it OK even if they do. Communicate to them that "no" is a valid answer that won't offend. And communicate it to yourself. There are so many reasons why people might not feel able to help and, if you've asked the right person, in the right way, you shouldn't be close to the top of that list. Stop making it all about you.

As we've probably all been told at one point in our career, if you don't ask, you don't get. One applicant was accepted to law school with a merit-based scholarship. He almost accepted that scholarship until Ruth encouraged him to ask for more. He asked, and within 24 hours, they increased their scholarship by 50%.

If you ask, you take the risk of someone saying yes. The worst that will happen is that you will remain exactly where you are now. And that's not so bad. All the high achievers Ruth studies repeatedly look at a challenge through a different lens. They don't wonder *if* they can overcome the challenge, instead, they focus on *how*. They ask themselves, *What is the strategy I have not thought of yet?*

The word 'yet' is critical. As Cornell University professor Vanessa Bohns shares in her research, people underestimate other people's willingness to help by as much as 48%.[188] This is especially true for those with higher empathy traits

---

[188] Bohns, V. (2016). "(Mis)Understanding our influence over others: A review of the underestimation-of-compliance effect." *Current Directions in Psychological Research* 25(2): 119–123.

who can appreciate someone's need for help.[189] A "no" isn't necessarily a rejection, but if you assume people will refuse and you don't ask, you almost certainly won't get the help that you need.

Even if we don't get all of the help we ask for from other people, just by being willing to ask for support, we will be more likely to gain. Robert Cialdini, well known for his work on how we influence others, tells us about the *rejection-then-retreat* technique.[190] Cialdini demonstrates how a refusal for a request is often followed by agreement to a request for something smaller. It is seen by the giver as a response to the concession made by the person asking, as they are prepared to settle for less.

You might notice that we haven't suggested that you ask people directly to be your mentor. There are times when this is appropriate but you have to be conscious of the pitfalls of a direct approach. Leadership speaker and author Dorie Clark has told us that asking someone to be a mentor is asking them to take on an added obligation. That may account for a lot of reticence when people are put on the spot.

Why would people help you?

Earlier in this chapter we argued that people will be more likely to want to mentor you if you already know them. If we want to feel confident approaching people to guide and support us, it's important to put ourselves in their shoes and understand *why* they would want to do so.

Generally speaking, there are three main reasons why people help others in a professional capacity:

- Because they have been told to
- Because there's something in it for them
- Because they like the person they are helping.

---

[189] Deri, S., Stein, D.H. and Bohns, V.K. (2019). "With a little help from my friends (and strangers): Closeness as a moderator of the underestimation-of-compliance effect." *Journal of Experimental Social Psychology* 82(2019): 6–15. Web.

[190] Cialdini, R.B. (1984). *Influence: The Power of Persuasion* Harper Collins.

In the first two cases, because people have been told to help or there's something in it for them, the key factor is what is known as *extrinsic motivation*.[191] They do it for the awards, rewards, promotions, or bonuses or even to keep their job. Not much of a long-term motivation tactic. It requires others to consistently judge you. These people will do as much (or as little) as they need in order to reach their objective. But they won't necessarily go further. When fuelled by extrinsic motivation, there is often little passion in the pursuit.

When we have a strong relationship with the person who needs our help, that motivation shifts. We no longer look for what we gain from the transaction, other than the enjoyment of seeing somebody we like or believe in succeed. That means that there is less of a cap on how much we'll commit to helping achieve that success and will be more invested in a positive outcome.

We say 'generally speaking' because mentoring is a slightly different case to other professional relationships. People do 'pay it forward' from an altruistic standpoint, wanting to give back, leave a legacy or simply boost the prospects of people whom they believe in or who might otherwise have been left behind, as we saw from Nicholas Davies in Chapter 5.

We can't rely on that altruism from our potential mentors though. If we can develop a strong bond with them, we can be confident that they will want to give more to support us, and we, in turn, will pay it forward.

Finding a mentor who *wants* to mentor you, rather than *has* to mentor you, will make all the difference. They will be fuelled by your success, assuming you show them you are putting in the work. They will be a guide by your side for the long term. There is no expiry date on mentoring, nor is it a life sentence. If it works out, then great. If it doesn't, you have others to go to for guidance.

---

[191] Deci, E.L. and Ryan, R.M. (1985). *Intrinsic Motivation and Self-determination in Human Behavior.* New York, Plenum.

CONCLUSION

Mentoring isn't just a concept; it's a powerful force for personal and professional growth that has the potential to transform individuals, organisations, industries and entire communities. Throughout this book, we've explored the multifaceted world of mentoring, delving into the intricacies of effective mentoring relationships, the importance of mentorship support networks and the broader impact of mentoring beyond the individual.

Now, the pivotal question arises: "What can you do next?" We believe this is the moment where the true value of this book comes to life. Let's break it down into the three key topics we've explored:

1 Look at how effective you are as a mentor

The first step in becoming a more effective mentor is self-reflection. We encourage you to review your existing mentoring relationships, whether they are formal or informal. Are you offering enough guidance and support to your mentees? Are you truly making a difference in their lives and careers? Are you willing to adapt and grow as a mentor?

Consider mentoring opportunities beyond the traditional model. Look around your organisation or community for potential mentees who may benefit from your knowledge and experience. Remember, mentorship knows no boundaries; it's about sharing and uplifting others.

2 Are you getting the mentoring support you need?

Effective mentors need guidance and support too. Identify your formal mentor if you have one and ensure your objectives are clear. Track your progress and communicate your needs to your mentor. The mentor–mentee relationship is a two-way street, and it's crucial that you receive the support you require to continue your growth and development.

Additionally, recognise the value of your mentoring team. These are the individuals who can offer diverse perspectives and advice, no matter your level within the organisation. Harness the power of your mentoring network and tap into their collective wisdom. Remember, mentorship isn't limited to a one-on-one dynamic; it thrives in a supportive community.

3 What can you do to encourage mentoring in your organisation, industry, or community?

By now, you've hopefully witnessed the transformative potential of mentoring. Now, it's time to pay it forward. Consider taking part in organisations that actively promote mentoring including those within your industry associations. Consider celebrating 27th October as National Mentoring Day[192] around the world. We are delighted to be partnering with National Mentoring Day in their quest to amplify, celebrate and promote mentoring on a broader scale. Be a role model in your organisation, industry or community by actively engaging in mentoring relationships and showcasing their positive impact. Don't be shy about it!

Furthermore, consider joining organisations like the Association of Business Mentors to connect with like-minded individuals who are passionate about mentoring. Together, you can work to create a mentoring culture that fosters growth, learning and collaboration.

And keep a look out for other similar initiatives that might be local to you, or more widespread, such as National Mentoring Month in the US.

This isn't just a call for individual action. In September 2023 The Association of Business Mentors launched a call for political and business leaders to work together to boost the uptake of professional business mentoring. They suggested five actions to make mentoring mainstream:

---

[192] https://nationalmentoringday.org

CONCLUSION

BUILDING MOMENTUM BEHIND MENTORING TO DRIVE BUSINESS GROWTH

FIVE RECOMMENDATIONS BY THE ABM

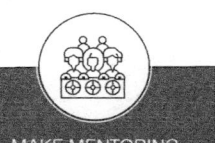

MAKE MENTORING MAINSTREAM

Successful businesses have mentors. Mentoring should be acknowledged as a valuable, necessary and indispensable function of daily business life, driving positive outcomes for businesses and growth.

Awareness needs to be made of the impact of business mentoring by demonstrating these positive outcomes to leaders and decision makers who can embrace mentoring within their own businesses.

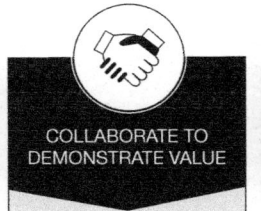

COLLABORATE TO DEMONSTRATE VALUE

The business support community has a powerful and influential voice, particularly where businesses are struggling, or recognise their need for guidance, but are unsure of what's available.

Working together, we can speak with a shared voice that promotes the value of mentoring and guides ambitious business owners and leaders to seek professional support.

PROVIDE PARTNERSHIP PROGRAMMES

Successful business support partnerships are already delivering programmes with significant impact.

Strengthening these partnerships will ensure these initiatives continue and evolve, delivering accessible mentoring opportunities and further growing the mentor community.

Funded or subsidised mentoring opportunities can be a powerful incentive for first-time mentees.

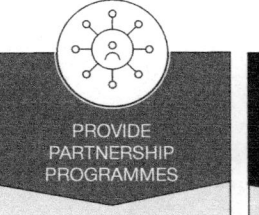

RAISE THE STANDARD

Voluntary and paid-for mentoring should meet an acceptable industry standard. By providing a recognised professional framework for formal programmes and individual professional business mentors, we will elevate sector capabilities and drive excellence across the profession.

Mentor skills, experience qualifications and commitments to continual professional development should be encouraged and transparent.

ADDRESS TOMORROW'S NEEDS, TODAY

As business and economic growth patterns evolve, so will the business mentoring landscape.

Researching the impact of business mentoring on the success and health of businesses will ensure that mentoring advances to reflect the needs of tomorrow's business, economic climate and UK long-term growth ambitions as well as the opportunities and challenges presented by advancing technologies and other developments.

This book, *The Financial Times Guide to Mentoring*, is not merely a book to be read and put aside; it's a call to action. It's an invitation to reflect, evolve and inspire. Mentoring has the power to shape not only your destiny but also the futures of those around you and the broader world. So, what can you do next? The answer lies in your commitment to embracing mentoring as a powerful force for positive change. Start today, and let the ripple effect of mentoring create a better tomorrow.

We have created a quick assessment to help you reflect on how you can increase the impact of your mentoring relationships, whether as a mentor or mentee. Go to ftmentoring.scoreapp.com or scan the QR code below to take the test and get some immediate advice to help you plot your path forward.

If you enjoyed this book, we would be grateful if you would tell your colleagues, mentees and broader network, leave a review where you bought the book and on readers social networks like Goodreads, as well as request that your local library order it so that others can enjoy it as well. And please feel free to reach out to us, either at authors@mentoring-guide.com or individually at andy@mentoring-guide.com or ruth@mentoring-guide.com. You can also find the resources mentioned in this book at mentoring-guide.com.

Ruth Gotian:
The Success Factor, Kogan Page, 2022

Andy Lopata:
Building a Business on Bacon and Eggs, Life Publications, 2005
. . . and Death Came Third! The Definitive Guide to Networking and Speaking in Public, Rethink Press (2nd Edition), 2011
Recommended. How to Sell Through Networking and Referrals, FT Prentice Hall, 2011
Connected Leadership, Rethink Press, 2020
Just Ask. Why Seeking Support is your Greatest Strength, Rethink Press, 2020

Andy is also the host of The Connected Leadership Podcast, available on all major streaming platforms.

INDEX

academic medicine 5–6
Academy for Chief Executives, The 170
accountability 93–5, 109, 134
accreditation resources 48
action learning sets 21
active listening 103, 106, 121, 126
adaptability 46, 69, 80, 88
ADHD 88, 90
advantage blindness 83
advocacy 29, 56, 60, 74, 85, 141
aging research 57
aide memoire 95
Airbnb 72
altruism 185
Antetokounmpo, Giannis 110–11
appraisal process 137
artificial intelligence (AI) 112, 154
Association of Business Mentors 44, 45, 179, 188
assumptions 183
asynchronous communication 99
asynchronous mentoring 98–100
attention, giving full 70

backgrounds 153, 174
Bader, Dr Mortimer 92
Baker, Chelsey 60–1
Baker Tilly International 46
Bandura, Dr Albert 116
benefit of mentoring
　to both mentees and mentors 7
　broader 7–8
　to wider society 7
benign envy 85
biases 131
Birsel, Ayse 177
black women 12
blogging 99
Bohns, Vanessa 183

bonus programmes 136
boundaries, setting 126
Boys and Girls Clubs (USA) 5
Brawn, Professor Miranda 174–7
breaks 127
Brookfield, Dr Stephen 107, 163
Brooks, Alison Wood 85
Brown, Peter 154
bullet points 95

Calendly 99
career guidance 47
Carnegie, Dale 91
Center for the Improvement of Mentored Experiences in Research (CIMER) 45
challenges and accomplishments capture grid 109
challenges
　faced by mentees xxxviii–xxxix
　faced by mentors xxxv–xxxvii
　faced by organisations xxxix–xli
check-Ins, scheduled 99
Chernett, Brian 170
Cialdini, Robert 184
Clark, Dorie 184
CoachAccountable 112
coaches vs mentors 43–5
coaching, definition 39
cognitive diversity 130
cognitive load 81, 124
co-mentoring 21
communication
　asynchronous 99
　lack of xxxviii
　skills 29
　styles 153
　unclear 133–4
communities of practice 32–3
compacts 34

competence 86
complacent mentoring relationship 122
confidence 70-1
conflict of interest 151, 176
Connected Leadership Podcast 106
constructive-developmental theory 117
consultants 41
contracts 34
conversations, mentoring 104-13
　accountability and empowerment 109
　analogue or digital? 111-13
　capturing challenges and accomplishments to review
　establishing connection 105
　listen for, not to 106-7
　parking your ego 107-8
　providing a helicopter view 110-11
Covey, Stephen: *Seven Habits of Highly Effective People* 106
COVID-19 pandemic 3-4, 124
credibility 86
Critical Incident Questionnaire 163
Crosby, John C. 39
cross-sector mentoring 30-1
cultural challenges 152-3

Davies, Nicholas 55-7, 185
Devereaux, Shonali 51
Directors Guild of America Episodic Television Mentoring Program 168
discourse 99
distraction, avoiding 70
diversification of mentoring team 57
Diversity, Equity and Inclusion (DEI) programmes 7, 8, 10, 150
doers 94
Doodle 99
Drago-Severson, Dr Ellie 116, 117-18
dreamers 94
Dropbox 99
Dunbar, Robin 177
Dunbar's Number 177

Edmondson, Amy: *Right Kind of Wrong* 84
effect of mentoring 123-7

effectiveness as mentor 187
ego orientation 110
Ehie, Dr Odi 65, 100
Elevate 30, 145, 146
Ella Forums 170
Email 98
empathy 29, 127
employee engagement 6
Employee Resource Network (ERG) 28, 142, 150
encouragement of mentoring 188
ERG 8
Erikson, Erik 57
ethnic minorities 11, 28
ethnic networks 142
exit plan 28
exiting from mentoring 28, 155
expectations, failure to manage 134-5
experiences 153
experiential learning 79
external objectives 54, 60-1
external organisations 145-7
extrinsic motivation 185
eye contact 103

Facebook 33
false platitudes 134
Farson, Richard 106
Fast Forward 15 51
fast-track programme 10
feedback 93-5, 96, 162-3, 181
Fellows, Max 145, 146
first-generation college students 11, 55
Flanagan, Caroline: *Be the First* 53
flash mentoring 22
flexibility 80
focus, ensuring xxxiii-xxxiv, 126
Fordham, Simon 3-4, 44
formal mentoring 16, 33-6
Forzoni, Roberto 110
friendtors 20, 81
future of mentees 100-1

Generation Z 24, 88
generational differences 24, 87-8

INDEX

Generative AI 154
generativity 57
Girard's Law 176–7
GlaxoSmithKline (GSK) global talent programme 58–9
goals, realistic 126, 158
Goldsmith, Dr Marshall 96
Goodreads 190
Google Docs 99
Gordon, Patrice 24, 25
Gotian, Ruth: *Success Factor, The* 168
Grainger, Dame Katherine 93
gratitude 181
group mentoring 12, 136
guidance, giving 91–3

Hall, Vanessa: *Truth About Trust in Business, The* 86
hallway mentoring 22
Heffernan, Margaret 36, 37
Heiser, Dr Deborah 57
helicopter view of career and performance 110–11
help, reasons for giving 184–5
hidden curriculum 55
Hiew, Samantha 88, 89, 90
Homer, Andy xxxviii
honesty 127
Honeycutt, Jay xxvi–xxvii
Human Resources 142, 150
humility 107
humour 105

IBM 11
ICE CREAM mnemonic 71–3
  Introduce 71
  Connect 72
  Engage 72
  Create opportunities 72
  Reply 72
  Encourage 72–3
  Amplify 73
  Motivate 73
importance of mentoring 3–13
impostor syndrome 52–4, 100

indiscretion 71
informal mentoring 16, 31–2
in-house mentoring programmes 29
Institute of Leadership and Management 45
Instrumental Knower 117–18, 119
integrity 86
intrinsic motivation 73, 120
inverted pyramid 44

journalling 99
junior-senior framework 19

Kall Kwik 3
Kegan, Robert 117
key power skills 29
Kilpatrick-Liverman, LaTonya 45–6
knowing 117–18
Kobilka, Dr Brian 108
Kolb, David 79
Kram, Kathy 47, 57

lack of engagement 116–21
Lagerberg, Francesca 46–7
Landherr, Daniela 106
laughter 105
Lawal, Ronke 9
Learning and Development (L&D) 142
  fast-track scheme 28
learning preferences 153
learning rapport 115
learning style inventory 79
Lefkowitz, Dr Robert (Bob) 58, 91, 108
  Funny Thing Happened on the Way to Stockholm, A 92, 105
letting go 172
leverage discussion 107
Lewis, Matthew 58–9
LGBT+ network 28, 55, 142
limitations, mentor 67–8
line management 136
  role of 144–5
LinkedIn 33, 105, 179
Loom 99
Lopata, Andy: *Just Ask* 22, 85
loyalty to employer 6, 10

malicious envy 85
Managing Partners Forum 30
marginal mentoring 28
Marion, Annetta 167–8
mastermind groups 21, 22, 23
matching mentors 61–2, 152
matchmaking xxxv, 129
meeting, mentoring 154–5
   planning 96, 97
   summary 112
Melville, Dr Heather 12
Mensah, Melissa 8–9, 10
mentee, selection of 61–3
mentor, origins of term xxxi
Mentor Match programme 30
Mentor Project, The 32, 57
mentor selection table 174, 178
mentoring 8–10
   definitions 39
mentoring agility 79–81
mentoring agreement 35–6
mentoring circles 21, 22
mentoring culture 135–7
mentoring cycle 122–3
mentoring environment 98
mentoring platforms 99
mentoring support 187
mentors vs coaches 43–5
Merryck xxxviii
Messaging Apps 99
Microsoft 99, 137
Microsoft Teams 99, 112
milestones 69
Millennials 24, 88
Mini-Me Trap 62
minority representation 7
minority tax 11–13, 35, 60, 142
Miranda Brawn Diversity Leadership Foundation 174
mirroring 83
mission statement 104
momentum of relationship 133
Murray, Andy 110

National Mentoring Day 61, 188
National Mentoring Month (USA) 188
Nazarene, Olivet 31
Nebula 12
neurodivergent mentee 88–90
neurodiversity 88–90
Noakes, Mel 145, 146
note taking 94, 111–12
Nwankwo, Chloe Petrovna 66–7

objectives 69
   personal 54, 55–8
   organisational 54, 58–60
   external 54, 60–1
OneDrive 99
Online Discussion Forums 99
Oprah Master Class series 167
organisational culture 15
organisational objectives 54, 58–60
organisational trust 25
Otter.ai 112

Pachulia, Zaza 15, 110
participants in programme 149–50
passive mentoring 133
peer group mentoring 21–2
peer mentoring 11, 16, 20–1
peer-to-peer mentoring 149
perceived vulnerability 182
Perry, Tyler xxxix
personal objectives 54, 55–8
personal profile 151–2
perspective blindness 31
Pixar (Disney) 'plussing' approach 120 95
planning, poor 133
PM Forum Mentor Match 179
Pollak, Lindsey 87–8
   Remix, The: How to Lead and Succeed in the Multigenerational Workplace, 87
Post-It note 113
praise 114
praise sandwich 95–6
Prince's Trust, The (UK) 5

psychosocial support 47–8
pushback 121–2
PwC 11

Queen Mary's University mentoring project 56

rapport 81–2
recognition 114
reflection, creative 127
Reitz, Megan 96
  Speak Up 83
rejection 130–1
rejection-then retreat technique 184
reluctance in seeking help 180–3
remuneration 34, 136
resentment 136
respect 85–7
responsibilities
  to employing organisation 73–4
  for formal mentoring programmes 28
  to mentee 65–73
retention of employees 6, 7
retirees 176
reverse mentoring 11, 16, 22–5, 59, 149
rising leaders programme 58
Rogers, Carl 106
role models 40–1, 57, 104
Royal Bank of Scotland 11
Rumball, George 3–4, 10

safe space for mentees 84
safety checklists 18
Sandberg, Sheryl: *Lean In* 22
sector-wide mentoring 29–30
Self-Authoring Knower 117–18, 119
self-belief 116
self-care 126
self-confidence 160
self-development programme 133
self-efficacy 116, 160
self-reflection 187
Self-Transforming Knower 117–18, 119

senior executive, relationship with mentoring 10–11
senior internal mentors 45
senior management, role of 135, 143–4
Shared Document Collaboration 99
Sharpe, Fay 51
Signoretti, Luca 18, 82
Sinek, Simon xxxiii
Slack 33, 99, 112
social mobility 8
social pain 180
Socialised Knower 117–18, 119
Sony Mobile 145
sophisticated barbarian 111
speed mentoring 130, 154–5
sponsorship 41–3, 73
Start Up Loans finance scheme (UK) 60–1
statistics 6–7
status threat 180
Still: A Michael J. Fox Story 167
stories 91–3, 107, 143
Stott, Nicole xxvi–xxvii, xxxi, 8
strain, handling as mentor 125–7
strategic thinking 170
streamlining matching process 151
success, measuring 157–61
  competency and knowledge 160
  goals 158
  measuring success 158–9
  performance in role 160
  professional network growth 161
  promotion and career progression 160
  relationship between mentor and mentee 161
  self-confidence and self-efficacy 160
  skills development 160
  value the programme and support 161
success, mentee 108
Sun Microsystems 7
superiority illusion 83, 84
support 126
Syed, Matthew 37
  Rebel Ideas 31

Task Management Tools 99
task orientation 110
teams, mentoring 36–8, 67, 149, 154
technical support 153–4
texting 98
time management xxxiv–xxxv
tired mentoring relationship 122
title of mentor 32
Tourette's syndrome 88
tracking
 maintaining 69
 progress 94, 109, 159, 187
traditional-hierarchical mentoring 16–19, 67
training for mentees and mentors 45, 48, 131–2
transparency 86, 127
Trello 99, 112
trust 70–1, 85–7
 types of 86
Twitter 179
types of mentoring 15, 16–25

Uber 72
under-utilisation of mentoring 9–10

Vallely, Vanessa 60
value, delivering 113–14
values 66, 104, 153
veterans 11
video messages 99
Virgin Atlantic 24
voice messages 99
voluntary mentoring programmes 33
vulnerability 82–5, 182–3

We Are the City 60
WhatsApp 33, 99
Winfrey, Oprah 40
Wisdomwins 170
women 11, 30, 33, 55
women's networks 28, 142
Wooten, Dr Lynn Perry Wooten and Erika James 20, 21
 Prepared Leader, The 20
 Success Factor, The 20
work–life balance 104

Young, Lord David 60–1
youth, mentoring 5

Zoom 112, 154

Printed in Great Britain
by Amazon